LEXINGTON
Queen of the Bluegrass

Thoroughbred Park at Midland and Main Streets. A bronze sculpture grouping by Gwen Reardon honoring the Kentucky tradition of thoroughbred racing with portrayals of the best jockeys in the world wearing silks from Kentucky horse farms: Greentree (Willy Shoemaker) and Fourth Estate (Randy Romero) tie for first place, followed by Calumet (Pat Day), Overbrook (Jerry Bailey), Lane's End (Craig Perret), Hagan (Don Brumfield), and Claiborne (Chris McCarron). (Photo by Richard Greissman.)

LEXINGTON
Queen of the Bluegrass

RANDOLPH HOLLINGSWORTH

ARCADIA

Published by Arcadia Publishing
Charleston SC, Chicago IL, Portsmouth NH, San Francisco CA

Printed in Great Britain.

Library of Congress Catalog Card Number: 2004107921

For all general information contact Arcadia Publishing at:
Telephone 843-853-2070
Fax 843-853-0044
E-Mail sales@arcadiapublishing.com
For customer service and orders:
Toll-Free 1-888-313-2665

Visit us on the Internet at http://www.arcadiapublishing.com

CONTENTS

FOREWORD

I was born and raised in Lexington, Kentucky. This is a good conversation starter for me at parties around here since most people are always astonished to meet a "native." My small-talk skills could use some improvement, so I often rely on this strategy in groups of non-natives. It gets them going. Most all of my friends and acquaintances love living in Lexington and yet, paradoxically, they are quick to describe how they are not yet comfortable saying in public that they are "from" Lexington. The pressure from the older families is too intense when the "newcomer" is exposed as having lived in Lexington for only a generation or less. The cultural identity of old town Lexington is palpable. Since I have a bilineal name I tend to be even more sensitive to heritage. Even after I grew up and went away from home, casting away my Lexington heritage (I thought) forever, I carried it with me. My friends up north and while teaching in Africa called me "Kentuck." Of course, "Kentucky bred" is a coveted descriptor for a thoroughbred in a racing program, but for a young woman searching for her new professional identity in the wide world, this is not always a moniker of esteem. Nevertheless it is something unique in the world, and Lexington is at the heart of what makes Kentucky what it is.

Scenes of my life in Lexington (so far) can be described in snapshots. A big barn where we would brush the horses before riding through a field with the Red Mile track lights in the distance defined a wonderful farm nestled on what was then the outskirts of Lexington. Mother working on a quilt with her mother and aunt from Virginia who visited our small house built from a G.I. bill loan and a handshake. The wonderful smells and sounds of Keeneland and the horsemen talking with Grandfather on a cold April morning—the puffs from the flaring nostrils of horses as they gallop. Seeing his brothers in their cars as they came in from Scott County to bring my cousins to school, Father would compete to be the last one of the drivers to put on his brakes as we went down Short Street, trying to catch the lights just right—sometimes using the rear bumper of the car in front to stop so the brake lights wouldn't betray him. Sneaking in the Old Sayre building's great front door when my uncle, the headmaster, wasn't looking (or a worse fate, being caught by any of my aunts who worked there) to get to class on time. Walking from Sayre School to ballet lessons at U.K. or choir practice at Christ Church Episcopal all by my grade-school self. My sisters and I picked out the best dresses we wanted at Wolf Wiles because we were going to hand out trophies at the Junior League Horse Show. We would play hide-and-seek in the empty offices of the *Blood-Horse* while waiting for Father to finish writing an editorial and take us home. My team never won playing field hockey with the "Old Ladies" at Transylvania University. Cotillion dances led to debutante balls at Idle Hour and Lexington Country Clubs where I was glad to rely on my handsome older brother as a dancing partner when all of a sudden I was without one. I had refused to have a "coming out" of my own much to my tolerant parents' amazement. No, I was going to Vassar College and have a great career in New York—never coming home, except for maybe being in Grandmother's wonderful plays we put on every Christmas at her horse farm, The Hollys.

Well, of course I came home after ten years of exploring the world and got a job at U.K. My artistic side had to have an outlet and I got a role as Pitti-Sing in *The Mikado* at the Opera House—it reminded me of the wonderful times as a child when I would go with Mother and my aunts to the Lexington Music Theatre's productions of Gilbert and Sullivan operettas. The scandals in the athletic world that rocked U.K. and ousted a wonderful president seemed too distant to me as I worked hard at getting young Kentuckians to pay attention to their history lessons. My little brother with his cool bandana dodged mall-patrolling police using acrobatic skateboarding skills, and I knew something of the world that captured the attention of younger folks. At a multi-cultural training workshop, I heard stories from my dean who spoke of growing up in a black community in Lexington—it was a very different Lexington from what I remembered growing up in! Steve Kay and Rona Roberts started the wonderful "Lexington Speak Out!" series of forums, and my husband and I helped facilitate several neighborhood and school-based sessions where we learned of the great variety of people and lifestyles in what we had always thought was a very provincial town. There were also many opportunities lost as the city and university seemed to go their separate ways, and the downtown area struggled to find meaning for itself. Traffic snarls in the main arteries going out of town became the topic of whole conversations, and "green belt" has come to mean something very real to this horse lover and her daughters. Keeneland is still a place to bring children, and like my parents before me, I teach my girls that burgoo and red-hots are good for you because we're at the tracks. Lexington.

ACKNOWLEDGMENTS

Writing this book has been a labor of love. That is, I could not have succeeded in this labor without all the generous love that I so undeservedly receive. I am deeply indebted to my wonderful family and to those of my colleagues who may admit to having some regard for me. Much of the research work reflected herein comes from the blood, sweat, and tears of others who forged ahead in mining the rich local history records of Lexington. I have always, to great profit, relied on the kindness of our librarians and archivists, and in particular I would like to thank the Lexington Public Library and the University of Kentucky Special Collections and Archives. My thanks also for the help I received from the Kentucky Virtual Library and its wonderful Kentuckiana Digital Library to get me going. Thanks go as well to the U.K. Audio-Visual Archives, Transylvania University Special Collections, the Kentucky Historical Society, the Keeneland Association Library, and Harold Barker of Lexington Fayette County Urban Government's Records and Archives. Several of my historian colleagues whose generosity to me in sharing of their time and energy as I puzzled over some of these themes need to be mentioned: Jim Prichard of the Kentucky Department of Libraries and Archives, Ken Williams of the Kentucky Historical Register, Nancy O'Malley of the U.K. Anthropology Museum, Glenna Graves of Inter-Cultural Connections Inc., Rebecca Hanley of the Junior Historical Society, Jake Gibbs and Rick Smoot of Lexington Community College, and Terry Birdwhistell of the U.K. Oral History Program. I relied also on my past students' oral history tapes of members of Lexington's black community, and I thank them for doing history so well. Melanie Beal Goans, Kentucky historian at the University of Kentucky, meticulously edited my original drafts, and when you find errors it is because I did not follow up on one of her terrific suggestions. My gratitude also must go out to those who gave me the time out of their busy days to share wonderful insights from their own recollections and perspectives on the history and future of Lexington: Ed Bowen, Joe Graves, Pat Green, Rudo Greissworth, Bill Hanna, Preston Madden, Guy Mendes, Pam Miller, Helm Roberts, Gerald Smith, and Tom Underwood.

INTRODUCTION

A native Lexingtonian knows these things: how to lose money on a horse race gracefully, how to craft a business deal while presenting a good "poker face," how to drink bourbon, and how to give a rousing long toast at a dinner table. Judge James Hilary Mulligan, son of one of Lexington's first Tammany Hall–type city bosses and well respected on his own merits for his oratory skills, gave a speech at a banquet for a group of Kentucky legislators at the Phoenix Hotel on February 11, 1902. He used the occasion to debut his poem "In Kentucky" that can be identified with the benefits of living in Lexington even today. The night was so spectacular and so indicative of the splendors of Lexington at the heart of Kentucky that the *Lexington Leader* put the poem on its front page the next day. The newspaper described the debut of Mulligan's famous toast:

> At the close of an unusually brilliant and witty toast he drew from his pocket, as if drawing a deadly weapon, a dangerous-looking type-written manuscript, and, peering over his glasses with a smile of satisfaction that amounted almost to a leer, read a poem which he said he wrote himself and was willing to take responsibility of its authorship. Without excuse or apology, and with very little warning, he read the following, which was constantly interrupted by applause that burst into a grand napkin salute at its close . . .

"In Kentucky"

The moonlight falls the softest
  In Kentucky;
The summer's days come oft'est
  In Kentucky;
Friendship is the strongest,
Love's fires glow the longest;
Yet, a wrong is always wrongest
  In Kentucky.

The sunshine's ever brightest
  In Kentucky;
The breezes whisper lightest
  In Kentucky;
Plain girls are the fewest,
Maidens' eyes the bluest,
Their little hearts are truest
  In Kentucky.

Lexington

Life's burdens bear the lightest
  In Kentucky;
The home fires burn the brightest
  In Kentucky;
While players are the keenest,
Cards come out the meanest,
The pocket empties cleanest
  In Kentucky.

Orators are the grandest
  In Kentucky;
Officials are the blandest
  In Kentucky;
Boys are all the fliest,
Danger ever nighest,
Taxes are the highest
  In Kentucky.

The bluegrass waves the bluest
  In Kentucky;
Yet bluebloods are the fewest
  In Kentucky;
Moonshine is the clearest,
By no means the dearest,
And yet, it acts the queerest,
  In Kentucky.

The dove's notes are the saddest
  In Kentucky;
The streams dance on the gladdest
  In Kentucky;
Hip pockets are the thickest,
Pistol hands the slickest,
The cylinder turns quickest
  In Kentucky.

Song birds are the sweetest
  In Kentucky;
The thoroughbreds the fleetest
  In Kentucky;
Mountains tower proudest,
Thunder peals the loudest,
The landscape is the grandest
—and Politics—the damnedest
  In Kentucky.

Chapter One

KENTUCKE

Lexington was built in a beautiful area of central Kentucky called the Bluegrass: one of the most unique geographical areas in the United States. A large basin of Ordovician limestones lies under it, which by all accounts explains the beauty of its greenery and the strength of the great thoroughbreds bred and raised within a forty-mile radius of the city. Before the city was built, visitors traveled through a hardwood forest of walnuts, sugar maple, oaks, ash, and beech, and the rustling canebrakes in which wild game and hunters could easily hide. The bluegrass (poa pratensis) for which this part of Kentucky is named did not arrive here until the 1700s. No one is sure how it got here, but it became the landmark sight for those who came out of the woods into the beautiful meadows of central Kentucky.

Before then, the people who came through this area generally did not stay for long, and any settlements were sparse and easily abandoned. Up until about 500 C.E. the human travelers who left evidence of their passage through the Lexington area were probably hunters and gatherers. The Mount Horeb Earthworks provide the best evidence that a sophisticated prehistoric culture lived in the area near Lexington. The Adena people lived near major rivers and streams of central and eastern Kentucky during the Woodland Period and had developed well-organized societies that left behind large burial mounds and other earthworks. The Mount Horeb complex includes six archeologically identified sites, two of which were villages surrounded by earthen embankments and stockades. The most intriguing site features a perfect circle with a central platform and single entryway—no mound was built on the platform of this enclosure but once a wooden, unroofed structure stood there. Archeologists conjecture that it was a ceremonial or social center of those villagers who lived nearby. It is likely that the people who lived there were highly skilled stoneworkers, and the villages were an integral part of a larger Adena exchange network.

While the great Hopewell and other Woodland cultures of the midwest and southeast flourished, this area mainly served as a hunting area or stopping point for the manufacture of hunting tools. Whitetail deer, bear, and turkey were plentiful as were herds of buffalo. The fertile area, abundant with natural springs, streams, and ponds, provided an abundance of river mussels, fish, and turtle. It also yielded nuts, seeds, fruits, and squash, which were important to the diet of these seasonal hunter communities who could forage while pausing at a processing camp.

Lexington

Sometime between 900 to 1700 C.E., during what archaeologists call the Late Prehistoric period, enterprising settlers in the area introduced corn, beans, and other crops, and more permanent villages surrounded by stockades appeared. However, the devastation from European diseases and inter-tribal warfare over hunting grounds combined to limit the development of large settlements in this area. Though most Native Americans considered this area to be no one particular people's land, by 1750 the Shawnee considered central Kentucky as part of their territory. The last known large Shawnee settlement, Eskippakithiki, thirty miles east of Lexington, housed approximately 800 people in a stockaded stronghold and over 3,000 acres were cleared for agricultural purposes. The inhabitants abandoned this town soon after 1754, probably due to the continued attacks from enemies, and the town was burned. Later European settlers took advantage of the cleared farmlands and settled there, calling it the Indian Old Corn Fields. The Shawnee continued to hold claim to these disputed lands despite the many treaties and negotiations the Europeans conducted with the Iroquois and Cherokee.

Hunters served as explorers and guides for land companies and speculators, though the Shawnee whom they encountered did not know this. The "long hunters" would often spend months in the central Kentucky area processing their kills and packing up the hides for their return to the east. If they were caught, they were treated as unwelcome intruders: often the Shawnee warriors would confiscate their valuable deerskins and simply warn them not to return.

The colony of Virginia had begun soon after the French and Indian War to grant military land warrants to veterans, but the British king's Proclamation of 1763 prohibited white settlement west of the Alleghenies. Surveyors came to Kentucky from along the Ohio River and approached the Shawnee at their large town of Chillicothe, promising to pay them for the land south of the Ohio and to continue to allow them to hunt there. A series of treaties were drawn up between the various Native American nations and European trading companies who hoped to purchase the rights to the Indian land protected by the Royal Proclamation. But the Shawnee refused to recognize the agreements the English gained from the Cherokee from the southeast and the Chickasaw from the southwest. They soon began to see that the rising tide of Virginian, Pennsylvanian, and Carolinian settlers were intending to stay, and the colonial firepower was killing off the game too quickly. They guessed correctly that, despite the promises of the whites, the land was not going to be shared with them as a seasonal hunting ground.

Virginia created the County of Fincastle (which included present-day Kentucky) in December 1772, and during the following year many private investors commissioned surveys in the hopes that they would soon be authorized to file land claims with the official surveyor, Col. William Preston. Some regular surveys, by Colonel Preston's appointed deputies, led by John Floyd, were authorized in that year, but both the private and state authorized surveyors were at risk from hostile Shawnee protecting their claims to the land.

After a powerful stand at Point Pleasant at the mouth of the Kanawha River in October 1774 against the larger forces sent in from Virginia, Shawnee troops under the command of Cornstalk decided to negotiate a peace. At this treaty negotiation the Shawnee leadership agreed that the British could travel the Ohio River and live in the territory south of the river. However, the Shawnee people did not all agree, and the dissenters often waged their own separate wars against the settlers brave enough to bring their families and belongings down the river.

In 1775 more and more colonists built settlements in Kentucky County and created a patchwork of conflicting land claims. Few surveyors in Kentucky had an education, and their results were often guesswork at best. The settlers who hired them to validate their claims came to central Kentucky either through the Cumberland Gap or down the Ohio River to Limestone (near present day Maysville). The pioneers like the "land jobbers" before them traveled into Kentucky on many of the existing trail systems that had been used by animals and Native Americans for hundreds of years. Then in 1775 the Transylvania Company commissioned Daniel Boone and twenty-eight axmen to blaze a trail along the south bank of the Kentucky River: the Wilderness Road. The Virginians established Logan's Station, Harrod's Station at Boiling Springs, and Boonesborough where on May 23, 1775, the settlers' leaders enacted new laws to govern the county of now approximately 300 whites and their slaves.

That same year, William and Francis McConnell led a land-hunting party from Pennsylvania down the Ohio River and up the Kentucky River to the Elkhorn. There they met up with others, including John Maxwell, who were building cabins on the North Elkhorn. The legend is that while they were camped at a sinking spring near the Middle Fork, they talked about the recent news of the battle at Lexington, Massachusetts that spring and thereafter thought of the area as Lexington, in tribute to the birth of the American Revolution and the "shot heard round the world." This small hunting party did not stay in the area; however, for most Lexingtonians of today, their historic campsite marked the true founding of Lexington.

In December 1776 Virginia's legislature dissolved the county of Fincastle and a part of it was taken to form Kentucky County, which followed roughly the state's present boundaries. This not only allowed for the settlers to have more say in the government but also offered new opportunities for squatters who had already made "improvements" of corn fields and cabins. Land courts were set up to clear the claims made prior to 1778, and the settlers arriving in the new county of Kentucky after January 1778 and before May 1779 could purchase 400 acres at the state price of £80. So, in April of 1779 Robert Patterson, a young ranger and Indian-fighter from Pennsylvania, came to central Kentucky to erect a garrison. Under the orders

Lexington

of Captain Levi Todd stationed at Fort Harrod, he was to build fortifications north of the Kentucky River. The idea was to support Gen. George Rogers Clark's campaign to halt the combined Anglo-Indian attacks on the Kentucky outposts. Patterson was experienced at hand-to-hand combat but knew little about the strategic placement of military fortifications, or else the settlement there at the Middle Fork of the Elkhorn might not have taken place at that time. Placing the blockhouse on the stream near where McConnell's party had camped was more for the purpose of marking off tracts of land than for military defense. On a flood plain trapped between two inclines, they built a little log structure at what is now the southwest corner of Main and Mill Streets. It served as a bunkhouse for men to scout out the area and start planting the requisite corn acreage for settlement (400 acres) or "improvement" and gain pre-emption (plus an adjoining 1,000 acres) rights to the land. Later Patterson confessed to being a land speculator himself; he had made twenty "cornpatch and cabin" improvements on the best lands in order to then sell the rights to the claim.

The first cabin built by the settlers in the Lexington fort was for John Morrison's wife and children. About thirty acres were cleared to plant corn, and during the summer of 1779 the Morrison family and twelve men built three more cabins and worked the fields. More settlers came to the area that fall, but the winter snows were harsh that year, and the lack of enough food for the whole community together with the cramped conditions made the living conditions brutal. Most of the pioneers relied completely on the wild game in the area, mainly buffalo and wild turkey. Talk around the evening fires turned to politics and land ownership, and on January 25, 1780, the small community signed a "citizens' compact."

This document delineated the creation of eighty-seven in-lots of one-half acre each. Most of the city blocks were five in-lots each, and the out-lots were five acres each. The shape of the town followed the Town Branch (the fork of the Elkhorn) and all the streets and the town commons were laid out in a grid pattern generally based on the line of the stream banks. Qualifications for ownership were detailed in the citizens' compact: each man over twenty-one who had been a resident of Lexington for six months, or who had raised a crop of corn, could draw for one in-lot and one out-lot. Women who were the heads of household or in legal terms, femme sole (for example, widows), were also eligible. Though a drawing for lots had been held during the previous year, the consensus was that this one was fairer. The town trustees were also elected, and eventually John Higbee's tavern on the southwest corner of Mulberry (now Limestone) and High Streets served as the gathering place for them to conduct town business. By April, they had built a stockade around several cabins and the blockhouse. Meanwhile, several stations around Lexington experienced regular attacks by Native Americans and British mercenaries, including Bryant's Station only five miles away.

Kentucke

The Virginia Assembly divided Kentucky County into Fayette, Lincoln, and Jefferson counties in November 1780. Lexington served as the county seat for Fayette, and Governor Thomas Jefferson appointed John Todd the county lieutenant for the regular militia. Todd had served as one of the first Virginia burgesses representing Kentucky County and introduced bills to emancipate slaves as well as to set aside land grants for education. He served with Gen. George Rogers Clark in 1778 and was appointed the first civil governor of Illinois, though he left most of his duties up to deputies. He earned the rank of colonel (second in rank only to Gen. George Rogers Clark), Daniel Boone was appointed lieutenant-colonel, and Thomas Marshall surveyor of the county. Todd recruited a large body of men after the winter of 1780–1781 to build a fort that would protect the settlement against the British and Spanish artillery in the hands of the Native American raiding parties.

Like many other frontier villages, the early settlers worked all the land together without particular regard to ownership at first. In a letter to the governor, Colonel Todd explained how he built the fort:

> Lexington, 15 April 1781 . . . I laid off the fort upon the simplest plan of a quadrangle, and divided the work among four of the most pushing men, with a bastion to each, authorizing them to employ workers from this and the neighboring stations, and assuring them of their pay myself. On the faith of such assurance, considerable sums of money had been spent and advanced to the workmen, so that the work in about 20 days has been nearly completed, in a workman like manner. The gate is nearly finished and the magazine contracted for. The whole expense amounts to £11,341.10s. I believe four times the expense never before made for the public a work equal to this."

A second, smaller but cannon-proof fort was built a few blocks to the west in the summer of 1782. The only house in this fort belonged to a Mr. January, who was 105 years old. An abundance of cane grew around both the forts where there were no trees. John Filson, a teacher, surveyor, and cartographer, described this central Kentucky grass variant in his pamphlet on "Kentucke" published in 1784:

> Here is great plenty of fine cane, on which the cattle feed, and grow fat. This plan in general grows from three to twelve feet high, of a hard substance, with joints at eight or ten inches distance along the stalk, from which proceed leaves resembling those of the willow. There are many cane brakes so think and tall that it is difficult to pass through them. Where no cane grows there is abundance of wild-rye, clover, and buffalo-grass, covering vast tracts of country, and affording excellent food for cattle.

Lexington

Perhaps it is this vista that inspired the early migrants to settle here, too far inland for efficient use of a river and too exposed for a military fortification. Besides the building projects and drills, Colonel Todd kept the men busy with such entertainments as horseracing and plenty of whiskey.

Nevertheless, the intense fear of Native American raids held sway, and in early March these fears were realized when a work party out gathering logs was attacked. One workman, John Wymore, was killed, and in revenge the settlers took the scalp of a downed raider and hung it on a pole "to mortify the Indians." The dead enemy's head was cut off and placed in a nearby cherry tree. Town records do not show that any other people were killed within the town boundaries by the Indian war parties.

Josiah Collins, an early settler, told John Dabney Shane in an oral history interview in the 1850s that he thought the reason the Indians did not attack Lexington as often as the outlying stations was because the men so frequently shot off their guns in raucous celebrations.

Though the fort was not as large as the original stockade, the settlers seemed more confident in its ability to protect them. Twice more the settlers retreated to the fort upon hearing of Indian raids in the area. They chopped out all the cane around the fort so that marauders could not hide in them. Even though the canebrakes provided better fodder for the settlers' cows, the resulting bluegrass meadows around Lexington provided the distinctive vista that so charmed visitors from the east then and today. Eastern speculators and traders typically spent the winters in the fort and went back east in the spring before raids began again.

The settlers sent a petition to the Virginia Assembly in April 1782 to establish the town. Only one month later, on May 5, Virginia created the Town of Lexington as the county seat of Fayette. The Virginians named the county for General Lafayette, a popular French ally in the Revolutionary War. The act to create the Town of Lexington assigned 710 acres to the town trustees, who then granted deeds to the owners of the lots already assigned. That summer, the British-Indian war parties continued to harass outlying settlements and Colonel Todd along with many other community leaders died in a disastrous skirmish at Blue Licks (now Robertson County), the worst military disaster for the settlers in Kentucky. The citizens of Lexington blamed General Clark for not preventing the attack in the first place, and when Virginia refused to allow Clark to retaliate, the anger and frustration against easterners grew.

The county courthouse, a two-story log building with a board roof built on the northwest corner of Main Cross (Broadway) and Main Street, served as the center for both economic and political gatherings. Court Day was the one day of the month when the county court was held, and farmers—both black and white—came to the county seat to sell their produce and buy supplies. Horses and lawyers abounded, and Court Day gave the community members many opportunities to watch exciting, death-defying horse races and hear political debates or flowery speeches in court during sensational lawsuits. Many of the political speeches led later to fights and even duels over personal honor. Politics was much more of a body-sport then than now.

In the 1780s the farmers in this area invested heavily in high quality breeding stock, especially mules, cattle, and horses. Following in the cultural norms of the great family farms of Virginia and the Carolinas, and looking toward the beautifully constructed barns and stud farms of the English gentry, the wealthier settlers became obsessed with horses of good pedigree, or "blooded" horses. Joe Estes, editor of the *Blood-Horse* magazine, wrote, "When there were no Indians to be chased, there were arguments to be settled, and in Kentucky it usually takes a horse race to settle an argument." By 1785 only fifty-five cabins had been built outside the walls of the fort, but the Fayette County tax rolls of 1789 listed 9,607 horses and fifty-six stallions. In 1791 Lexington began the annual three-day race meets in October, and six years later Kentucky's first Jockey Club (modeled on the English Jockey Club) was organized at John Postlethwaite's Tavern as a way to standardize the rules of racing and identification for breeding. When in 1793 the town trustees complained of "dangerous racing through the streets," they admitted they had no authority against it and so requested an election of the town citizens to give them the power to regulate racing in the town. The result was that racing was confined to the lower end of the Commons (west Vine Street) where stud horses were shown.

By the mid-1780s Lexington was a thriving hub of roads from the countryside to the rivers and from there on to the Mississippi. Stores, inns, and taverns sprang up to meet the needs of a mobile population willing to gamble on the growth of a new town. The first water mill in Kentucky was built in 1788 to use the waters of the Town Fork of the Elkhorn. Lexington's first entrepreneurs were daring: John Findley and then James Wilkinson traded Kentucky agricultural products in the markets of New Orleans. Wilkinson pushed for the free use of the Mississippi River for Kentucky produce as he conspired with the Spanish to build an empire in the west. The settlers were producing a wide variety of articles that could be traded at the Lexington merchants' stores: whiskey, hemp bagging and ropes, tobacco, pelts, sugar, linsey and wool cloth, ginseng, butter, lard, eggs, and fruit.

The first uniformed militia company west of the Alleghenies, the Lexington Light Infantry, included nearly every merchant in Lexington. They elected the dashing Wilkinson as captain in 1789. This elite group of citizen-soldiers wore blue pantaloons and red-collared blue coats with cuffs and bell buttons. They wore their soft black hats with the left side turned up and with a red plume. It is likely that many of them were also members of Lexington's secret order of Freemasons started that same year. In the spring of 1790, John Bradford organized the first regular fire company, "Union Company," which raised money for equipment and supplies by giving fancy balls. Other fire companies were "The Kentuckians," "The Lion Company," and "The Resolution," and they competed violently among themselves in responding to fire alarms. All of these groups conducted public parades and displays that bolstered the spirits and patriotism of the local community.

Two-story log houses, fine Federal-style brick homes, and warehouses began to outnumber the rough shelters and single room cabins, though forests of huge bur oaks and black walnuts still surrounded the town. The pioneer families wanted to form a model community of free citizens in these last days of the Revolution, and they sent their children to a school in the public square. This school had started as early as 1781. In 1783, the story goes, schoolteacher John McKinney fought off a wildcat attack and strangled it with his bare hands. This was the first of a whole host of schools and academies that boasted their teaching skills in the fine arts, sciences, and languages.

Transylvania Seminary, chartered by the Commonwealth of Virginia in 1780 to serve as a "public school" for the male citizens of Kentucky County, offered its first classes by the great Presbyterian freethinker and Princeton graduate Rev. David Rice. Rice, an early abolitionist preacher, taught in his log cabin in Mercer County from 1785 to 1789, when the school was moved to Lexington. A group of Lexington businessmen sponsored the construction of a two-story brick building between Second and Third Streets, and they offered the building and the lot to the school trustees for free to locate the school permanently in Lexington. By 1799 the Commonwealth of Kentucky merged Transylvania and the Kentucky Academy, a Presbyterian school nearby at Pisgah, and the Episcopal priest, James Moore, served as the first president of the new university. The medical department boasted such prominent scientists and practitioners as Dr. Samuel Brown, whose talents included the development of a steam method of distilling alcohol for the production of whiskey and the immunization of Lexingtonians against smallpox.

Night schools for adult learners advertised in the *Kentucke Gazette* early in the 1790s. The town included approximately 1,000 people and twenty businesses, and basic skills were in high demand. The night schools offered training in accounting, navigation, and mathematics. Also, keeping up with the great female academies of Philadelphia and New York, Lexingtonians could boast of at least three schools for girls before 1800. In 1793 Mrs. Ann Walsh advertised in the *Gazette* that she had opened a school to teach girls spelling, reading, and needlework. In 1797 Mrs. Lucy Gray established an academy at her home "four miles from town" at which she taught Italian and arithmetic, among other disciplines. In 1798 Mr. James W. Stevens started a school for young ladies "in order to prevent an indiscriminate intercourse of the sexes so injurious to the morals and incompatible with the delicacy of the 'fair' [sex]"—and this careful training would result in a degree in classical education.

The first library in Kentucky was created in 1784 when the Transylvania Seminary's board of trustees imported a collection of books from the Rev. John Todd of Virginia, Colonel Todd's wealthy uncle, who was the first minister to preach in the Lexington fort. By 1795 the Lexington Library Company was formed to organize a plan to bring in more books for the scholars at Transylvania. In only a few days they had raised the staggering sum of $500 to be sent east. After nearly a year the books arrived, with even more coming in the following two years. The Library Company voted to house the library downtown rather than in the Transylvania Seminary. In November of 1800 the library was moved into the lower floor of a building on Market and Short Streets where Andrew McCalla, who offered to serve as librarian, also housed his drug store. By 1801 the library owned 750 volumes, and in 1803 the Library was moved to the second floor of the Old State House. It served as an important symbol of Lexington's insistence on the Jeffersonian values of an educated electorate.

Another important aspect to building and maintaining the new republic was to keep the citizenry informed on the work being done by their delegates in Danville to gain Kentucky's independence from Virginia. Lexington settlers John and Fielding Bradford agreed to take on the task of publishing the debates and decisions at the constitutional conventions. They traveled to Pennsylvania to learn how to operate a press and brought back to Lexington the type that would produce the first issue of the *Kentucke Gazette* on August 11, 1787. It was printed in the back room of the Fayette County Courthouse, and probably very few copies were made since none of this first issue are known to exist. The Bradfords determined after this first attempt that they needed to have an experienced printer take over the production process, and they found Thomas Parvin in Clark County whom they persuaded to join them in their enterprise. They established their own post rider system to gather news and distribute the paper. Since there was no post office in Lexington at this time, the *Gazette* riders served also as the delivery system for local letters and packages. This business proved so successful that the Bradfords were able to move in 1795 to the brick market house on Main Street and there continued publishing the *Gazette* for forty years. John Bradford served as an important community leader and sponsored literary and publishers' meetings to support the growth of a free press and a critical literary community in Lexington.

Lexingtonians boasted of being a center of culture and the sciences even in these early days. Dr. Robert Peter, a professor at Transylvania in the mid-nineteenth century, listed great inventions by early immigrants to Lexington. Edward West, the first watch-maker to settle in Lexington, developed a pistol, a nail-cutting machine, and a hemp-braking machine before he became a silversmith. He constructed a model steamboat, which he demonstrated in the Town Fork in 1793, the first ever placed on American waters. His received his patent for this invention in 1802, a year before Robert Fulton's. John Jones created a stone-sawing machine as well as a spindle speeder. Joseph Bruen of Lexington created the first railroad and the first locomotive to run on it ever constructed west of the Alleghenies. Nathan Burrows invented a machine for cleaning hemp in 1796, and Kentucky soon became a leader in twine, rope, and bagging production.

Lexington

Lexington was well on its way to becoming a new manufacturing center, and black labor was key to the success of the emerging town. Lexington slaves built houses, roads, bridges, and fences. They worked in the taverns, warehouses, stables, nail factories, tanneries, woolen mills, carding factories, and brickyards. African Americans, both free and enslaved, were mail carriers, furniture makers, cobblers, blacksmiths, tobacconists, weavers, barbers, gardeners, chefs, butchers, healers, jockeys, preachers, musicians, and even lawyers. In 1795 there were two brickyards in Lexington with 281 African-American workers. A scene in which vegetables and crafts were bought and sold at the local marketplace should conjure up a picture comprised mainly of people of color. Slaves were hired out for domestic service as well as agricultural work, and they sometimes had a say in where they worked. Leased slaves were important especially for manufacturers who did not have to spend much in supervising, housing, and feeding their workers. The greatest number of urban African-American workers (even young children) were employed in the hemp industry. Slaves worked in the rope walks and bagging factories and learned important skills that could be utilized in other venues.

Urban slaves in Lexington lived in cabins behind the slaveowner's house that often faced a back alley that cut between the original town lots. This created many small villages within the town and in close quarters with the white residents. In contrast, the outlying farms often included segregated areas to house the black field labor in flimsy shacks, but more substantial brick or stone cabins for the "house servants" still exist near old farmsteads in Fayette County. These buildings often included the work areas for the more skilled crafts produced by a Bluegrass farm and sold at market.

Because most Kentuckians used the task system to harness their slave labor, many local bondspeople were able to earn cash by working at different jobs once their assigned tasks were done. The more ambitious people worked long and hard hours to keep their extra jobs. Though the wage was often a fraction of what a white laborer received, it could serve as enough of a start for a truly entrepreneurial spirit. Some African Americans in Lexington speculated in housing and even purchased their own slaves in an effort to make their fortunes.

Free African Americans possessed little more freedom than slaves, but it is likely that they maintained an elite status in the community through the use of personal contacts with landed and professional-class whites. Every month, in almost every session of the Fayette County Court, a slave received his or her freedom. It was easier to emancipate a slave in Kentucky than in the deep south, and the Kentucky Court of Appeals tended to rule in favor of freedom during contested cases in these early days of Kentucky slavery. Few laws targeted free blacks specifically since color, rather than bondage, determined the type of regulation. For example, blacks could not own weapons, testify in court against whites (though there were some exceptions), or even be suspected of trying to fight against whites. In 1798 Kentucky passed its first slave code that required slaves who were away from residences for longer than four hours to have a pass. According to this law, a slave who was caught without a pass could be turned over to a sheriff for ten lashes—in Lexington, the town trustees increased this punishment to thirty lashes at the public post in the courthouse yard. Any African American without proof of freedom, such as a certificate of emancipation or testimony of white friends, could be sold into slavery.

Nevertheless, Lexington's black communities thrived. Enough so that the Lexington trustees passed a resolution on July 8, 1800, hiring a city streets patroller to watch for large numbers of blacks in Lexington, especially on Sundays, since the large gatherings had "become troublesome to the citizens." In 1801 the Kentucky legislature protected free blacks by making it a crime to kidnap them and sell them into slavery. The principle of the law was clearly to keep the peace rather than give any special protection since later, in 1808, Kentucky passed an anti-immigration law prohibiting the entry of free blacks from other states. Even so, Kentucky blacks maintained as strong a commitment to their families, communities, religious worship, and education as the whites.

Organized religion served an important purpose in the growing community, and at the same time, Lexington harbored religious leaders who were persecuted by the established churches in the east. In 1783 the Baptist elder Lewis Craig left Virginia where he had been jailed for his denunciation of the newly formed Episcopal Church there, and he relocated a Spotsylvania County Baptist congregation on the South Elkhorn at Craig's Station. The first Baptist Church in Lexington was built on Main Street under the leadership of Elder John Gano and Edward Payne, though most Lexington Baptists attended Town Fork Baptist Church on the Frankfort Pike. Peter Duerett, a freedman from Virginia known as "Old Captain," established the first African-American church in Kentucky during the mid-1780s when he began holding informal services in his cabin. He baptized converts despite opposition from the white Baptist association, and in 1801 he started Lexington's First African Baptist Church. Under the leadership of London Ferrill, a former slave also from Virginia, the First African officially split from the original white church at the "Head of Boone's Creek" and in 1824 gained acceptance as a separate church within the Elkhorn Association. It became the largest antebellum church in Kentucky with nearly 2,000 members by the 1850s. During the controversial split, however, the remnant Baptists who did not follow the conservative Ferrill kept the name "African Church" until 1829 when it took the name Pleasant Green Baptist Church.

Another Christian denomination that flourished in the south and the new west, the Methodists, relied on circuit preachers and no permanent structure was established in Lexington for this group until 1819. Lexington Presbyterians invited the Rev. Adam Rankin of Virginia to come to Kentucky in 1784, and he started a small church called the Mount Zion Presbyterian Church at McConnell's Station. This served as the core of what later split into two important churches in Lexington history: the First and Second Presbyterian Churches. The Baptists and Presbyterians both were vocal advocates for freedom and served as some of the earliest abolitionists in an area where slavery was perceived as an important symbol of socio-economic status and potential prosperity. They also fueled the great revivals that swept this area at the turn of the century, and were the catalyst for the nation's Second Great Awakening. Lexington served as the seedbed for the rise of a new American denomination, the Christian Church—which eventually merged with another new church of the Restoration movement, the Disciples of Christ.

The early Episcopalians formed as a separate denomination from the English Anglicans in 1789. Some of Lexington's most powerful citizens were Episcopalians even though their politics were seen as Royalist, and they held services as early as 1794 under the auspices of the "Episcopalian Society." Two years later, they had begun to hold services in a small structure on Market Street, the site of today's Episcopal Christ Church Cathedral. Christ Church was the first Episcopal congregation west of the Allegheny Mountains. Like the Anglo-oriented Episcopalians, the Catholics in this area met under a cloud of suspicion: they were seen as possible spies for the Spanish, French, or their Native American allies. Father Stephen T. Badin, a refugee of the French Revolution's Reign of Terror, came to Lexington in January 1794 and served the few Catholic families in this area until he returned to France in 1821.

Kentucky gained her independence from Virginia in 1792. New migrants were still vulnerable to frontier violence if they settled in isolated areas. Lexington benefited from its central location and with every ox cart or riverboat came new skills, trade materials, and innovative ideas. So the first meeting of Kentucky's legislature was held in Lexington's new Market House. The inauguration of the first governor, Isaac Shelby, included a parade by the Lexington Light Infantry and a welcome address by John Bradford, town trustee.

The legislature appointed five men to research where the state capital should be located and this commission visited many settlements that seemed able to contribute to the construction of the first capitol building. Among them were Frankfort, Leestown, Louisville, and Boonesborough. Andrew Holmes, a Lexington land speculator who controlled the vast holdings in Frankfort once owned by its founder, Gen. James Wilkinson, partnered with eight Frankfort businessmen to woo the legislature. They came bearing gifts for the legislators and offered to give to the state the general's own house for seven years, half of the proceeds from city lot land sales, warehouse receipts, and cash up front. The commissioners were split on their decision between Lexington and Frankfort and in December 1792, the deciding vote for Frankfort came from Robert Todd, the Lexington representative, who feared he might be accused of favoritism.

Kentucke

Meanwhile, Lexington's businessmen chafed under the Federalist Party and President George Washington's insistence on neutrality in the international controversies between France and Spain. Gen. Anthony Wayne sent an open letter published in the *Kentucke Gazette* warning citizens to be neutral in these controversies, and he felt compelled to specify that Kentuckians should not join in any expeditions against New Orleans and the Spanish possessions in the Mississippi River area. The Democratic Society of Lexington, founded in the summer of 1793, wore tricolor buttonieres and raised a Liberty Pole on Main and Cheapside Streets in honor of the French revolution and their fear of a return to an unfettered monarchy. In 1794 when Gen. Charles Scott brought nearly 1,500 mounted Kentucky militiamen to join Gen. Anthony Wayne in his campaign against the Native Americans, it is not known how many Lexingtonians were in his company. A first-hand account described the Kentucky Volunteers' dress as "a hunting shirt and leggings, with rifle, tomahawk, knife, pouch and power horn." It is not likely then that these volunteers were Lexington businessmen. Nevertheless, Lexington's business clearly benefited from Wayne's success at the Battle of Fallen Timbers, which effectively ended twenty years of Kentucky's warfare with the Native Americans.

In 1797 Thomas Hart, a prominent merchant in the rope business, formed the Lexington Immigration Society with John Bradford as secretary. They published tracts and magazine articles to attract eastern farmers to the Lexington area. The tax books show there were twenty-eight retail stores in Lexington by then, and the county's white population over sixteen years old was little more than half the number of slaves. A census was taken of the town inhabitants in 1798 that recorded a total of 1,475:

Males above 12 years	462
Females above 12 years	307
Whites under 12 years	346
Negroes	360
TOTAL	1,475

Compared to the county population of only 772, this shows the importance of this new urban area. Of the surrounding counties, only Bourbon and Scott reached more than 1,000 but still not near the size of Fayette County.

The town was bustling with business and the claims on land were more strident than ever. The surveying had been conducted so haphazardly that over twenty-four million acres had been issued in grants—even though the state itself contained fewer than thirteen million acres. By 1800, only half of Kentucky's heads of household owned any land in the state. In addition, the landownership had become increasingly unequal so that by the turn of the century a small percent of Kentucky's citizens owned one-third of the land. Lexington served as the place of hope for those small landowners who might find an advocate who could help them keep their property.

Lexington

The culture of the new republic encouraged the entrepreneurial farmer and artisan to speak out against the inequities of an entrenched establishment and find a strong foothold on his personal ladder of success on behalf of his family.

Few records exist to help an interested researcher find out much more about pioneer Lexington. Besides the oral histories preserved by a few historians interested in transcribing the stories of some of the original settlers, the *Kentucke Gazette*, the Fayette Circuit Court, and some memoirs and letters are all that are left. Many valuable resources, including the records of the Fayette County Court and the county tax and marriage records, burned in January 1803. Levi Todd, the clerk for the Fayette County Court, had kept them in his private office situated at the back of his home, Ellerslie, one of the earliest mansions in the area. Though it was speculated that settlers without legal title had set the fire, those who benefited by the destruction of these records were those who could bring in their copies of deeds and get oral testimony recorded as to their land claims. The homesteaders lost claims to land that the local gentry or their land-jobbers had more carefully documented.

The local feuds over land were influenced by the political conflicts of the day. Valid claims depended on the support of prestigious lawyers and politicians, and if a claimant had not been careful in garnering the right sort of support for a land case, he might lose based simply on which lawyer he had chosen to defend him. The Alien and Sedition Acts of 1798 caused an uproar in the frontier town; these laws postponed citizenship (and thus voting rights) for immigrants and gave the President the power to imprison or deport aliens suspected of activities posing a threat to the national government. The Sedition Act forbade spoken or written criticism of the government, the Congress, or the President and virtually nullified the First Amendment freedoms of speech and the press. Five thousand people attended a protest against these Federalist initiatives on August 5 in the streets of Lexington. When their own John Breckinridge introduced the radical Kentucky Resolutions in response to these new federal laws, Lexingtonians celebrated with a bonfire, parade, and free drinks in the inns.

In the fall of 1797, Henry Clay left his law practice in Virginia and came to Lexington. He soon thereafter became very successful in lawsuits over land claims, especially when acting on behalf of the local gentry. In April 1799 he married Lucretia, the daughter of the wealthy Thomas Hart. In that year, Clay began his long campaign for the gradual emancipation of Kentucky's slaves when he spoke out in the campaign for election of delegates to the Kentucky constitutional convention. Lexington had too much to lose already if she freed her slaves, and the Kentucky constitution of 1799 clearly cemented the right to own slaves and denied basic rights even to the few free African Americans in Kentucky. The issue of slavery would prove to be Lexington's downfall, yet Clay's future role in the national debate would be one of her finest legacies.

Chapter Two

ATHENS OF THE WEST

> Lexington contains 104 Brick, 10 Stone, & 187 Frame and log Houses, a Court-house, Jail, Market-house, and four places for public worship; an handsome Lodge for Free Masons; an Insurance Office; the Transylvania University—this seminary has five Professors, and is governed by a board of trustees; a public Library, containing several hundred volumes of the most valuable books, stands on a corner of the public square. Messrs. Todd and Jones, two ingenious mechanics, have erected machinery for carding, roving and spinning cotton—Mr. Todd's contains 188 spindles—Mr. Jones' 144. Extensive works are now erecting by Mr. Todd for carding and spinning hemp, by machinery. Mr. Hunt's Duck manufactory keeps 40 or 50 hands employed.
>
> Lexington Directory, taken from *Charles's Almanack* for 1806.

By 1810 the Bluegrass region of central Kentucky was not altogether frontier and not yet fully developed. It was Kentucky's first extensively settled region due to the predominance of major river systems: the Salt, the Kentucky, and the Licking. Lexington was Kentucky's first city. Its literate citizens both rural and urban were convinced that Lexington was a new Philadelphia, a cultural mecca of civilization at the heart of the new republic's farmlands and mineral resources. Her population had jumped from 1,800 in 1800 to over 4,300 in 1810; the sales of some merchants surpassed $1 million per year, and annual incomes reached $60,000. Between 1808 and 1809, for example, the value of William Leavy's mercantile holdings nearly doubled from $25,817 to $46,710.

Lexingtonians were so sure of their role in the new nation that they embraced ostentatious dress and pious church going, sumptuous banquets and outdoor barbecues, dancing and duels, horseracing, whiskey, and torchlight parades. With the rise of the lawyer, merchant, and banker in Lexington came an extension of commercial networks that tied Lexington's elite to a national ruling class. The emerging professional class of the new city intermingled with the old Virginia and Carolina landowner families, and a new gentry with Old World ways greeted the surprised visitor from the east.

The fashion of the day was to write exotic travel books, and Kentucky was a popular place for easterners and Europeans to visit. The old buffalo traces and Indian warrior trails afforded access to the more romantic views that avid readers could see in their imaginations. From a settler's perspective though, the Wilderness Road was

Lexington

dangerous as they attempted to bring in their livestock, household goods, farm equipment, and meager reserves. The Ohio River seemed a better bet after the 1790s, and it could take only a week to pole a flatboat down to Maysville from Pittsburgh. Though this small village was the most important port in the west, it was small and poor. It was originally named Limestone and served as Daniel Boone's home when he was a tavern-keeper and trading-post owner supplying food to Native American prisoners. By 1810 it was a bustling port: keelboats left every four weeks from Pittsburgh filled with merchandise from Baltimore, Philadelphia, and New York City. Travelers disembarking from the riverboats used an old buffalo trace to find their way to the heart of the Bluegrass. Farmers had settled along the trace, and small villages had grown up along what had become a main artery into Kentucky.

The Maysville Road, as it came to be called, led the nineteenth century travel writer from a backwoods scene to where, according to Fortesque Cuming, the road became "very wide and fine with grazing parks, meadows, and every spot in sight cultivated." Within a hundred-acre area, the preponderance of brick and white limestone houses revealed the new city's cosmopolitan charm. Cuming described Lexington's main street, running south-east from Frankfort toward Boonesboro, "about eighty feet wide, compactly built, well paved" and lined by brick walkways. Even as the naming of Lexington symbolically linked the founding of the new republic to the new city in the "wilderness," this new Athens of the West proudly embodied the principles of the Enlightenment's natural laws and liberty. Its strong belief in republican political institutions was reflected in the clear sense of cultural superiority that the city exuded. Here Jefferson's "natural aristocracy" could rise and lead a new nation. The strong ties between the Virginia and Carolina leading elite and Kentucky's wealthy landowners reinforced this belief.

Since few of the nation's internal improvements before the War of 1812 included the west, Lexingtonians and their war heroes felt they deserved more. From the 1790s on, the members of the Lexington Democratic Society argued that their economic success depended on the free and open access to the Mississippi River and the New Orleans markets. Many Lexington merchants had business partners in the east and sent their sons to New Orleans and Natchez markets. Their mistrust of the federal government was only slightly allayed by the news of the Louisiana Purchase of 1803. The Maysville Road was the lifeline to the Ohio and the Mississippi Rivers, and it was cleared and maintained by the local communities. As a consequence the quality of the road was very uneven—there were few bridges and in some places an old buffalo trace was all the travelers had to go by. Kentucky's frontier roads, like the streets of Lexington itself, depended on citizens to provide the labor and paving materials. Few felt strong ties to a national economic or political entity.

Certainly, early Lexington's society was not a democracy. The only citizens who could exercise the right to vote for or serve as town trustees were those who owned valuable land within one mile of the courthouse. In 1804 this meant that out of Lexington's 298 heads of household, only 133 could vote. It was not until 1811 that the General Assembly overrode the town's suffrage law and granted suffrage to all free white male town lot owners of at least eighteen years of age. In Lexington, the type of businessmen Lexington historian George W. Ranck called the "Money Kings" ruled. A good example was Peter January, an early settler from Pennsylvania who was in the mercantile business with his son Thomas. January's two-story brick home is said to be one of the first brick buildings erected in Lexington, sometime before the year 1790. Thomas January was a successful businessman, a justice of the peace, a state representative, and philanthropist. He served as one of the promoters of the Lunatic Asylum of Lexington, which in 1816 was the second public institution of its sort in the United States His hemp industries, ropewalks, and bagging factories took up much of the inner city area near Transylvania University.

In 1808 the state assembly had forbidden the migration of free blacks into Kentucky, yet Lexington and the surrounding villages of the Bluegrass served as home for a large number of freemen. Unlike Louisville, where the small free black population lived in segregated enclaves, Lexington's black population lived in homes scattered among white residences. In 1810 white Lexingtonians created havoc after hearing rumors of a slave uprising. Several slaves were tortured and jailed but nothing transpired. Nevertheless, Lexington trustee George Trotter Jr. ordered William Worsley, captain of the night watch, "not to disturb the white citizenry—but to apprehend and secure all verry [*sic*] suspicious blacks who may be found on the streets in doubtful situations—and keep them in custody—until they can be delivered to the civil authority."

Besides the fears of the enemy from within, around 1810 Shawnee attacks from the north and along the Ohio River renewed and Lexingtonians took up the battle cry again. It was the passion of his fellow Lexingtonians that shone in Henry Clay's speeches when he was elected to the U.S. House of Representatives for the first time in 1811. Along with his compatriot Richard M. Johnson of Scott County, Clay became one of the "War Hawks" who believed that war with Great Britain would preserve the overseas markets of American staple producers. Clay soon thereafter was elected speaker of the house, a post he served in longer than anyone else in the nineteenth century. Lexington raised six companies amid triumphant speeches and parades. Clay assured the nation that Kentucky's militia alone could conquer Canada.

Henry Clay had by this time already gained prominence in Kentucky and was considered to be an important voice for the elite Bluegrass society in the national scene. He was twenty when he came to Lexington in 1797—right after he had been given a license to practice law in Virginia. He had studied under the great statesman George Wythe and apprenticed with Robert Brooke. Admitted to the bar in Lexington in March 1798, he set up an office on N. Mill Street; due to good connections through Colonel Thomas Hart, his father-in-law, Clay honed his talent as a criminal lawyer. His persuasive abilities in a jury trial were so powerful that he never lost a case. Clay was successful in both civil and criminal cases, even taking such high-profile cases as that of former Senator Aaron Burr. Like most Jeffersonians and most Kentuckians, Clay believed that Burr's treason trial was part of a Federalist conspiracy. Unbelievably, Clay's reputation was unsullied even after Burr's intentions to create a personal empire in the American southwest had become widely known. Clay joined the Lexington Lodge No. 1 F&AM, taught law at Transylvania University, and invested in land and businesses in the area. More importantly, he spoke out often against the Alien and Sedition Acts, which was a very popular stance to take in Lexington. In 1803 he was elected to represent Fayette County in the Kentucky House of Representatives, and so began his forty-year span of public life.

Clay greatly enhanced his political image when he challenged the hot-tempered Federalist Humphrey Marshall to a duel in 1809. Ostensibly the argument was over the Jeffersonian embargo and Clay's proposal that Kentucky legislators and their families should wear homespun in protest of British oppression on the seas. Marshall called Clay a liar, a "poltroon," and—what was perhaps worse—he criticized Clay's oratory as being the "language of a demarogue [*sic*]," which is probably what began a round of fisticuffs in the Kentucky House of Representatives. Since dueling was illegal in Kentucky, the contestants crossed the Ohio to the Indiana shore, just below the mouth of Silver Creek (now in New Albany). They exchanged three rounds at only ten paces, and finally Marshall landed a shot in Clay's thigh whereupon the seconds halted the duel. The House of Representatives censured both men even though the resolution included a commendation on their bravery. That Clay, the outsider, did not back down before Marshall, a renowned duelist and orator, turned the wound into a badge of honor among Kentucky gentlemen. Thereafter, Clay openly condemned the tradition of dueling, though it remained an important status symbol among Kentuckians for yet another generation.

Clay began acquiring property on the south side of the Boonesborough Road leading eastward out of Lexington in 1805. In 1809 his large family moved out of Lexington to their two-story brick country home called Ash Land to which four years later he added two wings designed by Benjamin Latrobe. Though today his home is considered not far from downtown, it was once the centerpiece of a 600-acre farm where his farm managers handled some of the best bred stock in the country: sheep, cattle, horses, mules, and other farm animals. He and his wife Lucretia Hart Clay had eleven children of whom only four outlived them. The Clays entertained such notables as Daniel Webster, General Lafayette, President Monroe, Martin Van Buren, various ambassadors, and many other dignitaries.

Henry Clay's rise in the national political scene came at the end of the War of 1812. By late January 1813 Lexington learned the news of the defeat at Frenchtown in Michigan Territory near the River Raisin and the massacre of prisoners including native sons Captain Nathaniel G.S. Hart and Major Benjamin Graves. This did not stop the outpouring of volunteers who then joined Governor Shelby in the summer of 1813 to support Gen. William Henry Harrison's campaign against the British and Native Americans. Kentuckians under Colonel Richard M. Johnson, yelling "Remember the River Raisin!" attacked the great Shawnee warrior Tecumseh. Perhaps it was Johnson who killed the charismatic Indian leader, but no one knows for sure. The horror of war was brought home in the form of human skin stretched and tanned and proudly handed down to the soldiers' descendants as Tecumseh's own flesh. Lexington celebrated in February 1815 the victory at New Orleans and the Treaty of Ghent, at which events Lexingtonians had played important roles:

> To the Citizens of Lexington. Fellow-Citizens, We are at last officially informed of the successes with which it has pleased the Almighty to crown the American arms under the command of Major Gen. ANDREW JACKSON. After events so cheering and gratifying, so vitally important to the interest of the whole Western country, and so honourable to the patriotism and valour of the gallant Jackson and his army—it is believed that we should be doing injustice to our own character and feelings, if we fail to notice them in a conspicuous manner—To do this there must be an expression of the united sense of all our townsmen: To combine which, the Trustees of the town have passed the following resolution:—At a called meeting of the Board of Trustees, on the 18th February, 1815, Resolved, That the Citizens of the Town be requested to attend at their respective houses of Divine Worship, on WEDNESDAY next, (being General WASHINGTON's birth-day) to render homage to the Supreme Ruler of the Universe, and to express their gratitude to Him for the signal success with which He has been pleased to crown the American arms under the command of Major-General ANDREW JACKSON—And that it be further recommended to the Citizens to ILLUMINATE three hours on the evening of the same day. . . . (Fowler McCalla and Cloud will make other necessary arrangements and an oration delivered at Courthouse 3 o'clock same day). Kentucky *Gazette*, Monday, February 20, 1815.

After the War of 1812, America turned her back on Europe and found she had an identity problem – what made Americans American? The rise of a two party system was in part a way to answer this question. From 1816 on a series of tariffs and Supreme Court decisions emphasized a national commitment to internal improvements such as chartered banking, harbor and port facilities, roads, industry, mono-crop agriculture, mining, public education, business corporations, civil defense, and policing. Lexington was at the heart of the new nationalism that swept Kentucky and the rest of the nation during Monroe's presidency. The celebration of a true independence from Great Britain included a federal program for the second National

Bank, high tariffs to protect domestic industries, and federally funded "internal improvements" that promised to meet the needs of all the regions of the United States. This new political agenda, coined the "American System" by Henry Clay, looked very much like what Lexington's elite had been advocating in the state for years. Clay's role models as he aspired to the presidency were great constitutional scholars like John Breckinridge as well as the slaveowner Robert Wickliffe and Benjamin Gratz, a prominent Jewish hemp manufacturer.

The golden age of stagecoaches bloomed during this time, and Lexington was at the hub of a trans-continental migration. The great diversity of people who came through the "Athens of the West" added to her wealth in more ways than one, for the Money Kings were also involved in the lucrative business of road building, especially toll-collecting turnpikes. The first stage route ran from Lexington to the elite spa Olympian Springs in Bath County beginning in 1803. The Lexington-Maysville turnpike was chartered in 1818 for sixty-four miles: the macadamized road, thirteen tollhouses, and six covered bridges cost $426,400 to build. Since Lexington was the distributing post office for the states of Kentucky and Tennessee, this road was an important route for stagecoaches carrying mail. All the mail from Washington, D.C. and the east came by stagecoach to Lexington where it was then sent by the many "star routes" to the rest of the state and beyond. Two more turnpikes chartered that same year included the Lexington-Danville-Lancaster and the Lexington-Harrodsburg-Perryville roads, each covering forty-two miles. In 1817 Colonel James Johnson started a coachline west from Lexington to Louisville, and Abner Gaines started the line from Lexington north to Cincinnati in 1818.

Edward P. Johnson and Company held the most important mail stage route in Kentucky: starting with the Zanesville post office at the end of the National Road, down the Maysville Road through Lexington, then south through Nashville to Florence, Alabama. There the mail was put on a steamboat for New Orleans. Interestingly, the carrier pigeon system of communication grew alongside the stagecoach lines. The carrier, or "homing" pigeon, transmitted important messages for the post office, army, and navy before the telegraph was introduced. For example, Lexington learned of the battle of Buena Vista during the Mexican War—and the death of Henry Clay's son—by a report that came by way of pigeons: from Mexico to New Orleans, then Lexington, and on to Washington. The largest pigeon "loft" in the United States was in the top of the stage barn on Limestone Street in Lexington. Here there were cages for the birds that were trained to find Washington, Knoxville, Zanesville, and Cincinnati, among others. The breeding and training of these birds was as important to the stagecoach company owners as were their horses. The training of homing pigeons became a sport for elite central Kentuckians and some long-time Lexington residents still carry on the tradition today. Charges for transmitting a message by pigeon at that time contributed handsomely to the fortunes of Lexingtonians. The predominance of Lexington in the era of the stagecoach mail routes lasted through the age of steamboats—the Ohio River steamboats proved too costly and too slow for long distance mail distribution. The improvement of the central Kentucky railroads in the mid-1850s, especially the Lexington & Frankfort and the Lexington & Maysville lines, put the principal stagecoach mail delivery routes out of business.

In the brief boom time after the War of 1812, Americans began to move west in huge numbers looking for cheap farmlands to grow cash crops. The rise in speculation and demand for credit enticed the professional class to gamble in a growing banking system. The Kentucky Insurance Company, started by prominent Lexingtonians and incorporated by the state legislature in the year 1802, was the first banking institution established in Kentucky and in Lexington. However, its charter was due to run out in 1818. The Kentucky legislature then chartered forty-six independent or "wildcat" banks. These banks printed their own currency, which was traded in the local communities as notes. With the increase in land speculation and business, more and more banknotes were issued in a frenzy of lending—without the gold specie to back the loans. Some banks would cash some banks' notes but not others: the face value of the notes came to mean little and the Panic of 1819 hit Kentucky hard. Prices on land, cash crops, and slaves dropped; in Lexington, homes were put up for auction and unemployment rose. The Athens of the West was under siege.

The hemp industry suffered a terrible blow from the return of British competition to the market after the War of 1812, and by the middle of 1815, all fourteen ropewalks in Lexington had shut down. Most did not reopen or, if they did, started up again on a much smaller scale. President James Monroe, accompanied by the war hero Andrew Jackson, visited Lexington on July 2, 1819 and bolstered the spirits of Kentuckians. He spoke at Transylvania and was entertained at Mrs. Keen's Tavern and at Major William S. Dallam's beautiful home on Grosvenor Avenue (now known as the Pope House). Though Kentucky had been heralded until 1815 as the richest and most promising state west of the Alleghenies and Lexington was at the center of the economic prosperity, the bubble had burst. Most Kentuckians were now debtors—during a time when imprisonment was still the penalty for debtors. The republican ideology of the day equated debt with dependence, an abhorrent condition for the ambitious, law-abiding citizen.

By 1820, Lexington's manufacturing interests were in a major depression and the simultaneous collapse in commercial volume crippled the aspirations of the new professional class. The legislature passed laws revoking the charters of the "wildcat" banks and giving debtors the right to not pay off their debts for one year—two years relief if the creditor refused to accept Bank of Kentucky notes. They also created the Bank of the Commonwealth of Kentucky to bolster the old state bank, but no one out of the state would accept the new bank's notes. In 1823 the Kentucky Court of

Lexington

Appeals declared that the relief laws were unconstitutional. Governor Joseph Desha, who accused the leaders of Transylvania University of being elitist and had pulled their state funding, dissolved the Court of Appeals and created a new court. The old court's records were confiscated, but the judges continued to meet. Kentucky now had two supreme courts, neither recognizing the authority of the other. The Old Duke of Fayette County, Robert Wickliffe, became the spokesperson for the "Old Court" and trumpeted the Breckinridge-Jeffersonian values of limited government. The governor and legislature could not take on the responsibilities of the judicial branch without upsetting the balance of power. By steady pounding during stump speeches on the rights and liberties of a true republic, Wickliffe led the state to repeal the New Court by 1826 and defeated the popular pro-relief faction. It was not coincidental that he was supported by friends like John Wesley Hunt, probably the first millionaire west of the Alleghenies, who was president of the Farmers and Mechanics Bank of Lexington, one of the few banks to remain solvent during the panic of 1819–1820. The Money Kings still ruled the Athens of the West.

Meanwhile, Lexington kept her tradition of political newspaper publishing alive. William W. Worsley and his brother-in-law Thomas Smith published one of the three newspapers in Lexington after the War of 1812: a weekly (and later semi-weekly) called the *Lexington Reporter*. In addition the printers published pamphlets, almanacs, religious tracts, and several books during the years 1816–1819, including Robert McAfee's *History of the Late War in the Western Country* and Michael Smith's *Narrative of the Sufferings in Upper Canada, with his Family in the Late War*, which are considered valuable pieces of early Americana.

Transylvania University served as the intellectual and cultural center of Lexington with its amateur theatrical performances, open lectures, and lyceums. The main building of the University was finished in 1816 and featured three stories crowned by an elaborate cupola. It was designed by a Lexington architect, Matthew Kennedy, who chose to combine a classic style with Georgian Baroque. Horace Holley, a great Unitarian minister and orator in Boston, came to Lexington in 1818 to serve as the institution's third president. He recruited an excellent faculty in the liberal arts, medicine, and law. Charles Caldwell of Philadelphia was a noted phrenologist who came to Transylvania. He was sent to Europe with $11,000 to purchase books and apparatus that helped Transylvania's library become one of the best medical libraries in the country. The law department was one of very few in the United States and the first in the West. The faculty included Judge George Robertson and the chief justice of the Kentucky Court of Appeals, a notorious duelist, Thomas Marshall.

The Transylvania Literary Institute was a private organization that included the president, professors, trustees, and friends; it met regularly in the members' homes where papers were read and dinner served. The Transylvania Botanic Garden Association started up with subscriptions procured by Professor C.S. Rafinesque in

1824, with the great landowner Robert Wickliffe elected president. The site was a ten-acre lot leased from Joseph R. Megowan opposite his house on east Main Street. Rafinesque planned for the construction of an octagonal brick building with a greenhouse, museum, library, and seedroom. But most Lexingtonians did not want to bet on Rafinesque as a businessman and the grand scheme failed. Many of the nation's future leaders attended Transylvania, such as Jefferson Davis, Stephen Austin, Richard M. Johnson, and John C. Breckinridge.

Private academies flourished in Lexington and their students often attended the open lectures at the University. It wasn't until 1834 that a public city school opened, but by 1853 public school enrollment was close to 1,500 white students—this eager trend toward public education became a hallmark for Lexington. An Irish immigrant, Dennis Mulligan, came to Lexington in 1837 to work on one of the many large-scale railroad projects and attended night school at the Phoenix Hotel. There he learned basic business and accounting procedures well enough to become successful in the mercantile trade and an important politician in post-war Lexington. African-Americans had few opportunities for academic education even though, unlike most other slave states, Kentucky did not forbid teaching slaves to read and write. Private schools sprang up with both black and white teachers where neighborhood black children were taught during weekdays or nights. Jane Washington, one of Kentucky's first black educators, ran a day school for black children in Lexington just before the Civil War. Some whites, like Colonel Robert Patterson, organized Sunday afternoon schools to teach basic literacy and some vocational skills to free blacks or those who were willing to leave and help colonize Liberia. In 1816 Transylvania University allowed for a white women's group to teach black women, and it is likely that Mary "Polly" Todd Russell, heiress of Colonel John Todd, was a leader in this effort.

In 1808 Luke Usher opened a theatre seating as many as 500 in the second story of his brewery between Vine and Hill (now High) Street. The scenery was painted by George Beck, an English landscape artist, who with his wife Mary had opened an elite school for girls a few years earlier. John Vos from Montreal played the lead in Shakespeare's *Macbeth* in 1810, which many claim was the first Shakespearean production in Kentucky.

Many talented musicians were attracted to Lexington. Anthony Philip Heinrich, a Bohemian musician, recruited enough musicians to present a grand concert on November 12, 1817, at Keen and Lamphear's Assembly Room in Postlethwait's Tavern (later the Phoenix Hotel). The program's first piece was the "Sinfonia con Minuetteo" by Beethoven, his First Symphony—and Lexingtonians were the first in the West to hear this piece and only the second audience in the United States. That winter some members of Christ Church Episcopal performed Handel's "Messiah," a tradition still continuing at this venerable institution. James Moore, first rector of Christ Church and first president of Transylvania University, was a flute player and lover of music. His home "Vaucluse" included a special room designed for musical performances. Craftsmen such as Josiah Green and William Thompson had manufactured pianos locally since 1805. Music teachers flourished in Lexington, advertising their talents to teach a variety of subjects including vocal music, piano, violin, guitar, flute, and harp. By the 1830s William Ratel had organized bands in Lexington and neighboring towns and composed music for the numerous parades and assemblies.

Dancing schools were very popular, and most of Lexington's elite homes had ballrooms. Like the Tidewater planters, the Bluegrass elite competed on the dance floor as much as on the racetrack. Even children as young as five or six were taught the essentials of waltzes, gavottes, and reels. Hotels provided the larger rooms for public dances; one of the most popular dancing rooms was on the second floor of a confectionary owned by Monsieur Mathurin Giron. It was seven bays long with a high frescoed ceiling, and the outdoor balcony running along the length of the building was decorated by an ornate iron railing. Gambling, card games, and billiards were common sidebars to the dancing, and the stakes were often very high leading to brawls and duels.

Perhaps because Lexington served as the center for dancing and public assemblies—where her citizens dressed in their finest—artists came from near and far to capture this elegance in a thriving portraiture trade. Lexington attracted George Jacob Beck and his wife Mary, both accomplished painters from England. The Becks attracted other great painters and sculptors, and many Lexingtonians became noted artists. Matthew Harris Jouett tried to study law at Transylvania but gave up and in 1815 became a painter, against his father's wishes. He studied in Boston under Gilbert Stuart and returned to Lexington to paint portraits of such notables as Henry Clay, Mrs. Benjamin Gratz, John C. Breckinridge, and the Marquis de Lafayette. He would travel down the Mississippi River every winter to paint the wealthy families of Louisiana and Mississippi. Since he did not sign his work, no one knows how many portraits this prolific painter completed, but some estimate that he produced more than 300. Edward Troye, the Swiss-born equine artist, came to Lexington in the early 1830s and began his career as America's thoroughbred bloodstock artist. Joel T. Hart of Clark County came to Lexington to work in a marble factory and began experimenting in carving marble busts. He set up a studio on West Second Street and sculpted the busts of his affluent patrons: Cassius M. Clay, Henry Clay, Dr. Benjamin Dudley, Rev. Alexander Campbell, John J. Crittenden, and Robert Wickliffe. He also sculpted romantic pieces of female beauty and basing his art on the phrenological science of the physical ideal, he created works that inspired poets.

One of the most beautiful pastoral scenes in Lexington even today is the Lexington Cemetery, created in 1849 out of a forty-acre woodland belonging to Thomas E. Boswell on West Main Street, which grew to 169 acres by 1930. The day it was dedicated, June 25, 1850, was declared a holiday in Lexington. All the businesses closed, and a huge procession including the Masonic and all the other fraternal orders of the city, along with students from Transylvania University, began the ornate ceremonies.

With all the excitement of fancy balls, the fine arts, and belles lettres, Lexington attracted the kind of entrepreneur who might not make it in the jaded eastern cities. Coupled with the readiness of financiers to gamble on a good investment, the high-minded society of the Athens of the West proved a fertile ground for new endeavors. The new emphasis on an American System of internal improvements and independence from European markets buoyed the spirits of the manufacturers willing to take a chance in the west, and manufacturing took off early in Lexington. Men like Lewis Sanders, owner of one of the largest woolen and cotton factories in Kentucky, and the Prentiss brothers, Thomas and James, bankers, encouraged others to come and join in the new world of the western entrepreneur. The comparatively low cost of living in the new urban center encouraged workers, both skilled and unskilled, to gather here looking for jobs. When boarders paid only $1 to $2 per week for room and board, a single journeyman could go a whole week with one day's labor. The expanding population and the need for master craftsmen of all types meant that Lexington had plenty of jobs paying good wages. At the same time, however, Lexington was growing around a cash-poor economy and land ownership remained firmly in the hands of the elite. Workers often did not get paid what they demanded (or were originally offered), and with no property to invest in and keep them tied to the locale, the urban population was mostly transient.

James and Thomas Prentiss came to Lexington from New England around 1805 and built an entire manufacturing center called "Manchester" on the western edge of town. It included a woolen factory and paper mill as well as company housing for the workers in an area that later became known as "Irishtown." Ebenezer Hiram Stedman, son of a paper manufacturer in Massachusetts who came to Lexington's Manchester, wrote a memoir that chronicled the issues facing the working class in Lexington. He came to Lexington as a boy in 1815 with his family. His trip down the Ohio River included his first view of a steamboat, and upon landing at Maysville, he saw a group of African-American women washing clothes on the bank. "I was So Scared That I could not walk. . . . I Recollect after Getting up on the Bank the negros Saw how frightened I was, Came to whare Mother was and you may Be Shure I was Close by hur side and wanted to passify Me in ofring me a Big lump of white Shugar… Mother often Say that She was near as Much frightened as the Rest of us."

They lived in a company house and yet Stedman remembered that his father had "the Finest Firniture that Could be Got at that time." In particular, he remembered a large sideboard that was always kept full of different kinds of whiskey and wine—"thare it was free for anny one to help themselves." He remembered that it was at this sideboard where he first saw Henry Clay and the Trotters. The Trotter brothers, Samuel and George, were owners of a large mercantile firm and were stockholders of the Prentiss paper mill and the Lexington White Lead Manufacturing Company. Samuel also ran a gunpowder factory on his farm two miles west of Lexington. Stedman remembered that his father and his friends "woold Ride out after Banking hours to Se their Factory was getting along, alwais have company with them & as Drinking was the order of that Day, they alwais Stopt at the Side Bord to Drink for thare ware plenty of Fine Havanas on the Bord." The paper mill's main building was 300 feet by 60 feet and five stories high. Outside the main building were the engine and boiler house, the dry house (for the paper) and a dye house. The first floor was used for paper, the second and third for wool, and the fourth and fifth for cotton. All the machinery was run by a steam engine, "the first large engine that had bin made in pitsburg;" the boiler was thirty feet long and six feet in diameter. They burned seventy-five cords of wood daily. With 300 hands at work in the factory and all the teams hauling wood, "it made things lively." Stedman's father was a Free Mason and so was very close with the owner of the White Lead Manufacturing Company, a chemist from Massachusetts, Mr. Anson Turner.

Master craftsmen prospered in Lexington during the early nineteenth century, especially those who contributed to the building of houses and furnishings for elite manors. Many local residents brought considerable experience and expertise with them when they settled in the growing town. David Sutton, a large landowner and manufacturer, designed the new Fayette County courthouse. John McMurtry, a Lexington carpenter, studied architecture under Gideon Shryock and assisted in the construction of the Greek Revival building, Morrison College, the central building at Transylvania University. Old Morrison stands today as one of three National Historic Landmarks in Lexington. McMurtry's first major commission was St. Peter Catholic Church on North Limestone, which was completed in 1837. His Italianate-style buildings dominated the Lexington landscape by the latter half of the nineteenth century.

Henry Clay's brother, Porter Clay, produced fashionable furniture out of the walnut and cherry that was so plentiful in this area. Silversmiths converted old coin silver into flatware, julep cups, pitchers, and tea sets. Samuel Ayres was the most popular silversmith for the prominent families during the Federal period (up to 1800), producing primarily spoons, ladles, and sugar tongs. The Empire period (1810–1840) was led by Lexington's Asa Blanchard, the greatest of these craftsmen in the early days. Blanchard took on many apprentices who went on to become renowned silversmiths themselves. His shop on the corner of Mill and Short Streets prospered during this era. Whitesmiths, producing ornate ironwork such as special hinges, fences, railings, arched doorways, and grills, were in huge demand. In 1818 Joseph Bruen built a foundry to mechanize the process. It was in Bruen's foundry that

Thomas Harris Barlow constructed his steam locomotive and two-passenger car in 1827 and ran them on a specially constructed track.

Elisha J. Winter, a merchant, started the Lexington & Ohio Railroad, becoming its first president in January 1830. He had the foundation of the road laid with long limestone blocks for the rails to run on. It ran between Lexington and Louisville, and at first horses drew the cars. For a short time, the railroad directors used the steam engine designed and built by Barlow and Bruen, but it proved to be inefficient and they replaced it with engines manufactured in the northeast. By 1834 the track reached Frankfort; however, technical problems and financial mismanagement halted any further developments until the 1850s. Lexington's traditional rivalry with the river city, Louisville, may also have hindered the railroad's progress. Meanwhile, in 1835 Lexington built a long, two-story depot at Mill and Water Streets designed by John McMurtry—the first railroad depot built west of the Allegheny Mountains. By 1838, Julius P. Bolivar Mac Cabe wrote in the preface to his City Directory for Lexington: "From the Charleston, Louisville and Cincinnati Rail Road the most benificial [sic] results maybe expected, by affording facilities for the transportation of the manufactures and produce of this country to the Southern market."

Alongside the growth in transportation came the importance of large agricultural fairs that facilitated livestock breeding and trading. Lexington was becoming an important stop for the Western plantation owners looking for stock to take with them down the Ohio and across the Missouri Rivers. By 1817 Fowler's Gardens had become an important part of the Lexington scene. Captain John Fowler, an early settler and local businessman, provided the land on the eastern side of town that probably covered twenty-five acres from Walton Avenue to Race Street and was bounded by East Main and Fifth Streets. This park was the site for fairs organized by the Kentucky Society for Promoting Agriculture. Here farmers could bring in their best livestock, garden produce, and manufactured products such as woven cloth or whiskey. Mule breeding was a big industry at this time as was the breeding of Merino sheep and Hereford cattle. Robert Wickliffe experimented with the breeding of buffalo with his cattle to produce a larger hybrid he called cattalo.

Stallions with an English-Arab pedigree were confined to a specific area for viewing and assessed for their virtues as stud for valuable broodmares. Dr. Elisha Warfield, known today as the "Father of the Kentucky Turf," was a professor of surgery and obstetrics at Transylvania University and had helped found the Lexington Jockey Club. In these early days of crafting the best pedigree of blood-stock for turf racing, he bred his finest broodmare, Alice Carneal, to the great stallion Boston. The result in March 1850 was a bay colt who came to be known as Lexington, the most famous of the great Kentucky-bred thoroughbreds. Warfield leased him as a three-year-old to a former slave and great horse trainer, Harry Burbridge. Burbridge won some high profile races and the thoroughbred caught the attention of prominent

Lexington

horse breeder Richard Ten Broeck. Ten Broeck bought the colt from Burbridge and Warfield and named him Lexington. Upon the loss of his sight, Lexington was retired to stud. R.A. Alexander of Woodburn Stud bought him for a record price of $15,000 and by 1861, Lexington topped the American Sires List. Lexington was the leading sire sixteen times, fourteen of them consecutive—longer than any stallion in history.

The Kentucky Association began sponsoring the fairs when racing became the predominant feature for the crowds that attended, and the race meets were moved from the west side of town to an area just north of Fowler's Gardens where a formal racetrack was built. By the 1850s, the fairgrounds were moved away from the track to land next to the Maxwell Spring Company. The company had been incorporated in 1850 and purchased the city's park, "Maxwell's Spring," where city residents traditionally gathered for Fourth of July celebrations and speeches by Henry Clay or William T. Barry, and where the Lexington "Old Infantry" drilled. The Kentucky Agricultural and Mechanical Society's first president, Benjamin Gratz, raised the money to build a two-story amphitheatre there with an 800-seat capacity, an octogonal building called Floral Hall that still stands today. He also led the way for the race courses for Standardbred trotters and pacers nearby—still operating today under the name of Red Mile.

Fowler's Garden and the Fairgrounds were not used only for business. Here the new American democracy sprang into action. Lexington's political energy during this period could not be contained in the courthouse yard. The Jacksonian Democrats and National Republicans began developing their political identities in this era, and Lexington was the birthplace for the types of county and district clubs where modern American politics was born. Barbecues accompanied the inevitable political orations that could last hours. In this spirit, Henry Clay stepped up his campaign to get federal funding of internal improvements and to bolster the business and industry of the new West in partnership with the financial and manufacturing leaders of the northeast. He changed his mind on the role of a national bank and pushed for its support. It was not coincidental that his friend Colonel James Morrison, a Lexington hemp industrialist and benefactor for Transylvania University, was president of the branch of the Second Bank of the United States.

The national scandals surrounding the election of 1824 with the Jacksonian partisans charging Clay and Adams with crafting a "corrupt bargain," were tame compared to the verbal battles, tricks, and violence in Lexington. A particularly memorable event from this time was the "brick-bat war," which raged one day on the streets of Lexington. Men, probably drunk on the whiskey proffered by both parties, taunted each other to the point that they began tearing up the street pavement with crowbars and picks and were throwing the rocks at each other. Finally, Robert J. Breckinridge and Charlton Hunt, two opposing candidates in the local election, walked arm in arm, each waving a white handkerchief, down the embattled street between the combatants. The battle died away as the combatants saw the two young lawyers joining together to end the violence.

A slightly less violent episode happened after the Old Duke, Robert Wickliffe, celebrated at the closing of the polls after his win with the traditional "big treat" for his loyal constituents. The Old Duke placed a barrel of punch in the middle of Limestone Street and a National Republican partisan, ever thereafter known as "Doctor" Napper, slipped tartar emetic into the punch. The vomiting began almost immediately and the party-goers soon dispersed. As William Leavy described later in his memoirs:

> Such a scene as ensued beggars all description, and could hardly be limned
> with the pencil of a Hogarth. The retching and heaving, the sputtering, and
> spewing, and spouting with the two and seventy stenches, All well defined,
> and several stinks, which assailed the olfactories of the passers-by was due
> notice to give the participators in the debauch a wide berth. That was the
> last general political treat given in the interior of the state.

Besides horse racing, one of the more famous political feuds between Henry "the Great Compromiser" Clay and Andrew "Old Hickory" Jackson was the dispute over the funding for the upgrade of the Maysville Road. In 1830 Richard M. Johnson of Scott County (who was a Jacksonian supporter but like many of the elites in central Kentucky favored the American System), sponsored the Maysville Road Bill in a second attempt to extend the National Road from Zanesville, Ohio, to Lexington. Johnson insisted that federal funds should support this highly traveled road and thus "promote the common good" by providing north-south arteries to the great road that currently went only east-west. The bill had failed by one vote in the Senate in 1828, but under the leadership of Henry Clay, it passed in 1830. Jackson vetoed it for purely partisan reasons: it would have advanced the Whigs' American System. He also emphasized his belief that federal support for internal improvements was unconstitutional—sharpening the differences between Whig and Democratic political platforms and putting central Kentuckians into a quandary.

The 1830s proved to be an important watershed for Lexington. The Kentucky legislature appointed Transylvania University president Alva Woods and the Rev. Benjamin O. Peers to write a report on the state of Kentucky's educational needs. In November 1833 an education convention in Lexington drew up plans for a statewide common school system. The state made history when it allowed Lexington's female heads of household to vote in elections for school boards and school tax issues. It authorized the formation of two professional firefighting companies in 1830, and the business community felt well protected against the devastation of fire. In 1832 Lexington paid for a city marshal and more watchmen, and in 1835 they added a poorhouse to the workhouse and moved the joint institution to buildings on Bolivar

Street. The professionalization of organizations that provided these important city services did not take the place of private fire companies, volunteer patrollers, or benevolent societies, but firmly established the role of the city as keeper of the peace. The county government was insufficient for Lexington's growing needs, and rather than relying on the state-level representatives to pass special legislation, Lexington needed its own city government. The act to incorporate the city of Lexington passed successfully in the General Assembly on December 7, 1831. The system of city trustees changed to institute Lexington's first mayor, Charlton Hunt, who served as the city's executive officer as well as a chief judicial officer. Throughout the United States the largest cities were financing their own internal improvements such as the creation of waterworks, sewer systems, and large-scale municipal parks. Lexington was right in step. The separation from the old county court system was made clear in the original charter that gave city taxpayers immunity from county taxes and established a city court.

In Kentucky the county courts were the focal point of local government; if one faction controlled the county court, then that faction's members were assured the lucrative and politically powerful appointed offices such as sheriff, county clerk, and constable. The feud between the county and city heightened over the constitutionality of the City Court of Lexington. At first a suit by county residents successfully challenged the constitutionality of the City Court; however, city residents achieved a legislative triumph with a law that validated the court. However, in the face of continuing challenges, the city incorporation charter was amended to create a separate judge for the City Court. The twelve city councilmen were to be elected from six wards—two each—who would appoint the mayor and the city judge.

By 1833 Lexington had grown to more than 6,000 residents; that spring, as usual, the Town Branch overran its banks with the heavy spring rains. A cholera epidemic that reached from New York to Maysville the year before finally showed up in Lexington. Bourbon County lost eighty out of 1,200 people. In Scott County's Blue Springs it spread through the Choctaw Academy, taking ten Indian boys and fifteen slaves of Colonel Richard M. Johnson. The doctors were confident though that the disease could not invade Lexington, claiming that it was located in the midst of a beautiful, high, rolling, well-drained country. Dr. Drake of Transylvania distributed a broadside claiming that cholera was not catching: instead, he said, the disease was caused by some poison in the air from which one could not run away.

It started in the densely populated downtown area around the Town Branch, and half the town's population fled to their farms or those of relatives in the surrounding rural areas. The faculty of the Transylvania Medical Department bravely stayed behind to fight the outbreak, but their remedies were often more harmful than the disease itself. A recommendation for treatment for cholera symptoms was published in the Lexington *Observer and Reporter.*

Sir: We have succeeded in three cases amongst our servants with mustard and salt given in warm water as a puke. A Tbl of salt and the same of best sifted mustard infused into a half pint of warm water, taken when nausea of the stomach takes place; when puked take 25 grains of calomel and 25 grains of rhubarb and give as a purge. If patient is cramped rub with hot brandy and cayenne pepper, keep patient warm. We have not failed in a single case where properly attended to in time.

Dr. Dudley was the only one of six professors at Transylvania Medical School who never became ill throughout the epidemic. Of the twelve doctors in the city, three died within twenty-four hours of each other and three medical students lost their lives, including Alexander McCord from Alabama. In later histories, Dr. Drake blamed Lexington's high mortality on the doctors' large doses of calomel.

The dead were piled in front of the cemeteries in sheets or boxes, and there were not enough gravediggers to do the job. The Right Rev. Benjamin Bosworth Smith, the rector of Christ Church and newly consecrated first Episcopal bishop of Kentucky, along with the free black Baptist preacher Rev. London Ferrill of the First African Baptist Church, were among the few ministers who would tend to the job of shrouding the bodies and burying them. William "King" Solomon was an alcoholic vagrant whose labor was sold at public auction in 1833 to a free black business woman, whose name to readers of James Lane Allen's short stories was simply "Aunt Charlotte." He became a hero when the cholera epidemic hit the day after the auction and he began voluntarily digging the victims' graves. He died at the poorhouse on Nov. 22, 1854, and the whole community paid for a casket and later a monument.

Nearly 10 percent of the population of Lexington was wiped out; more than 100 white children were left orphaned and homeless. That summer, a group of elite Lexingtonians raised $4,400 to start the Lexington Orphan's Home. The home of Dr. James Fishback on West Third Street was the first site for this benevolent endeavor for poor white children who otherwise would have been roaming the streets. The management of the home relied on the fundraising efforts of prestigious women and young ladies of Lexington who served as its Board of Directors. The effects of the plague were devastating to the growth of the new city. Between 1830 and 1840 the population of Fayette County dropped about 2,000, and though this population loss was gained back in the next decades it was not enough to create the center of business and industry that the city promoters had envisioned.

Chapter Three

LEXINGTON, SLAVERY, AND

NATIONAL LEADERSHIP

Kentucky as a whole was not unlike the rest of the nation in that it was, in the main, a rural society. Kentucky farms were rarely more than 600 acres and relied on a diversified crop yield. By the 1840s, for example, Kentucky was second in the nation's corn production at the same time that Kentucky farmers and manufacturers produced one half of the national yield of hemp. Kentucky's slave population was larger and more widely distributed than in other "border" states. Kentucky gained its reputation, however, mainly as the major supplier for the U.S. domestic slave trade: an estimated 2,500 slaves per year were exported from Kentucky during the 1830s–1850s. This was even more remarkable since from 1833 to 1850 Kentucky made the importation of slaves for the purpose of selling them down south illegal.

Fayette County was the state's leading hemp producer, and one of the highest concentrations of slaves lived in that county. In fact, by 1860 Fayette County's population was only slightly more white than black. The tradition on Kentucky's farms was to use the task system; that is, the landowner or driver would list tasks to be completed by individuals or small groups, usually without direct supervision. When the slave accomplished these chores, the rest of the day was his or her own. Typical tasks were to hoe and weed a half-acre of tobacco, milk the cows, or exercise and groom the horses. It was not uncommon for slaves to take on additional tasks for their own profit, or to spend time learning valuable skills or crafts. Some farmhands could, during the off seasons, live in town and hire out their time. Examples of uses for farmhands in Lexington included labor in brickyards, in ropemaking or bagging factories, and as grooms at the racetrack. Once hired out, the slaves paid their owners the majority of their wages but could still accumulate wealth over time. Some slaves owned their own businesses, homes, fine horses, and livestock. Some were able to eventually buy their freedom, and to avoid having to leave the state, some became slaveowners themselves. Most African Americans in Kentucky did not experience the tedium of work that characterized the gang system prevalent in the deep south.

Only 20 percent of Kentucky's slaves worked on large farms with twenty or more slaves. The average slaveholder in Kentucky held no more than five slaves, and the hiring of slave labor even by non-slaveowners was commonplace. Most Lexingtonians did not own slaves, but those few who did knew that possession of slaves served as evidence of wealth, class, and prestige. Many Lexington elites felt optimistic for their economic future after the success of the Mexican War and the acquisition of new lands for speculation by slaveholders and commercially-minded entrepreneurs. Slavery served as the economic backbone of all modern cities in the United States, both northern and southern, and Lexington stood firmly in its role as a financial and commercial center for the slave trade.

Urban slavery looked and functioned differently than rural slavery. Whether a child, woman, or man, a slave in Lexington had many opportunities to gain a valuable skill, become educated, get hired, and begin accumulating cash and material goods that rural slaves could not imagine. Living in close quarters with the white population, blacks learned at a young age to maintain a certain decorum and behavior that would keep them safely out of view. Any white person could have a black person arrested and punished for the slightest infraction. This was not much different from other Kentucky towns during the 1820s and 1830s. In fact, some surrounding villages had even larger percentages of urban black population than did Lexington at 40 percent. Versailles, in nearby Woodford County, and Frankfort, the capital city, were both 48 percent black. Georgetown, with its bustling mills, foundries, and breweries, was 60 percent black. Meanwhile, the Ohio River city Louisville was just starting to bloom as an international port of entry, and a mere 20 percent of its population was black.

Bluegrass planters relied more on hemp, supplemented by animal husbandry, than on the tobacco or cotton that dominated the economies of Kentucky's sister slave states. The expanding ship industry in the east and the need for bagging for cotton bales in the south provided growing demand for hemp, and Kentucky farmers produced more than any other state. By the early part of the nineteenth century, over 40,000 pounds of raw hemp fiber were annually exported from Kentucky to the lower south. Cotton bagging factories and ropewalks sprang up all over town. Like the textile factories built around the same time in Lowell, Massachusetts, the Lexington rope and bagging factories were long and multi-storied. Usually the first floor consisted of the ropewalk and a room for combing the hemp. On the second floor was a spinning room and sometimes sleeping quarters for the slaves; the third floor held the looms for weaving the bagging, and the fourth floor was where twine was spun. Hundreds of hired slaves worked in hemp and ropemaking factories. Through the antebellum years, the hemp industry in Kentucky was an important part of the economy and increased the city's reliance on slave labor.

History books teach our children that American slavery hinged on the cotton market, but for slaves in Kentucky cotton was a foreign crop and synonymous with the horrors of the gang system and the violence of the fields and plantation homes of the rural deep south. Harriet Beecher Stowe developed the plot of her novel *Uncle Tom's Cabin*, popular in the 1850s, around this idea. Her interviews with Josiah

Lexington

Henson, a Kentuckian on whom she based her saintly main character, and her visits to Maysville and the nearby village of Washington helped her craft the opening scenes of the book. Stephen Foster, a Philadelphia writer of sentimental plantation songs for the racist minstrel shows popular in the north, picked up on this theme and produced a draft that was originally called "Good Night, Uncle Tom." The plaintive notes of the state song "My Old Kentucky Home," still bring tears to the eyes of white Kentuckians as they sing of the weeping slave mistress and her guilt at selling bondsmen to the cotton plantations of the south. However, the black communities of Kentucky feel very differently when they hear the song, and the myth of Kentucky slavery being somehow more benevolent than that found in the lower south jars against the brutal reality of bonded service in the upper south.

The emancipation movement in Kentucky started early and coincided with the birth of statehood, but despite this few in Kentucky—or for that matter, in the United States—endorsed racial equality. Even the anti-slavery advocate and Presbyterian minister David Rice, who titled Kentucky's first antislavery tract in 1792 *Slavery Inconsistent with Justice and Good Policy*, included in his arguments his fears of race mixing. He wanted Kentucky to stop the importation of slaves since blacks would eventually take control over the lazy white man, "subvert the government and throw all into confusion." Rice never freed his own slaves—nor did Kentucky as a state. It took federal troop occupation and a constitutional amendment to end slavery in Kentucky.

Kentucky's brand of abolitionism went national with Henry Clay's rise in political stature. The Kentucky Abolition Society had formed in 1808 and though it died out in 1827, a bill was introduced in the Kentucky legislature the very next year to prohibit the importation of slaves into Kentucky. The Emancipation Society was organized in Lexington in 1830, and during the heated political debates between the Democrats and the Whigs, the moral implications of being a slave owner was often a topic of conversation. As the ideological heirs of Thomas Jefferson and George Nicholas, most Kentucky politicians believed in the abstract that slavery was immoral: as an institution inherent to southern agriculture and northern finances, it destroyed the white man's republican virtues of independence and liberty. Some even would agree that slavery was unconstitutional, but all politicians agreed that blacks were not fit for white society.

The American Colonization Society, founded in 1817, seemed to federal leaders to be an answer to the issue. The U.S. government purchased land on the west coast of Africa near the British colony Sierra Leone, and the new nation of Liberia (literally "land of freedom") was established. The capital was named Monrovia in honor of then U.S. President James Monroe. Though the African-American political leaders and many white abolitionists protested, the colonization movement gained momentum and by 1820, a group of eighty-six African Americans were deported to Liberia. Henry Clay was the president of the national organization by 1822; local colonization groups started up in Kentucky as early as 1823, and by 1832 there were more than thirty local societies. Robert S. Finley, agent for the Kentucky Colonization Society, had his headquarters in Lexington and was very successful in his appeals for funds, food, and clothing for deportees. However, the supporters of this movement often met with suspicion and controversy from their neighbors.

In 1829 the hot-headed first-born son of Robert Wickliffe, Charles, took offense at the way his father, the largest slave owner in Kentucky, was portrayed in the Kentucky *Gazette*. He stormed into the editor's office to demand the identity of the anonymous author of the offending article. When he did not get the information, he shot the editor. Robert Wickliffe, who was a Democrat, asked the leader of the Whigs, Henry Clay, also a family friend, to defend his son in court. The clever tactic succeeded: the local jury acquitted Charles Wickliffe of the charge of murder. However, later that year Charles challenged the editor's successor—also Charles's best friend, James George Trotter—to a duel. Trotter killed Wickliffe on the field of honor, but he fell into a deep depression. He was placed in the local Lunatic Asylum, where he eventually died. For Lexington's elite families, the politics of slavery and personal honor were intertwined.

Though anti-slavery sentiment took many different forms, white Lexingtonians could not accept any middle ground. Those who were against slavery violated the general order of society. Henry Clay's conservative approach served as the foundation of the Missouri Compromise of 1820 and again for the Compromise of 1850. This stance also influenced a young Republican of the 1850s, Abraham Lincoln, a Kentuckian by birth and Lexingtonian by marriage. However, for many Kentuckians this was not too unlike the more radical talk of Henry Clay's distant cousin Cassius M. Clay. "Cash" Clay insisted that white labor opportunities suffered due to the presence of slavery and advocated gradual emancipation—though never black equality, of course. The Presbyterians continued to hold a more moderate approach by urging state leaders to regulate the slave trade and exhorting the God-fearing elite who could afford to emancipate their slaves by way of the Kentucky Colonization Society to do so. The Rev. Robert Jefferson Breckinridge wrote long columns advocating this stance in the Lexington *Reporter* in 1830, even though it cost him re-election to the Kentucky legislature. In 1831 Breckinridge called together forty-eight slaveholders to meet in Lexington that September to form a society whose members pledged to emancipate the future offspring of their slaves when they reached twenty-one.

Race relations soured as the anti-slavery movement gained prominence in Kentucky. With the increasing reliance on slave labor in both rural and urban areas, the landless white male either raged against the vulnerable slave he hired or the free black he saw on the streets of Lexington. Opponents of abolition feared that freed slaves would take jobs away from white breadwinners, and many white Kentuckians like Cassius Clay who grew up in these times came to think of African Americans as competing with white laborers for limited resources. Many Kentuckians who were anti-slavery were also anti-black and simply wanted African Americans evicted from the state. Most Kentuckians, and certainly most Lexingtonians, were pro-slavery. Thomas R. Marshall, a professor of law at Transylvania University, believed that slavery was actually good for blacks. He was trained in the science of the day, which taught that Africans were of a flawed creation, and that the genesis in the Bible was describing the creation of white people. He thought of African Americans as the children of heathens and barbarians—they were naturally immoral and child-like in intelligence. Marshall helped to put down abolitionists by saying that public safety was more important than civil rights like freedom of the press. As did many pro-slavery Lexingtonians, he wanted stricter government control of newspapers and voting.

Free blacks helped to counter such stereotypes, even though their numbers were small. Except for restrictions on food and liquor retailing, neither the city nor the state government passed laws denying African Americans the right to pursue particular vocations. The 1838 city directory shows black men were joiners, masons, porters, hack drivers, whitewashers, painters, road workers, shoemakers, and coopers. Seven of the eight barber shops listed were black-owned businesses. Two of Lexington's livery stables and several groceries were owned by blacks. Rolly Blue owned a blacksmith shop on Water Street. Free black women took in laundry and sewing, or served as nurses.

The British travel writer E.S. Abdy wrote in his *Journal of a Residence and Tour in the United States from April 1833 to October 1834* about a free black man whose wife and children were slaves in Lexington. They lived together except for one child who was taken away by her master. The owner of this man's other children not only forced him to bear the cost of housing them, but also to pay the poll tax on them. Although African Americans had a vulnerable family life, some were able to find ways to stay together. Women accounted for 50 percent of the free blacks who were listed as heads of household in the 1820 census; even though this percentage decreased slightly to 45 percent by 1860, it seems clear that free black women tended not to marry as often as white women of the day. In 1850, according to Debow's *Statistical View of the U.S.*, the illiteracy rate for Kentucky free blacks over the age of twenty was 55 percent—in comparison to 20 percent for Kentucky whites. At the same time, the Fayette County 1850 census showed thirty-eight free black residents had attended school within the previous twelve months. Also, a school for free blacks existed as early as 1840 in Lexington, with B.B. Smith schoolmaster. By 1860, the number of free African Americans who had attended school within the past year dwindled to only eight. Finding the leisure time and safe environment to go to school was becoming harder and harder as race relations became more politicized. Unlike in many other southern cities, free blacks in Lexington mingled regularly with slaves and maintained a common sense of community. In May 1843 the Colored People's Union Benevolent

Society, No. 1 was started "to promote the happiness of our fellow beings; to disseminate, support and sustain moral principles; to foster and encourage civilization." Free blacks also attended the four African-American churches. By 1856 the First African Baptist Church had more members than any other church, white or black, in Kentucky. By the time of the Civil War, Kentucky's free black population ranked third among the slave states that remained a part of the Union in 1861 and seventh among all slave states and Washington, D.C.

However, with the fear of slave conspiracies like the Nat Turner rebellion in Virginia and the rise of radicals such as William Lloyd Garrison who advocated immediate emancipation, Lexington beefed up its patroller laws. Since the sons of the elite could often hire substitutes to take their place in the rolls, the men who became patrollers generally were from the working classes. They saw this as a way to help maintain order and control within their community, and the law was on their side. In Lexington, free blacks were required to carry their papers with them at all times. If any unknown African American could not produce these papers, he or she would be taken to jail as a fugitive—and if not rescued in time, could be sold at auction. Any slaves caught on the streets after the watch bell rang at 7:00 p.m. would receive thirty-five lashes on the bare back at the public whipping post. This post, at the northeast corner of the Fayette County Courthouse yard, was said to be twelve inches in diameter and more than seven feet high. By 1847 a new whipping post was needed, so the Fiscal Court ordered a three-pronged poplar tree in the yard to be officially established as the new one. A public whipping by the sheriff's men could bring crowds of spectators.

Unfortunately the patrollers could also use their power over slaves (and free blacks) for their own purposes. They spied on slaves, broke into their cabins to arrest them, raped women, and often beat the most vulnerable. When they went too far, however, there was often a price to pay. On February 27, 1831, the fiddler and erstwhile schoolteacher Henry Hensley hosted a dance for blacks in a rented building on a local farm. He was trying to make money since his school was closed on account of the winter snows. He either collaborated with the patrollers to close down the party at midnight—or he forgot to arrange it with them to continue past the legal curfew. Nevertheless when the captain of the patrol, Levin Young, heard about these "disobedient" African Americans who were out after curfew, he gathered his men and deputized more to create a posse of fifteen. They reached the old farm outbuilding at midnight, surrounded it, and ordered the dancers to surrender. The party-goers blew out the lights and tried to escape: some out the windows and others up through the ceiling to hide in the oats stored in the loft. The patrollers started after them, tying them up and shooting into the open windows. When all was finally calm, Young discovered among the many wounded that Charles, a slave owned by John Brandt, was dead. He had been killed by a gunshot wound to the head. Brandt sued in the Fayette Circuit Court and gained a $500 judgment from the owner of the farm where

Lexington

Hensley had his schoolhouse. Interestingly, the farm owner, Benijah Bosworth, won his appeal in Frankfort, claiming that he had had no prior knowledge of the party.

Some African Americans in the Lexington area went on to be famous in the anti-slavery circuit. Many of us today know about Josiah Henson, a Kentuckian from Davies County whose autobiography is said to have been the basis for *Uncle Tom's Cabin*. But during the nineteenth century, many Americans knew of William Wells Brown, a famous author and orator who had been born and raised in the Lexington area. In a narrative of his life as a slave, he wrote about his enslaved mother Elizabeth, who told him that she was a daughter of Daniel Boone and a slave mistress. She told him his father was a white slave owner, George W. Higgins. The family moved to St. Louis where he was hired out because of his embarrassing resemblance to his master's white nephew. In 1830 he worked for the abolitionist Elijah P. Lovejoy at the St. Louis *Times*. Later he was sold to a merchant and then to a riverboat captain.

Brown escaped in 1834 to Ohio where a Quaker by the name of Wells Brown helped him. After reaching Cleveland he became part of the anti-slavery movement, attended Black National Conventions, and began teaching himself to read and write. In one year he helped sixty fugitives reach Canada. In 1847 he and his wife Elizabeth (Betsey) Schooner separated and he moved to Boston with his two daughters. There he published his story of his life as a slave. The *Narrative of William W. Brown, A Fugitive Slave*, was first published in 1847 and expanded the next year to sell 8,000 copies in two years. Brown was one of several who represented the American Peace Society at the world Peace Conference in Paris in 1849. He remained in Europe for the next five years, researching in the archives of England and France and also visiting the West Indies. He also helped to found and run in 1852 the London newspaper *The Anti-Slavery Advocate*.

His novel *Clotel; or The President's Daughter*, published in Europe in 1853, was the first by an African American and scandalized the world with its barely fictionalized account of a biracial daughter of Thomas Jefferson. By putting the black offspring of President Jefferson at the center of his novel, Brown put in print what the Hemmings family alleged for so many years before DNA analysis of the Jefferson family's black descendants finally provided proof. But by the time it was published in the United States in 1864, all references to Jefferson had been removed from *Clotel*.

Published in 1863, Brown's *The Black Man*, a set of historical and literary essays, traced the African origins of black Americans in a heroic effort to explode contemporary myths of blacks' "natural inferiority." He included fifty-three biographical sketches of artists, teachers, actors, poets, preachers, lawyers, rebel slave leaders, and rulers of Haiti and Liberia. He portrayed Nat Turner as the model for action needed in the south during the Civil War. This book underwent ten printings in three years. For the rest of the nineteenth century Brown continued to write, producing more history books, a collection of songs, and many plays, one of which was published.

Lexington, Slavery, and National Leadership

In 1833 the General Assembly passed the Slave Non-Importation Law, which made it a crime to transport slaves into Kentucky. Any slave owners who immigrated to Kentucky after 1833 had to certify within sixty days that their slaves were "for their own use" and not for sale. In 1840, the Fayette County clerk recorded such a document in the Fayette County Deed Book:

> I, Tobia Gibson [of Louisiana], do solemnly swear that my removal to the
> state of Kentucky was with the intention of becoming a citizen thereof and
> that I have brought with me no slave or slaves with the intention of selling
> them, so help me God.

In the same year that the Non-Importation Law went into effect, the Kentucky Colonization Society's first expedition to Liberia began. Of the 150 freedmen who were sent down the Ohio River to New Orleans for their transatlantic journey, seven were from Lexington. Their story is worth telling. It begins with the story of Milly, a light-skinned African American born into slavery in the household of one of the founders of Lexington, Colonel John Todd. Colonel Todd was already dead in 1803 when Milly was born. Her mother Anaka was a slave of Todd's widow, Jane Hawkins Todd Irvine, and lived with her on a farm called the Pond Tract on the Boonesborough Road (now called Richmond Road) two miles east of the center of Lexington.

Jane had only one child of her own, Mary Owen Todd, who even as an infant was heir to the John Todd lands and one of the wealthiest people in Kentucky. Mary, fondly known as "Polly," married James Russell at age seventeen. Eleven months later her son, John Todd Russell, was born. After a few tumultuous years of marriage, Polly became a widow at the age of twenty and moved back into her mother's home. Milly probably grew up in very close proximity to her multi-generational white family in the two-story log cabin, eating and working side by side with her white masters.

Jane Irvine separated from her second husband and moved to Crawford County, Illinois to be with her Hawkins relatives sometime after 1808 when she emancipated Betty and Cynthia, Molly, and Jenny. According to the deeds surrounding the Irvine separation, Milly belonged to Jane's father and so was still a slave when she moved to Illinois with Jane. There she nursed Jane in her old age, learned how to read and write, and perhaps even dreamed of earning her freedom and being a teacher. In 1817, Milly had a baby and named him Alfred Francis Russell. Alfred was white to all who looked at him, but for those who knew he was the son of a slave—he was black.

Jane Todd Irvine died in 1822 and Milly still legally belonged to the household of James Hawkins, Jane's father. He also died in 1822, and Milly was put in the keeping of Littleberry Hawkins, James's grandson. In 1825 Littleberry sold Milly and Alfred to a slavedealer in Louisville, J.B.R. McIlwain, in order to settle James Hawkins's estate. Jane's daughter Polly privately bought Milly and Alfred for $650 from the slavedealer on April 8, 1825, and brought Milly and eight-year-old Alfred to her mansion Glendower, in Lexington.

Milly continued her studies this time with "Mrs. Polly." Polly was a very religious woman, an important founding member of the Presbyterian Church in Lexington. Her contributions to Lexington's society did not just include work for the education of blacks; she also contributed the land for the Lunatic Asylum that served as a refuge for people who were mentally unstable, impoverished, or others who couldn't stay in their families' homes because they were too disabled. In addition, she helped start an orphanage for the poor white children of Lexington.

In 1826 Polly married Robert Wickliffe, the largest slaveowner in Kentucky and the state representative of Fayette County. Wickliffe took young Alfred with him when he went to Frankfort for the political sessions. There, Alfred was exposed to the art of politics and learned how to take an active role in a democratic government. In September 1827 Polly Wickliffe transferred by a strawman tripartite transaction all her claims to her Todd estate lands and even relinquished her dower claims. However, she maintained her property right to seven of her slaves, including Milly and Alfred.

Probably under her strong influence, Robert Wickliffe agreed to serve as president of the Kentucky Colonization Society (KCS) in 1828. The idea was to send free and freed blacks to Liberia in order to help Christianize Africa, and at the same time the freedmen could create a new black nation separate from the whites who enslaved them. These sentiments abound in the KCS Annual Meeting reports. One resolution states: "that, in our opinion, the successful progress of African Colonization has established it as the best developed scheme of benevolence to advance and elevate the condition of the free colored population of our country in all the relations of moral, social and political life." In another resolution, the KCS affirmed "that since the cause of the American Colonization contributes emphatically and powerfully to establish and propagate civilization and Christianity in Africa, it should be dear to the friends of Christian missions."

In 1832 Polly finally promised the KCS that she would set her remaining slaves free and send them to Liberia. The trip cost approximately $25–$40 per person and it wasn't until 1833 that the Kentucky Colonization Society raised enough money to send 119 Kentucky African Americans to Africa.

In March of 1833, Milly and Alfred left Lexington along with their cousin Lucy Russell and her four children (Sinthia, Gilbert, George, and Henry). They had in hand their precious freedom papers; Milly probably had a Bible and maybe a daily devotional. They walked to Frankfort where they were put up for the night at Mr. Gray's. That night a friend of Polly invited them all to dinner, and afterwards Milly wrote a long letter of thanks to her former mistress. The letter reveals her fear of being one of two women alone with children—it was not until later that Milly's husband George Crawford joined them on the journey to New Orleans. (The letter has been transcribed as written, complete with misspellings common to most literate individuals in the antebellum era of Kentucky, whether white or black.)

March 10 1833 Saterday night

My Dear Misstress we have all arrived at frankfort in safety and health little George Lucy and all the children are well. My dear Misstress how shall we thank you for all your kindness too us. We sometimes despond being all females and children haveing no male protecter of our own. but we try to put our trust in the Almighty and go on in his srength. whatever betide us. My Dear Mystress you have done your whole duty. and may the [Almighty] bless and reward you a thousand fold. Lucy all love and thanks to you for your goodness care and kindness to us all. the children all desires me remember them to Mystress.

    Mystress we all desire you thank Mayster for his goodness and kindness to us. I hope the Lord will bless him give our love to miss Margaret miss Mary Mys Sally Wooly and all our friends. the Lord has raised up manny friend to us in fankford we are treated with so much kindness by all who see us. the gentleman at whose house we now lodge Mr Gray trets us with the utmost kindness—he had us all in his dining room prayed with and for us—the gentleman you wrote too received your letter recommending us to him he took us home with him gave us supper and we returned again mr grays you will hear again from us att Louisville May the bless preserve and reward you for all kindness is the prare of your unworthy but affecunate servant

Milly C

    The following day they traveled on to Louisville where they boarded a riverboat (the *Mediterranean*) and sailed down the Ohio and Mississippi Rivers to New Orleans. There they were joined by twenty-seven other emigrants from Tennessee, Ohio, and Louisiana.

    On April 20, 1833, they finally boarded the brig *Ajax* with many other deportees finally totaling 146—according to the ship's logs there were thirty-one men, forty-two women, and seventy-four children aged twelve and under. They were mostly farmers: 119 of them were from Kentucky and only sixteen were born free, the rest were freed. Together with the white missionary A.H. Savage and H.D. King, agent for the Tennessee Colonization Society, they finally began their sea journey. According to the Lexington *Observer & Reporter* of June 27, 1833, their number included "a female slave brought up by Mrs. Wickliffe, who possessed a superior education and gifted mind, and was intended for a teacher in Liberia. With her was her son Alfred who was to become a minister." The *Ajax* lost thirty to forty people to cholera while still anchored off New Orleans, and they were forced to stop after only two weeks at sea because of cholera, whooping cough, or bowel disorder, staying on a West Indian island. During the passage thirty people died, mostly children.

Lexington

They arrived in Liberia on July 11, 1833, after three months on the *Ajax*. They were immediately put under quarantine and eventually sent to Caldwell and Millsburg on the St. Paul's River (formerly Bassa country). Twenty-six more settlers died, two others returned to the United States, and one emigrated to the nearby British colony Sierra Leone. There were few houses ready for them to move into, not much food to buy, and no other doctors besides Dr. Mechlin, who was in charge of the whole colony.

Milly started a vegetable garden right away and soon her husband George joined her. Many of the immigrants died within the year. Lucy and all her children got very ill from malaria, and when they got better her daughter Sinthia, her two elder brothers, and Alfred got infected sores on their legs and arms. According to letters from Lucy, Sinthia did not keep her wounds clean and in 1836 the doctor felt he had to cut off one of her limbs in order to help her body heal. She died soon after the amputation. Lucy's sons were so sick that they could not work on a farm to support themselves. Lucy worked for a few months as a cook at Caldwell for a poorhouse and managed to feed and house her children; she cut up her own clothing to make new clothes for her family. Soon thereafter, she met a man she loved and married him. Her son Gilbert died in 1839.

The next year another Kentuckian, David Richardson (ex-slave of W.L. Breckinridge) sent a letter to his friend William Tucker in Lexington:

> I am very well pleased with this county and I believe we can make a good living here if we are industrious. We have settled on a ten-acre farm and are carrying on after the manners of the place—raising corn, potatoes, cassava, plantains and bananas which is very good food. I would advise anyone coming to this place to bring everything necessary, such as money, clothing and cheap cloth—knowing that in every new country these things are scarce and very dear.

Most of the settlers however simply traded with the native Africans for corn, wood, and palm oil, which they would trade again with the merchant vessels that came ashore. Few settlers worked at farming.

Alfred must have worked on a coffee plantation owned by Rev. Colston M. Waring, Baptist minister from Virginia, since he later tried growing coffee when he was a landowner himself. He hurt his leg somehow, maybe with a hoe, and the wound became so infected that he limped along with a crutch for several months. Although Mrs. Polly had sent money for Milly to use in Africa, the white minister who was the colony agent used it himself for needed equipment. When the equipment came by ship, it was stolen and Milly and Alfred never saw any of it. Lucy never received any of the money that Mrs. Polly sent her either. Milly and George made a living probably from farming and trading and kept Alfred in school to be trained as a teacher.

Eventually he was trained as a minister and went into the nations far inland to preach about Christianity "on the Goulab and Pessa lines." While he was away his mother Milly died in 1845 of "dropsy"—general swelling of the body due to kidney disorder. Alfred said in a letter to the Wickliffe family that his mother died of the "scours," which was the result of worm infestation of the lower intestines; either or both could have led to her death. A year later her husband George died suddenly.

In 1847 a constitutional convention removed the American Colonization Society from any official position in the Liberian government though missionary societies still held strong influences. Also by 1847 the Kentucky Colonization Society raised $5,000 to buy a new colony, forty square miles and fifteen miles from Monrovia on the north bank of the St. Paul River. They named it Kentucky in Liberia and Clay Ashland was the name of its capital in honor of Henry Clay and his farm. To help people live in the new colony, the society promised to pay not only for their transportation but also a living wage for six months after their arrival. Each head of a family was promised a building lot in the town along with five acres of land or, if the settler chose to live two miles from town, the society would provide fifty acres. If three miles, one hundred acres of land.

By 1855 Alfred Russell owned a beautiful 200-acre farm located on the St. Paul's River, and had built a brick house he called Russelton. The Old Duke wrote that year to Russell for the first time. Russell wrote back saying he was surprised to hear from him and sad to hear that "Mrs. Polly" had died. He wrote that he and the other children who came with him to Africa "had been reared like spoiled children and not servants, and if our parents or aney one else wated to give us a deserved whipping we flead to Mrs Polly, believing that the whole State of Kentucky could not take us from beside her chair. Who can forget that Blessed woman? her form and kindness is still fresh in our Memories." He told of his cousin Lucy who was sickly and unable to do much except knit. Lucy lived often with Russell but also lived with her son Henry who had built up a ten-acre farm in Caldwell, and with his brother George who ran a saw mill and made shingles for houses. He also grew sugar cane and sold the sugar for trade as rum. Henry had three children: Isaac, Lucy, and Alfred. His wife was "one of the descendants of the people sent out by the Breckenridge's, a girl born in the Atlantic." Henry also fought with the British troops against the Africans, going into battle at least eight times. George had four children and named the oldest girl Mary Jane Owen after the two women related to Colonel John Todd of Lexington.

By 1862 Russell was an Episcopalian minister and reported that there were 1,200 Africans converted by the missionary societies and that the churches and homes could not hold all the congregants who wanted to attend church. In 1877 Alfred Russell was elected vice president of Liberia under President Anthony W. Gardner. He was re-elected for a second term as vice president, and when Gardner resigned in 1883 Russell took over as the seventh president of Liberia. His term ended in January of 1884 and he died on April 4 of that year.

Lexington

Colonization efforts began to decline under the combined pressure of protest from the black political leaders and the rising costs of emancipation and emigration. Even with additional subsidies from the Kentucky legislature in 1856—an appropriation of $5,000 annually—the scheme could not be sustained. By 1859 the Kentucky Colonization Society disbanded: during the thirty years of its existence, it had sent only 658 settlers to Liberia. It is not surprising that Clay's dream of a compromise on the issue of black citizenship did not work. Lexington was at the center of the nation's slave trading business, and the mild effects of a colonization movement did not affect the larger trends of slave life in Kentucky. Lexington's landlocked location (in the center of the ten largest slaveholding counties of Kentucky) with armed patrols and slave jails all around made it an ideal spot for slave traders. A successful trader could clear $100 to $150 per individual successfully carried from Kentucky to southern markets like Natchez or New Orleans.

Lewis C. Robards was probably the most successful of the Lexington-based traders. He did most of his work from a long building of slave pens or "coops" on Broadway. The pens were eight feet square, seven feet high, with brick floors, small barred windows near the roof, and iron-grated doors facing Mechanics Alley. Other dealers opened slave jails in downtown Lexington: James G. Mathers had one on East Main Street and John Mattingly used Megowan's jail on the corner of Short and Mulberry (now Limestone) Streets.

The lucrative nature of the slave trade in Lexington resulted in fierce competition among dealers. They did not hesitate to take advantage of the helplessness of their victims: the more ostentatious display of African-American nudity, the more numbers of potential buyers would gather around. The slaves would be put on display outside near the auction blocks beside the county courthouse. Sometimes an enterprising slave dealer would use a more discrete environment for public viewings and physical handling of the slaves. Robards leased, then eventually bought the old Lexington Theatre on West Short Street and converted it into a slave jail. In an adjoining building he imprisoned selected female slaves in luxuriously decorated apartments where prospective buyers could interact with the women more privately. Senator Orville H. Browning wrote of his visit to these apartments:

> Many of the rooms are well carpeted & furnished, & very neat, and the inmates whilst here are treated with great indulgence & humanity, but I confess it impressed me with the idea of decorating the ox for the sacrifice. In several of the rooms I found very handsome mulatto women, of fine persons and easy genteel manners, sitting at their needlework awaiting a purchaser. The proprietor made them get up & turn around to show to advantage their finely developed & graceful forms—and slaves as they were, this I confess, rather shocked my gallantry. I enquired the price of one girl which was $1600.

This dehumanization and flagrantly inhumane treatment did not go unnoticed. It was the subject of many debates in Lexington during the 1830s and 1840s. When Robert Wickliffe, the Old Duke of Fayette County who served as the first president of the Kentucky Colonization Society, spoke before the women's auxiliary of the Lexington branch of the KCS, he praised the society for not interfering in the relationship between master and slave. Robert J. Breckinridge, a staunch anti-slavery proponent and Presbyterian minister, denounced the idea that the colonization movement could be neutral or that its members could remain pro-slavery. He described slavery as an evil that should be ended through gradual emancipation and then removal of African Americans to Liberia.

When others concurred with Breckinridge, Wickliffe left the society. In the summer of 1840 he resigned his seat in the Kentucky legislature as senator from Fayette County. He was disappointed about his repeated failure to garner enough support to repeal the Slave Non-Importation Law, and felt he should state publicly his opposition to the Whig clubs in his county who were tending toward the opinion of Henry Clay's advocacy of gradual emancipation. Clay had begun to promote the idea that if Kentucky got rid of slavery, then land values would rise, new jobs for white men would be created, and manufacturing would increase. Breckinridge delivered a speech in the Fayette County Courthouse yard in Lexington that celebrated Wickliffe's resignation, reiterated his position on emancipation, and with personal attacks on Wickliffe's administration of Breckinridge's father's estate, further inflamed the bitter feud between these two local pundits.

In an intensely personal series of public pamphlets, the two men continued to take verbal shots at each other. Sometimes issuing second printings of a speech, they would include depositions and additional evidence to bolster their claims. For two years they raged against each other in public and in print. They accused each other of being cowards, liars, and of being "amalgamationists" (urging racial unity through natural evolution or breeding). Breckinridge wrote: "Your charges, though utterly unfounded, were at first of a public character; but now they have degenerated into private accusations of a nature so scurrilous, that no gentleman should print them even if they were true; and being, to his own knowledge false, no man could utter them who was not lost to all sense of self-respect." Wickliffe responded in a speech and then wrote that Breckinridge "has after a period of nearly twelve months, by the instigation of the Devil, again brought himself into notice, not by meeting me, face to face, before the tribunal he once selected, but by meanly pouring forth his filth through the prostituted columns of the Lexington *Intelligencer* and the Louisville *Journal*. . . . I know, full well, that he that wrestles with a skunk must receive some of its odour." Breckinridge had the last word with his pamphlet with the following longwinded title: "The Third Defence [*sic*] of Robert J. Breckinridge against the Calumnies of Robert Wickliffe. In which it is proved by Public records, by the testimoney [*sic*] of unimpeachable witnesses, and by the declarations and oaths of the said wickleffe [*sic*], that his accusations are, within his own knowledge, destitute of truth."

Accusations of interracial mixing or "amalgamation" accompanied almost every conversation about ending slavery or emancipating individuals. Preoccupation with sex is not just a twentieth century phenomenon. The duels in Lexington were not only with words. The men of Lexington were ready to take up pistols at the proverbial dawn. Interestingly, the roles of women in these rituals were also important not only as objects of discussion within the language of honor, but also as participants crafting the rituals. A good example of how a Lexington woman functioned as an important political actor is in the story of the duel between Robert Wickliffe Jr. and Cassius M. Clay in May 1841. An important letter by Margaret Wickliffe Preston to her husband's brother-in-law, the famous A. Sidney Johnston, affected the outcome of the honorable exchange. She used her political skills not in the courts or elections but by clearly affecting the mainstream political outcomes. She brought in one of the most venerated warriors of southern culture. Johnston took charge of the ritual and so averted Cash Clay's usual reliance on fisticuffs. In the spring of 1841 Clay ran against Bob Wickliffe, "The Young Duke," in a race to represent Fayette County in the state legislature. In a public debate in late April, Bob Wickliffe referred to the antipathy of Cash Clay's own in-laws to his presumptions of abolitionism, and he implied that Clay was simply an ignorant dupe of northern agitators. Clay took exception to the mention of his wife as "inadmissible" and challenged him to a duel. Clay was renowned for his physical violence, and Margaret Wickliffe Preston knew that any male ritual to "save face" was not just a metaphor. She wrote to Johnston of her "unbounded confidence" in his "courage and discretion" and asked if he would function as her brother's "friend and adviser." She wrote to him, she said, "without consulting anyone" but she knew that her family would agree with her plea and feel gratitude for his presence as her brother's second.

Her brother would succeed if he showed not only superior marksmanship, but also his manly valor and cool demeanor under fire, his status in his choice of seconds and a negotiator whose version of the events afterwards would be acceptable to all. Wickliffe and Clay met at "Locust Grove" near Louisville; Colonel William R. McKee was Clay's second, and Johnston was Wickliffe's. According to Johnston's statement of events, the first shot "was exchanged which proved ineffectual." Clay insisted then that his honor was not restored, and he still demanded satisfaction for the insults he claimed he had received from Wickliffe during the public debate. Another shot was demanded, "which was promptly accorded."

While the seconds were reloading the pistols, they negotiated whether or not the "point of honor was satisfied." During this verbal exchange, they discovered that Clay was indeed satisfied "on the point in issue relative to the Father of Mr. Wickliffe Jr. but was not satisfied on an [*sic*] another point, namely the manner in which R.

Wickliffe JR had alluded to Mr. Clay's wife in public debate." In an addendum, Wickliffe wrote a long explanation that he had not known that a perceived insult to Mary Jane Warfield Clay was the point of honor since Clay had "not specified any particular ground for the challenge," and that had Wickliffe known this, he would never have exchanged shots with him but would have publicly apologized immediately for introducing a lady's name in public debate. Bob Wickliffe had assumed that the honor of his father was at stake, and he was ready to die for the reputation of the Old Duke—just as his older brother Charles had done in 1829. The men retreated from the field, but no verbal reconciliation between the two satisfactorily reestablished their honor. As Clay wrote about it forty-five years later, "we left the ground enemies, as we came."

The aftermath of the duel was as important as the exchange of shots and documents among the men present at the field of honor. Wickliffe wrote to William Preston, his brother-in-law, and assured him that he had defeated Clay and his political backers. By inference Clay had lost the challenge, both of the duel and of the political campaign, since he had not whipped his enemy but backed out of the duel: "even the bullies and blacklegs no longer speak of him as the 'Little Black Bull with hair on his back three inches long.' " Bob Wickliffe alluded to his reverence for A. Sidney Johnston and that there was still evidence of portending violence: "The question to be decided at the next election is one of 'victory or death' and I intend to be prepared at all points."

In June he wrote a triumphant letter to Johnston telling him that the statement of events had been signed by John Rowan Jr., his other second, but more importantly to relate to him "the best thing that has ever been said of the difficulty between Clay & myself." He wrote that during a large gathering of elites from central Kentucky, the details of the duel were being discussed and a "lady with great naiveté" spoke out: "La! Isn't it strange that Mr. Clay did not think of his wife until after the first shot? I think he ought according to every rule of gallantry to have fought first for his wife and then for himself. Now suppose Mr. Wickliffe had shot Mr. Clay, why then Mrs. Clay's honor would have been unavenged!" Clay was thus publicly exposed, and the duel continued in the sense that a woman implied that Clay was a trickster, a sly manipulator, a man without honor. This elite woman's public speech had humiliated Cash Clay, and Bob Wickliffe was exultant. Not coincidentally, Wickliffe won the election; Mag Preston masterfully orchestrated the cast of characters in the duel and perhaps it was she who had landed the final blow with the clever quip at the assembly. The Wickliffe-Clay duel involved not just the exchange of bullets, but also the verbal record that Johnston constructed. And Johnston would not have been there without Margaret Preston's letter. The men involved in this elite ritual knew of the importance of women in its full performance in the public realm of an exclusive and elite world.

The presidential elections of 1844 were bitter campaigns and Lexington celebrated with barbecues, assemblies, and torch-light processions. On Saturday, July 20, the

Lexington

Democratic Party organized a grand procession through the streets of Lexington complete with militia in full regalia, bands, banners, "polk-stalks," and "game roosters" who were in charge of putting up the tall hickory pole in memory of the liberty poles of the Revolutionary era. The parade was crowned with a long series of speeches by such great orators as Senator John Pope and Chief Justice Thomas F. Marshall. The very next Saturday the Whig Clubs of Fayette County organized a grand "tableaux" parade with floats that depicted each of the local businesses and industries that supported the expansion of Clay's American System. The Whig Ladies Clubs could participate in these tableaux, and the costumes must have been spectacular. It would have been quite exciting for Lexingtonians to watch with all the flags, the drums, and shouting, "Hurrah for Clay!" This parade ended with an elaborate ceremony in which the Whig Ladies presented banners to the male leaders of the Clay clubs. Clay's loss of the presidential elections was a bitter one, and his supporters were sure that the old charges of political corruption from his first presidential candidacy in 1824 had followed him through the second race in 1832 and again in 1844. In a speech in Lexington on September 9, 1842, Clay had expressed his anger at the negative campaigning by his rivals and the power of this old charge: "My error in accepting the office tendered me arose out of my underrating the power of detraction and the force of ignorance, and abiding with too sure a confidence in the conscious integrity and uprightness of my own motives."

His less famous distant relative Cassius M. Clay tried to establish himself in Lexington as a newspaper editor. Cash Clay was an anti-slavery leader who had supported the Non-Importation Act of 1833 and helped turn back efforts to repeal it. Nevertheless, he refused to allow anyone to call him an abolitionist—he was famous for his eye-gouging, ear-biting fights where he might pull his bowie knife on his opponents. Clay accepted the legality of slavery and was a slave owner himself, but denounced the "peculiar institution" because he thought it was destroying Kentucky's economy, particularly for nonslaveholding whites. He used statistics extensively in his many speeches to show how Kentucky's economic development was lagging behind free states such as Ohio. He focused in particular on the role of female slaves as producers of future slaves, and advocated the cause of gradual emancipation of African-American women by 1860 (later he changed this deadline to 1900).

A personal story explains best, however, how he really felt about black women slaves. When his young son suddenly became ill and died after three weeks of terrible suffering, Clay suspected the boy's slave nurse Emily of poisoning his child. Emily lived under the suspicion of murder for two years before being indicted—she was constantly watched and often accused of other crimes by her masters. While she awaited trial, Clay, convinced of their guilt too, sent her mother, brother, and sister to the New Orleans slave market. In spite of the general feelings against her, a proslavery jury found Emily innocent, but Clay sold her south anyway.

His fear of skilled and articulate African Americans was one of the main thrusts of his newspaper *True American* in its first issue on June 3, 1845. He warned that slave insurrections would destroy Kentucky and that Kentuckians had to rid themselves of their dependence on black labor. He suggested easing the conditions for Kentucky's slaves and granting political equality to free blacks. His articles described his opinions about many specific Lexingtonians whose livelihoods relied on slaves, and the personal attacks were most likely his own undoing. While he was ill with typhoid fever in mid-July, a mob gathered around his office on North Mill Street to destroy his printing press. He had anticipated Lexington's response to his new paper—he had a long history of being attacked during his fiery speeches in many communities—so he had equipped the building with small cannon, guns, pikes, and even a keg of powder to blow up the building if necessary. However, his feebleness from the fever emboldened his opponents, who feared his deadly anger.

Professor Thomas F. Marshall of Transylvania, a strong pro-slavery advocate and a Kentucky chief justice, made a long speech to the crowd. Marshall defended the suppression of the newspaper by saying public safety was the superior law (above the Constitution's Bill of Rights regarding freedom of the press). He said that Clay had become the tool of northern abolitionists and that outsiders should not run Kentucky affairs. "Such a man and such a course is no longer tolerable or consistent with the character or safety of this community. . . . the negroes might well, as we have strong reason to believe they do, look to him as a deliverer. . . . A Kentuckian himself, he should have known Kentuckians better." A committee of men from both political parties approached his sickbed and served him with a writ of seizure. He had no choice but to give them the keys to his office. They then, under protection of the Lexington police and the city marshal, dismantled and safely packed up his press and—all expenses paid—shipped it to a particular house in Cincinnati that Clay had requested of them. Clay was able to sue the committee members and won a judgment for $2,500, which was then paid by several local political clubs. However, Lexington's black population was not treated so royally. The day after the *True American* was dismantled, several of Lexington's free blacks were brutally attacked by white mobs who supported Professor Marshall's ideas.

All the African-American population of Lexington knew how easily they could fall prey to a mob determined to keep fear in their hearts and submission in their demeanors. All knew the tightrope they must walk to keep safe as slaves or free persons in a slave owning state. At some point, however, the siren call for freedom entered everyone's mind. It was just a matter of timing, good connections, and incredible luck to answer the call. One of the more famous Lexington escapes happened in 1844. Though many focus on the role of the white abolitionists who helped orchestrate the charade that started the fugitives on the road, the story is best told from the vantage point of the people who "stole" their own freedom from their slave owners.

Lexington

Lewis Hayden was born into slavery in 1816 in the household of Rev. Adam Rankin of Lexington. His wife was Esther Harvey, a slave of another Lexingtonian, the merchant Joseph Harvey. When she became pregnant, Harvey and her son were sold to Henry Clay. Soon thereafter Clay sold Esther to slave traders and she was never seen by Lewis again. He met and married Harriet Bell, also a slave in Lexington who had a young son, Joseph. Meanwhile he was bought and sold himself several times to other Lexingtonians of the mercantile class. Finally he was hired out as a waiter to John Brennan, the owner of the elegant Phoenix Hotel in downtown Lexington. There he was able to make enough money from tips to take his wife and seven-year-old child out of Kentucky. He also was able to make important acquaintances and carefully ask the right questions of travelers in order to understand what roads led to freedom. He learned that simply running north across the Ohio River was not enough and that he had to connect with the right people to make good his family's escape. He and Harriet decided to take the quickest route to reach the best conductors in the Underground Railroad and to cross the border to Canada.

In September of 1844, Lewis Hayden met with Delia Webster and Calvin Fairbanks to plot his family's escape. Webster was probably a regular at Brennan's establishment: she was a schoolteacher from Vermont who was the principal for a girls' school (which later came to be known as the Sayre Female Academy). Webster introduced Hayden to the minister from Ohio, Fairbanks, whose activist energies were fueled by his connections with abolitionists, black and white, at Oberlin College. Hayden hired Fairbanks to scope out the Maysville Road for safe resting places, to assess the security measures at the thirteen toll booths they would need to pass through, and to find the famed Underground Railroad conductors in Ripley, Ohio.

They left by carriage on a Saturday, two days before Hayden's lease with the Hotel was to expire. They at first pretended to be Webster's servants, but when they crossed the Ohio on the ferry, Hayden was the driver and his wife stayed in the carriage with her face veiled and their son hiding under the seat. They headed to the home of Eli Collins and then on to the village of Red Oak where the abolitionist family of Archibald Hopkins helped put them on the "road"—traveling by wagon hidden under farm produce or in a false-bottom wagon bed—to Lake Erie. There they paid their way across on a steamboat and found freedom at Amherstburg in Canada. Hayden wrote a letter to one of his former masters in Lexington, exactly four weeks after the Haydens had crossed the Ohio River:

> Mr. [Lewis] Baxter,
> Sir you have already discovered me absent. This will give you notice where and why—I never was a great friend to the institution of robbing and crushing slavery and have finally become sick of the whole concern and

> have concluded for the present to try my freedom and how it will seam [*sic*] to be my own master and manage my own matters and crack my own whip. . . . I also at length concluded to try how it will seem to walk about like a gentleman, my share of the time I am willing to labor but am also desirous to act the gentleman with all the important mien that attaches to a man who is indeed a truth, himself, the self, identical to the very living Being of whom Lock wrote in his essays. . . . So farewell—Any communication after this had best be sent to the British North American Institute on River Sydenham, the Colored People's College.

Hayden went on to become an important activist in the abolitionist cause. He served as a stationmaster on the Underground Railroad, facilitated the rescue of the escaped slave Shadrach in Massachusetts, and participated in the conspiracy that culminated in John Brown's raid at Harper's Ferry, Virginia. At the start of the Civil War he worked to recruit soldiers for the black regiments. His son Joseph, who had enlisted in the Navy, was killed in action.

One of the greatest ironies of United States and Kentucky history was the declaration of war against a democratic Mexico in May 1846, not long after the newly independent Mexican government had abolished slavery. White Kentuckians saw the Republic of Texas as an important part of their American Dream. They might want to go west someday and claim the land as their own for economic advancement or just to have their own large farm denied to them by the Money Kings of Kentucky. The war fever was high: the excuse was that the Mexicans had attacked a detachment of troops under Gen. Zachary Taylor, a Kentuckian, at the Rio Grande. Governor Owsley proclaimed that Kentuckians should organize militias and in answer to his call, Lexington formed two companies of cavalry. The blustery orator Cassius M. Clay was voted captain of one of the companies, and was promptly captured with ten of his men when they reached Mexico. Clay spent his time in Mexico in prison. Many of the Kentuckians were killed at the Battle of Buena Vista in February 1847, including Henry Clay's son, Lieut.-col. Henry Clay Jr. For the funeral procession in Frankfort that next summer, Theodore O'Hara wrote the "Bivouac of the Dead," which is today printed in the Lexington paper every year on Veteran's Day.

The conquest of Mexico only intensified the debate over slavery and Kentucky served as a cross point. In 1848, seventy-five slaves escaped from Lexington and the surrounding farms and headed for the Ohio River and freedom along with Patrick Doyle, a Centre College student. A $5,000 reward was offered for the runaways, and soon nearly one hundred men were chasing after them. With reinforcements, they surrounded the fugitives in a hemp field in Bracken County only a few miles from the river. Doyle was brought back to a Lexington jail in irons, and the slaves were imprisoned in Brooksville, the county seat where they were captured. Doyle was sentenced to twenty years of hard labor in the state penitentiary.

Lexington

By 1849 the debates in Kentucky abolitionist and pro-slavery camps had escalated to the constitutional convention where Kentucky's third constitution was being drafted. There the state legislature repealed the Non-Importation Act of 1833 and bowed to the slave-trading lobby. The Kentucky Constitutional Convention conceived of a new statement for the 1850 constitution making ownership of slaves "an absolute property right . . . the right of property is before and higher than any constitutional sanction, and the right of the owner of a slave to such slave and its increase is the same and as inviolable as the right of any property whatsoever." Free blacks, mulattos, or any freed persons were to leave Kentucky or go to jail. Many slaves who were freed thereafter were not given their freedom papers so that they could stay in Kentucky; many freed bondspeople bought relatives so they could remain in the state as slaveholders themselves.

The Fugitive Slave Law signed by President Millard Fillmore on September 18, 1850, meant that free blacks were at an even greater risk of being kidnapped and sold to the cotton fields. For African Americans in Lexington and the surrounding areas it was often an advantage to stay where all in the community knew them. In 1850 when Kentucky had nearly 211,000 slaves, only ninety-six fugitives were reported; in 1860, with more than 225,000 slaves the reported fugitives numbered 119. Alongside white abolition societies, a multitude of African-American self-help groups geared up to oppose the effects of the new federal support for slaveowners. The age-old vocation of bounty hunter gained new importance as a patroller could solicit the help of federal marshals to capture an African American who was identified by the patroller as a runaway slave.

A new interest developed in Kentucky-bred bloodhounds used for hunting down people on the run. Some Kentucky farmers unabashedly began "breeding" slaves for the purpose of selling their children. Many of these unscrupulous men also had no problem selling their own children begotten from their raping of their female slaves. A famous episode occurred in Lexington in 1843 that highlighted this practice. Eliza, a servant who was "white with dark lustrous eyes, straight black hair and a rich olive complexion," stood on the auction block. Her mother was a slave in a Lexington household, and though Eliza had been given a good education, good clothing, and healthy food all her life, she was to be sold to the highest bidder. News of this potential sale was widely advertised and on the day of her auction, it is estimated that 2,000 people crowded into the county courtyard to watch. Calvin Fairbanks, a Methodist preacher and abolitionist activist from New York, bid for her purchase so as to set her free. His final competitor in the bidding process was a New Orleans trader who wanted Eliza for her value in the mulatto prostitute market down south.

According to the stories about this incident, there was a pause in the bidding around $1,450. The auctioneer was certain that he could get more money for her purchase price, so he pulled open the front of Eliza's dress to expose her breasts. The bidding continued half-heartedly to $1,475, then the auctioneer lifted her skirts to bare the rest of her body. He slapped her thigh and taunted the crowd to bid more for "this prize." Finally, the abolitionist Fairbanks won the bidding war at $1,485 and hurried her out of the view of the excited crowd. According to his memoirs, Fairbanks thought the sale of Eliza was one of the most extraordinary incidents in his work as an activist in Kentucky. He was acting on behalf of Salmon P. Chase, an ardent abolitionist who later served as Abraham Lincoln's secretary of the treasury, and Nicholas Longworth of Cincinnati, who authorized him to bid as high as $25,000 if necessary.

The Old Duke, Robert Wickliffe, had a carriage waiting and they were driven to a nearby house where her free papers were made out. It seems incredible that this wealthy slave owner would help a radical abolitionist in this quest. However, in his letters about this incident, Wickliffe expounded upon the immorality of slave trading and in particular the horrors of the dehumanizing use of African-American women's bodies for the titillation of the common man. Wickliffe claimed he never sold any of his slaves, and researchers have yet to find any evidence that he did.

The crafting of the Compromise of 1850, a part of which was the Fugitive Slave Law of 1850, proved to be the death of Henry Clay. He visited Lexington briefly during the summer of 1850 but upon his return to Washington, D.C. his health deteriorated rapidly and he died on June 29, 1852. The bells tolled in Lexington as soon as the telegraph was sent, and after a long funeral trip by train, his casket reached home on July 10. There a huge procession accompanied his hearse from Ashland to Christ Church and then on to the Lexington Cemetery. Every business was closed and the storefronts were draped in black. A huge golden eagle draped in black was hung high across Main Street with garlands and banners floating down almost to the heads of the marchers. The procession was accompanied by the firing of minute guns, the tolling of bells, and mournful band music. The glittering costumes of the Lexington fire companies, the Freemasons, the Odd-Fellows, Sons of Temperance, and the militia were in stark contrast to the somber dress of the clergy of all denominations, the state legislators and judges, lawyers, and school teachers. A few years later a huge monument including a column 120 feet high serving as a pedestal to his statue was completed in a central location in the Lexington Cemetery, and his body was reinterred there. The larger-than-life statue that faces back toward Lexington's downtown area can still be seen over the tall trees in the Cemetery's beautiful park-like venue.

The great divide over slavery was complex and Lexingtonians took many different stances. The status quo could not be maintained, and in the words of a great Kentuckian, Abraham Lincoln, the nation could no longer exist half-free and half-slave. In 1860 Lexington's population was counted at 9,521 within a county population totaling 22,599. A militia group called the "Lexington Rifles," first organized in 1857, were the first in 1860 to report to Governor Beriah Magoffin in defense of the state and as part of the state guard. The Lexington Chasseurs, another militia company, organized on May 9, 1860 in the grand jury room of the County

Lexington

Courthouse. On the Fourth of July, Miss Abby Stewart presented the Chasseurs with a flag and after the military review, the public was given a reading of the Declaration of Independence, a long speech, and a big barbecue.

David A. Sayre, a Lexington banker of humble origins, wrote to William Preston, the U.S. ambassador to Spain, on August 6, 1860 (the spelling is his own):

> You will feal my friend greatly greved in returning to your country and find it engaged in a wicked sivell war of the most Vishus kind—Our State as yet stands Nuteral and I hope will hold to her nuteralety and the only independent State that is North or South as we are yet free in Kentucky. As you pass thrugh New York and Washington lern all you can but do not make up or express your oppinions eather Union or Disunion but wate untill you get home and loock about you and see whare you wood wish to stand.

Preston was an appointee of the Democratic President James Buchanan, and with the contentious Presidential election of 1860, Kentuckians with any political ambition struggled to find a foothold. The States Rights candidate and current vice president was a Lexingtonian, John C. Breckinridge. He was a popular moderate who campaigned on an anti–Douglas Democrat, pro-Union, pro-slavery ticket. Though Lexington voted for Breckinridge, Kentucky went for the Constitutional Union ticket headed by John Bell of Tennessee. The Bluegrass elite did not represent the rest of the state, which firmly rejected any hint of secessionist sentiments that fall.

The Crittenden Compromise was one of several last-ditch efforts to resolve the secession crisis of 1860–1861 by political negotiation. Authored by Kentucky Senator John Crittenden (whose two sons would become generals on opposite sides of the Civil War) it was an attempt to resolve the crisis by addressing the concerns that led the states of the lower south to contemplate secession. "Congress shall have no power to abolish slavery in places under its exclusive jurisdiction, and situate within the limits of States that permit the holding of slaves." The Compromise, as offered on December 18, 1860, consisted of a preamble, six proposed constitutional amendments, and four proposed Congressional resolutions.

On December 28, 1860, Preston's nephew, William Preston Johnston, wrote to him about the bad conditions at home and urged him to return soon:

> Nobody is getting any money. The Banks are playing the devil. Trade is utterly prostrated. Everybody says disunion is inevitable. The most ultra Union men are now the loudest for secession. I knew it wd be so & have had no hope since August. You must come home immediately. This is the last money we can possibly raise I think. . . . South Carolina has seceded by ordinance. [Kentucky Governor] Magoffin is utterly unequal to the emergency. It was not until yesterday that he could be persuaded to call

together the Legislature to convene Jany 17th. He had an idea that this crisis was got up for his benefit, that the Deluge is a shower, and that he could settle the whole matter himself & be handed down as the Great Pacificator [Henry Clay]. You will see that he mistook the times & the man.

Lexington, at the crossroads of major turnpikes and on the L&O railroad line, in the heart of the most fertile land in this militarily strategic area, was at great risk. Yet her most passionate warriors soon left to join the action far away, and her merchants and bankers were left with only the inadequate local police force to protect their businesses. Her slave population both hoped for and feared the coming war: everywhere panicky white citizens were seeing insubordination and insurrection in the slightest reaction from an African American. It was a time of nervous expectation and fear that everything—and everyone—would change completely.

Chapter Four

CIVIL WAR, MILITARY OCCUPATION, AND "READJUSTMENT"

Like many in the border states, Kentuckians were divided in their allegiances as the events of the 1850s led toward secession. Political leaders on both sides of the impending crisis assumed that Kentucky was rich in supplies needed by soldiers, particularly in food, forage, and horses. As a crucial slave trade stop on the way west, Lexington relied on governmental support for slavery and internal improvements and could not afford to go to war. Her native sons continued to seek political solutions in the spirit of the Great Compromiser, Henry Clay. At the same time, the town's love affair with the pomp and honor of the military, an important part of every local celebration, fed the ranks of new military groups. Besides regular drilling to keep their movements sharp and snappy for public displays in their bright uniforms with tail coats, braided trousers, cross-belts, and fancy hats, the military companies sponsored banquets where speakers could expound their political views. They organized balls and assemblies where the elite could admire their costumes up close and talk informally about politics, the astonishing rise in the prices of slaves, and the stagnation of the hemp industry.

Three new companies formed in Lexington as the national political rhetoric about slave insurrections and secession heated up. The Lexington Rifles organized in 1857 and elected John Hunt Morgan as captain. They drilled in a city out-lot locally known as the "little college lot" near Transylvania University in an area still used by the city as a commons area, the Gratz Park. In 1859 the Ashland Rifles formed and chose as their captain Robert J. Breckinridge Jr., the son of the abolitionist Presbyterian minister. The Lexington Old Infantry, commanded by Captain S.W. Price, gained a political ally in the formation of the Lexington Chausseurs in 1860, under the command of Sanders D. Bruce. They drilled in the lot near the courthouse, at Cheapside. These latter two companies went mainly to the Union when the time came to choose sides, while the Rifles, almost to a man, joined with the Confederacy.

The Presidential election of 1860 put a Lexingtonian on the national ticket for the second time. John C. Breckinridge, a former Whig and popular orator on states rights, Kentucky-style, had served as the nation's youngest vice-president under James Buchanan. He was the favorite of the Southern Democratic delegates and tried in vain to get his rival Democrat nominee, Stephen Douglas of Illinois, and the Constitutional

Union nominee, John Bell of Tennessee, to withdraw. He hoped to merge the factions and find a compromise candidate who would unite them against the Republican candidate, Abraham Lincoln. Douglas, a favorite of the Northern Democrats, and Bell, elected by former Whigs and Know-Nothings, feared that their constituents would vote Republican rather than support a candidate who looked too much like a secessionist. Breckinridge, alarmed at the growing factionalism, held a barbeque at Ashland on September 5, 1860, and the crowds swelled to an estimated 15,000. He spoke for three hours, denouncing Douglas as an opportunist and the Republican Party for ignoring the principles of the Compromise of 1850 and the Supreme Court's Dred Scott decision. From his—and most Lexington voters'—perspective, the Southern Rights party held true to the original intent of the nation's Founding Fathers and thus the new Republican Party was the party of disunion.

In November Breckinridge came second to Lincoln with seventy-two electoral votes to Lincoln's 180. Though Breckinridge had won in Lexington, the Constitutional Union ticket won the popular vote in Kentucky. The powerful role of John J. Crittenden of neighboring Woodford County, a former governor and four-time senator for Kentucky solidified the Constitutional Union's message of patriotism and aloofness from party bickering. Crittenden served on the U.S. Senate's famous Committee of Thirteen, which could—like the House of Representative's Committee of Thirty-three—find no compromise to the growing sectional crisis. On December 18, 1860, only two days before the historic South Carolina convention's vote for secession from the Union, Crittenden proposed to re-invigorate Henry Clay's Missouri Compromise line of latitude (36°30') and the centerpiece of the Compromise of 1850, the Fugitive Slave Law. The proposal was defeated both in committee and before the whole Senate. In February of 1861, James Guthrie of Louisville, chairman of the compromise committee of the Peace Convention in Washington, tried to resurrect Crittenden's proposal but it was defeated there as well.

In April, Breckinridge spoke before the Kentucky legislature and called for a border state conference to find a way to appeal to moderates in the North and help halt the rising popularity of state conventions for secession. He had been elected to the U.S. Senate after finishing his vice-presidency and Lexington saw him as her most valuable orator in these contentious times. Before the convention could be held, however, Confederate forces in Charleston fired on Fort Sumter. The fort's commander, Major Robert Anderson, was also a Kentucky son and though he surrendered to the Confederates, he became a hero for Unionists. Governor Beriah Magoffin was a staunch Breckinridge Democrat, advocating stronger government support for slavery and emphasizing the constitutional right of a state to secede; when President Lincoln called for four state regiments from Kentucky, Magoffin refused. The Unionists of Kentucky agreed and Crittenden spoke in Lexington on April 17 endorsing neutrality for the state.

Lexington

In May, the Kentucky legislature adopted a policy of "armed neutrality"—holding herself independent of both sides, protecting her borders against both sides and asking them both to "respect the inviolability of her soil"—though Breckinridge was sure that it was both impracticable and indefensible. Nevertheless the State Rights advocates bowed to the active campaigning of the Unionists in the summer elections, and the total vote for a Union sweep of elective offices was less than half of the number cast in the 1860 presidential election. Recruits for both armies began quietly leaving Lexington in groups of two and three.

President Lincoln called for a special session of Congress to convene on July 4, and Breckinridge gave one of his most important national speeches that reflected well the beliefs of moderate Lexingtonians who feared the over-reaching powers of the Union's federal governmen:

> I think, sir, that this war is prosecuted, according to the purposes of a majority of those who are managing the legislation that leads to its prosecution, for objects of subjugation. I believe that, unless those States which have seceded from the Federal Union lay down their arms and surrender at discretion, the majority in Congress will hear to no terms of settlement, and that those who may attempt to mediate will speak to the winds. I believe, therefore, that the war, in the sense and spirit entertained by these gentlemen, is a war of subjugation. The eminent Senator from Ohio [Mr. Sherman], not less conservative than a majority of the organization with which he is connected, went so far, in the warmth of his feelings, the other day, as to declare that, unless the people of certain States in the South yielded willing obedience, he would depopulate them and people them over again. That I call not only a war of subjugation, but a war of extermination. . . . I know that the rampant spirit of passion is abroad over the land, and I know there are many here and elsewhere who have staked their all upon inflaming it, and keeping it inflamed to the frenzy point. The day is not yet, but it draws nigh, when a terrible accountability will be rendered by those who are plunging their country into the vortex of ruin, under the pretense of maintaining the Constitution and the laws. Peace, sir, peace is what we want for the restoration of the Federal Union and the preservation of constitutional liberty.

That same month, Simon Bolivar Buckner, a Kentucky legislator and leader of the Kentucky State Guard, traveled with Crittenden to Washington to get Lincoln to reaffirm his position that he would not invade Kentucky. They feared the U.S. government's Department of Kentucky would garner many recruits at the camps across the Ohio River: Camp Joe Holt near Louisville and Camp Clay near Newport. What they didn't know was that even as Lincoln promised that he currently had no intention of sending troops into the state, 5,000 "Lincoln guns" were on their way to loyal Unionist militia in Kentucky for distribution by Major Gen. William "Bull" Nelson. Buckner's State Guard had sixty-one companies but it was increasingly becoming associated with the States Rights Party, and the Unionists had organized a Home Guard that desperately needed federal assistance to survive. Lincoln knew that the best way to woo Kentucky was to give her federal assistance, and the Central Committee of the Union Party in Kentucky had Lincoln's ear. Richard M. Robinson offered the use of his farm at Hoskins Crossroads in northern Garrard County for setting up a recruiting station for the Union army, and General Nelson received the federal gun shipment at this site, named Camp Dick Robinson. Though the Garrard County residents generally accepted Union troop presence, Lexingtonians showed their displeasure at this violation of Kentucky neutrality.

On the morning of August 21, 1861, 200 federal cavalry under Colonel Thomas Bramlette rode into town from Camp Dick Robinson to receive the shipment of Lincoln guns arriving on the Louisville train. According to Reverend Pratt, who recorded the scene in his diary entry for that day, they stopped at Beard's stable on Short Street and a loud bugle blast sounded from the top of the armory of the Lexington Rifles. This signal was immediately answered by tocsins from rival companies of the Lexington Light Infantry and Chausseurs from the steeple of the courthouse, and instantly militia members rushed to their respective armories and mustered for a fight. Members of the Unionist Home Guards even brought out an old brass cannon that had served to this point for celebrations on the Fourth of July. The streets were full of people. Senator Breckinridge and the respected Lexington lawyer Madison C. Johnson spoke to the crowds and helped avert violence. The cavalry loaded their wagons and departed for their camp thirty miles away in Garrard County.

Kentucky as a state did not secede from the Union; however, sixty-three counties in western Kentucky tried—setting up a Confederate government at Bowling Green in the fall of 1861. Several Lexingtonians attended the meetings and Robert J. Breckinridge Jr. served as the Fayette County delegate. The Breckinridge family is a good example of the horrendous split among families over the impending war. Even though the Reverend Breckinridge had exemplified the Unionist feelings of many in the border states with his powerful speech on "The Day of National Humiliation" in Lexington on January 4, 1861, his sentiments did not necessarily influence his kin. On the Fourth of July that year his eldest son, Robert Jr., led the Ashland Rifles out of Lexington to form the first organized Kentucky volunteers for the Confederate States of America. A few months later his nephew John C. Breckinridge, former vice president of the United States, left to become a Confederate general and the secretary of war of the Confederate States. A year later his second son Willie left to join the South, as did two sons-in-law. Two of his youngest sons and three other sons-in-law joined the U.S. Army, thus exemplifying the horrors of "the Brothers War."

Lexington

Six military companies of the Bluegrass, which in 1860 had become the First Regiment of the State Guards, set up Camp Buckner at the old trotting track under the command of Col. Roger Hanson: Lexington Rifles, Lexington Old Light Infantry, Governor's Guard, Flat Rock Grays, Lexington Chausseurs, and the Bourbon Rangers. They paraded together, both pro-State Rights and pro-Unionist, on the Fourth of July with the old gusto—bayonets fixed, music blaring, and flags waving. At the same time, the first organized delegation of volunteers left Kentucky for Camp Boone in Tennessee: the Ashland Rifles became Company B, Second Kentucky Infantry, C.S.A.

The month of September, 1861 was an important turning point in Lexington's history. On September 19 her citizens observed the arrival of the first Federal troops, 1,500 strong. Under the command of Colonel Bramlette, they marched into town that morning and pitched their tents at the Lexington fairgrounds, a commons area that belonged to the Kentucky Agricultural and Mechanical Association, near the southern edge of town (about where the main administration building now stands on the University of Kentucky campus). Reverend Pratt wrote about them in his diary, describing them as "a hard looking set of creatures."

The next day, Col. Frank Wolford's regiment of Kentucky cavalry encamped on the outskirts of Lexington. Clashes between soldiers and citizens began to occur. A squad of union soldiers passing in front of the old Phoenix hotel was fired upon from an upper window. In a few minutes the hotel was surrounded by a battalion of infantry, a troop of cavalry, and several pieces of field artillery. They searched the building but did not find the shooter, according to an article in the *Kentucky Statesman*. The next Sunday, two men were wounded when they passed by one of the camps and shouted, "Hurray for Jeff Davis!" Orders soon came to disarm all the local militia—charging them for being disloyal. The federal officers accused those drilling in Lexington of "buying and stealing all the powder and lead they can get even tearing up lead pipes" from the streets. Union troops camped on the courthouse square and artillery was placed on the green at Cheapside.

That night, on September 20, Captain Morgan of the Lexington Rifles sent a few of his men to the armory as a decoy while the rest of the company quietly slipped out of the city with the arms packed into wagons loaded with hay. Tom Logwood told the story to Lexington historian C.R. Staples in an interview on May 22, 1930: "After we got clear of Lexington, we hurried on until daylight and then we went into a barn and stayed all day. We all agreed not to tell whose barn we stayed in." Early the next morning, a company of Union soldiers rode in from the fairgrounds to seize the arms of the Rifles. They were greeted by a crowd of hecklers, who taunted them when the armory turned up empty. Later that evening, Morgan and about twenty more of his Rifles left Lexington to support the formation of the provisional Confederate government in Bowling Green.

Civil War, Military Occupation, and "Readjustment"

Shortly thereafter the 14th Ohio, under Col. James B. Steadman, came into Lexington on the Kentucky Central Railroad—the first Federal troops from out-of-state to reinforce the Union troops in Lexington. They camped at Botherum, the house of Madison C. Johnson, a friend of Abraham Lincoln and lawyer for the Todd family. Confederate flags and emblems disappeared from the city streets for fear of being targeted as disloyal. Transylvania University's Morrison Hall, dormitories, and the Blythe house were used by the Union authorities for military lodgings and hospitals. The old medical hall was used for classroom space and only high school classes were offered for the duration of the war. Union commanders occupied the Bodley house in Gratz Park.

Lexington was under strict military rule. Martial law included denial of freedom of speech and of the press, the right of assembly, and the writ of habeas corpus; soldiers stood at the polls to prevent southern sympathizers from voting. The Democratic newspaper, the *Kentucky Statesman*, whose editor Thomas B. Monroe Jr. had served as Governor Magoffin's secretary of state, was shut down. Its last issue of September 24, 1861 was particularly caustic: "Who then has betrayed you? Whose minions flaunt their flags in your faces and shriek their partisan cries in your ears? Lincoln! Lincoln! Lincoln!"

Warrants for the arrest of pro–States Rights orators were issued. James Brown Clay, Henry Clay's second youngest son, had just lost the election for state office from Fayette County and finally left his wife and ten children to join his friends in the secessionist south. He was captured in Madison County. It was a somber moment for Lexingtonians of every political stripe when he was paraded through town along with 16 other prisoners from Camp Dick Robinson to the federal prison in Louisville. Reverend Pratt wrote in his diary: "I felt sad at the spectacle to see the son of the distinguished statesman brought through his mother city and not permitted to visit his family or to speak to anyone . . . but he had no business to defy his state or the military." In October Lieutenant Rittenhouse of the First U.S. Artillery opened a Union recruiting office on the corner of Short and Cheapside. Certain community leaders felt obligated to state openly their support for the office, including Madison C. Johnson, Hiram Shaw Sr., Sanders D. Bruce, Benjamin Gratz, David A. Sayre, Dr. Robert J. Breckinridge, Judge William C. Goodloe, and Dr. Ethelbert Dudley.

At the same time, opportunists welcomed Union occupation. Many Lexingtonians besieged the White House, hoping that their native daughter Mary Todd Lincoln would lobby on their behalf for presidential appointments. Mary Lincoln was our first "First Lady," so dubbed by the London *Times* for her "statesmanlike tastes." However, the fact that some of her Kentucky relatives, including several of her half-brothers, fought for the Confederacy, aroused suspicion against Mrs. Lincoln. Henry Clay's son Thomas successfully lobbied Lincoln himself for an appointment of Hiram Shaw of Lexington to serve as army paymaster.

Lexington

That winter, Lexington society seemed to enjoy the influx of new men and federal money. John Wilkes Booth starred in a run of performances of Shakespeare's *Richard III* at Lexington's Opera House, and the winter season of balls and assemblies bustled in both pro-Union and pro-Confederate homes. The women of Lexington did more than just dress up for social events, however. Their traditionally strong involvement in the community continued. For example, the "Union Ladies of the city" advertised in the *Lexington Reporter and Observer* for donations of clothing and supplies to the Soldiers Aid Society, and asked farmers for "a load of wood, potatoes, turnips, etc." for the wounded and sick who were filling up the military hospitals.

Union troops were encamped at "Pralltown" and anywhere else that had large trees and good fences that could be used for stove wood and campfires. Seventy-two African-American volunteers were quartered in the Clay engine house. The Union regiments stationed in Lexington were the 14th Ohio, 112th Illinois, 4th Ohio cavalry, 33rd Indiana, 48th Pennsylvania volunteers, 35th Kentucky U.S. infantry, 1st Ohio heavy artillery, 7th Rhode Island infantry, 22nd Wisconsin volunteers, 11th Michigan cavalry, 45th Ohio, and 11th Kentucky infantry. The violence inherent in armed men sitting idle most of the time in military camps soon evidenced itself. On the evening of December 18, 1861, the amphitheater at the fairgrounds was discovered to be on fire—rumored to have been started by recruits of Colonels Grisby and Anderson. A crowd gathered and a sentry approached a soldier in the crowd, Lieut. Joel D. Hickman of Mundy's cavalry, and told him to produce his pass. Hickman refused and started to tease the sentry, saying he was a "Secesh" and needed none. When the sentry challenged him again and received the same reply, he killed the lieutenant with a gunshot blast to the chest.

Francis Peter, daughter of Dr. Robert Peter, the Transylvania University professor who was supervising the Union military hospitals, was nineteen when she began writing her diary chronicling her observations of Civil War Lexington. She wrote in her entry for March 20, 1862:

> The secesh are getting pretty high here. The other day when some rebel prisoners passed through here, a great crowd of them went down to the cars & hurrad for Jeff Davis and made a great fuss over the scamps. It is said they expected them for some days & had even got a dinner ready for them. . . . The secesh ladies have also had a sewing society and have been supplying the rebel prisoners. Gen Halleck sent an order here that hurraing for Jeff. was not to be allowed.

Lexington was the hub of an Federal army supply route, and wagon trains traveled to and from the Cumberland Gap, sometimes as many as fifty wagons a day. It was also covertly serving the Confederate armies desperate for resources. The Union had shut down most of the Mississippi River trade, and the only railroad running north-south through Kentucky, the Louisville & Nashville, was totally unprepared for the increased traffic. Slave sales continued on Cheapside. Mule traders corralled large herds on Deweese Street between Main and Constitution Streets and used a paddock on Bruce Street for grazing.

Sometime during the spring of 1862, John B. Castleman organized a company of forty-one men at his mother's farm to join Confederate Captain John Hunt Morgan. As Castleman's men approached the Confederate camp in Tennessee, the legend is that the soldiers knew they were Kentuckians because, "they're all on Denmarks," the great foundation sire of the American Saddle Horse. Castleman was one of the great breeders of this distinctive riding horse—the breed's arched neck, high stepping gait, and calm intelligence were as highly valued as its renowned strength and endurance at high speeds over rough terrain. Morgan's own mount was the famous Black Bess, a beautiful mare whose pedigree was a cross between a Canadian pacer and a Kentucky Thoroughbred. Black Bess, like most horses in the Civil War, soon became a casualty, and the six-foot tall Morgan was given Glencoe Jr., a son of the great Thoroughbred Glencoe. His brother-in-law and second-in-command Basil Duke wrote: "Did you ever see Morgan on horseback? If not, you missed one of the most impressive figures of the war." Though Black Bess was reputably Morgan's favorite horse, the general is portrayed astride a stallion in the monument on the Fayette County Courthouse lawn. An interesting Lexington tradition for college boys in the mid-twentieth century looking for a prank was to paint the horse's genitalia red—perhaps in protest that Black Bess was not remembered instead!

Morgan's first Kentucky raid with his mountain squadron of about 900 troopers started out from Knoxville on July 4, 1862, and swept through central Kentucky. Union Gen. Jeremiah T. Boyle, the military commander of Kentucky stationed in Louisville, sent a wire to Mayor Hatch of Cincinnati: "Send artillery to Lexington and as many men as possible by special train without delay." By July 12 Mayor Hatch had sent 500 men. Brigadier Gen. William T. Ward, commander of Lexington, posted notices that read: "all able-bodied citizens of Lexington and Fayette County report themselves at the courthouse square forthwith. Those having arms will bring them; those having none will be armed." One thousand horses were impressed for mounted duty, taverns were closed, and merchants boarded up their shops. All citizens who sympathized with the southern cause were ordered to stay off the streets and remain in their homes. Major Bracht, provost marshal, wrote, ". . . everything here seems stagnant and three fourths of the stores and manufacturers are closed; every face wears a sickly, frightened look; men speak to each other of Morgan as though his name were to them what that of Richard the Lion Heart was to the Saracens. . . ."

On July 13, 1862, Lincoln sent a wire to the Union commander General Halleck, "They are having a stampede in Kentucky. Please look to it." The military rule tightened as Morgan took control of the villages around Lexington, recruiting local men, capturing Home Guards, stealing horses, destroying bridges, and looting government stores. Many of his unit were Lexingtonians who visited family members as they came through. But Lexington had about 3,000 troops under the command of Col. Leonidas Metcalf and Gen. Green Clay Smith, so Morgan turned south and avoided the city.

Reverend Pratt wrote in his diary on July 20, 1862: "The blockade has been enforced here for a week and no persons save the military are permitted to pass on the streets without a pass from the military authorities, or to go out of town. Soldiers and Cincinnati police patrolling the streets . . ." Stores were closed in midafternoon and all the saloons were closed. Mayor C.T. Worley urged all loyal citizens to join the 4 p.m. drills every afternoon with the Home Guards and most all the professional men of Lexington did—though many without guns. Suspected southern sympathizers, or any males not associated with a Home Guard, were not permitted on the streets after 4 p.m. The military provost-general, Maj. F.G. Bracht, issued an order by mid July that all homes should be locked up and lights out by 9 p.m. Military law remained in place until July 22.

These restrictions were not particularly out of order. General Boyle had already issued a proclamation that southern sympathizers in any county would pay for damages done to loyal citizens; the Kentucky General Assembly had passed many laws to restrict basic freedoms. Loyal oaths, for example, were required not only of public officials but also of teachers, ministers, and jurors. Both the Confederate and Union occupying forces used the oath as a loyalty test in Kentucky, and often in an arbitrary way. Gen. Jerry Boyle encouraged a thriving business in bribery when he insisted on oathtaking: civilians might have to swear their loyalty ten times a day and pay $1.25 for the privilege of having the provost hear it each time. The most despised loyalty policy in Kentucky was that which required tradesmen to pay 20¢ for a certificate proving they had taken the Congressional iron-clad oath. Franklin T. McCallie, who lived on Versailles Road, wrote in his diary on June 25, 1862: "Today I took the oath of allegiance to King Lincoln . . ." A descriptive phrase used for suspected southern sympathizers was "galvanized Yankee," that is, someone who had taken the iron-clad oath so many times that it was meaningless to them. Overall, it was clear to civilians—especially in towns—that taking the oath of allegiance would not insure they would be able to stay or that refusing to take it would automatically mean banishment.

Hostile crowds, perhaps also angry at the military restrictions on commerce in reaction to Morgan's raid, threatened to burn down the houses of Confederate sympathizers. Major Bracht let it be known that he could not protect the homes of Henrietta Morgan and her sister Eleanor Curd, female kin of the notorious Confederate raider, and that they should leave the state. But Morgan and his raiders had so fired the public's imagination that schoolchildren on both sides recited poems about them. The Unionist rhyme was: "I'm sent to warn the neighbors, he's only a mile behind. He's sweeping up the horses, every horse that he can find. Morgan, Morgan the Raider and Morgan's terrible men with bowie knives and pistols, are galloping up the glen." On the other hand, southern sympathizers' children chanted: "I want to be a cavalryman, and with John Hunt Morgan ride, a Colt revolver in my belt, a saber by my side. I want a pair of epaulets to match my suit of gray, the uniform my mother made and lettered C.S.A."

In late August, Cassius M. Clay, just called home from Russia where he had been American minister, came into Lexington where he heard of Confederate Gen. Kirby Smith's approach through central Kentucky. Clay held a major general's commission and he persuaded Gen. Lew Wallace (who later became famous as the author of *Ben Hur*) to give him two regiments still in Lexington, the 18th Kentucky and the 69th Indiana infantry, together with a section of Michigan artillery. Clay advanced this force as far as the Palisades of the Kentucky River north of Richmond. Gen. William Bull Nelson, who had established Camp Robinson, removed Clay from command and took charge of Lexington, establishing his headquarters in the Phoenix Hotel. This was an unfortunate decision since there was no telegraph line between there and Richmond, which left him out of direct contact with the rest of his troops in Central Kentucky and led to his disastrous loss at the Battle of Richmond.

By Sunday morning, the day after the Union loss at Richmond on August 30, 1862, the news reached Lexington. Morgan's men had already distributed broadsides encouraging the locals to rise up against the occupying troops: "AROUSE, KENTUCKIANS! Like of old, men of Kentucky, and our noble hearted women, arm their sons and their lovers for the fight! Better death and our sacred cause than a life of slavery!" Lexington's streets were filled with soldiers who had thrown away their guns, broken cavalry outfits, officers trying to rally their men who were deserting and trying to find their way home to Ohio and Indiana. Many Lexingtonians went by train to Louisville since they feared retribution for their Union sympathies. The Provost Marshal ordered that the town be evacuated; the banks emptied their vaults, and Dr. Todd the postmaster sent off the accumulated mail. Large quantities of guns and ammunition were broken and smashed; government stores were piled up and set on fire. The fairgrounds were abandoned with only about a dozen soldiers remaining to destroy the encampment.

The following Tuesday, September 2, under the command of Gen. Kirby Smith, the Confederate Army paraded into Lexington with flags flying and bands playing "Dixie" and the "Bonnie Blue Flag." They entered by way of Richmond and Tates Creek Roads, and central Kentuckians came from all over to line the roads and cheer. Caroline Preston, the daughter of a Confederate brigadier general, tore down a Union flag from a building on Main Street, and as the Confederates rode by she dramatically tore up and trampled on the flag. Not all Lexingtonians were glad to see them, however, and Frances Peter sneered in her diary entry that Smith's men "looked like the tag, rag & bobtail of the earth as if they hadnt been near water since Fort Sumter fell." Union flags and emblems disappeared from public display, and the pro-Confederate, Democratic newspaper the *Kentucky Statesman* started up publication again. The troops issued Confederate scrip and took over the foundry owned by Lanckhart and Mentelle to produce shot and shell for the Confederate Army. They hired one hundred girls to make cartridges.

On Thursday John Hunt Morgan returned to Lexington and led the parade down Limestone to Main Street, symbolically passing the old armory of the Rifles on his way to the former Union mustering grounds at Cheapside. Frances Peter wryly observed in her diary that the Morgan raiders tended to their horses' finery more than their own. She wrote, "The secesh ladies didn't seem to like their looks much more than we did. Some of them went & sat with Morgan's men in the courtyard, & all went about waving flags at the men & in the officers faces but when any common men came to their houses to ask for something to eat they had them taken in at the back gate to the kitchen and let the negroes wait on them." Gen. Kirby Smith made sure that his superiors knew of his exuberant entrance into Lexington and sent a wire to Richmond: "They have proven to us that the heart of Kentucky is with the South in this struggle." On a more practical note, Smith ordered the post office be closely monitored and Northern newspapers be confiscated. Anyone found reading Northern papers or speaking out against the Confederacy would be arrested. General Morgan made the offices of the *Lexington Observer & Reporter* his headquarters, and the presses were used instead for flyers, pamphlets, and military forms.

Confederate recruiting offices were opened in Lexington, but few recruits came forward. General Bragg issued several proclamations published as handbills and in newspapers, but to no avail. On September 29, Bragg urged: "As you value your rights of person and property and your exemption from tyranny and oppression, now rally to the standard which protects you and has rescued your wives and mothers from insult and outrage . . . this is the last opportunity Kentuckians will enjoy for volunteering. The conscript act will be enforced as soon as necessary arrangements can be made." General Smith commented in a private letter: "Their hearts are evidently with us, but their blue-grass and fat cattle are against us."

On October 2, 1862 Generals Bragg and Smith met in Lexington, and the next day they went by train to Frankfort for the installation of Confederate Governor Richard Hawes. By the afternoon though, the provisional government left town to avoid capture by Gen. Don Carlos Buell. On October 9, General Smith marched his men out of Lexington to meet General Bragg, fresh from the Battle of Perryville. Many men of southern sympathies who had been unwilling to take the oath of allegiance for the Union Army also left. In less than a week, the city was again occupied by the

Union, the mail restored, and Union military rule reestablished. Bragg took a sizeable plunder out of Kentucky with him: 4,000 wagons, herds of horses, mules, cattle and sheep, and vast stores of food, including country hams that many soldiers carried on their bayonets. According to the *Cincinnati Commercial* at least $1 million worth of property and guns, enough for 20,000 men, were taken by the Confederate Army from supplies captured at Richmond and Lexington. Morgan's first raid garnered him only 300 Kentuckian recruits instead of the thousands he had hoped for.

Major Charles B. Seidel's 4th Ohio cavalry entered Lexington; one company under Captain Gotwald camped at the courthouse as Provost Guard, while the rest camped at Ashland, the estate of James B. Clay, who had fled to Canada. Confederate flags were removed and the Union flag reinstated. Early in the morning of October 18, 1862, Gen. John Morgan, who had stayed at the rear of Bragg and Smith's army in their retreat from Kentucky, attacked the encampment at Ashland. After a short skirmish, the whole camp, some 500 strong, was captured by Morgan and his men. He took the captured horses, guns, and equipment and burned the government stables, railroad depot, and other buildings.

As Morgan's men triumphantly marched through the city streets they took down Union flags. Ella Bishop, the seventeen-year-old daughter of a hardware dealer, asked for and was given one of the flags. She then took the flag home for safe keeping and when the Confederates learned that she was a Unionist, they came to her home to retrieve it. According to the legend as told by Union Brigadier Gen. Green Clay Smith, Ella staunchly refused to surrender it and wrapped it around her body whereupon the Confederate soldiers gave in and let her keep it. Earlier that morning, three soldiers were dispatched to the home of U.S. Captain John B. Wilgus, a grocer and commission agent. His wife went to the door herself to give her husband time to escape. The soldiers tried to push their way in, but she struggled with them and got one of their guns away from them. She tried to shoot them with it but they got it back. An officer passed by on the street and, according to the diarist Frances Peter, he "swore at them and asked why the devil they didn't let the woman along & look for Capt Wilgus & one of them replied, that he'd better come & try it himself. That it was easier said than done." They then decided to look in the stables for him and she followed behind talking to them all the time and distracting them long enough for her husband to make his escape.

To prevent any further surprise attacks, Gen. Quincy A. Gilmore built Fort Clay on a hill overlooking the city near the Versailles Road (now the site of Stockyards). Fort Clay was a four sided earthworks armed only with sharp pointed stakes and surrounded by a ditch with a drawbridge. Inside was a magazine and a well. Another earthwork that was never used was constructed near the home stretch of the Kentucky Association racetrack in the eastern part of the city. No one was allowed to leave the city without a pass from the provost-marshall and merchants who refused to give the oath of allegiance to the Union (or didn't say it often enough for the military authorities) were shut down. There were many different forms of the oath of allegiance, depending on the provost-marshall of the region.

In January 1863, Lincoln's Emancipation Proclamation went into effect, and even though it did not legally affect any slave's status in Kentucky, the state's population was in flux. Lexington was filled with refugees from eastern Tennessee and many runaway slaves. Most regiments refused to keep the slaves, since it was against the law, but some, such as the 22nd Wisconsin Volunteers, did take them in. The families of Confederate officers were targeted for abuse and vigilantism. Margaret Wickliffe Preston, wife of Confederate Gen. William Preston, wrote from her mansion Glendower in Lexington to her sister in New York:

> I have just had a visit from poor Susan Shelby and am quite unnerved by it. The frantic grief was heartrending—The night her four children were dying, 13 Federal soldiers and murderers, demanded of her five hundred dollars or her life, and the young man who protected her was shot, and her clothes bespattered, and her dying boy, said Mother, dont weep for me, you will be murdered on your own floor, and why should we grieve to leave such a wicked world. He was just one year younger than my Wick [Margaret's son] – she is going South in a week and if you will write to William, and enclose the letter to me I will send it by her.

Skirmishes between the Home Guard, the State Guard, wandering vigilantes, and occupying Union troops were more frequent than any battles against the Confederacy in Kentucky. Frances Peter wrote in her diary on Friday, July 3, 1863, about an attack on a train traveling from Louisville to Lexington the previous morning. She had heard from the passengers that a squad of nine or ten guerillas led by Confederate Captain Thomas H. Hines of the 9th Kentucky Cavalry had boarded the train looking for loot, then burned the cars and overturned the locomotive:

> The daughters of the rebel Gen Wm Preston were on the train returning from paying a visit to a relation in Louisville, and had in their trunks besides a quantity of new things they had purchased a good deal of jewlry and other finery which their relatives had given them. . . . The guerillas destroyed the Misses Prestons baggage with the rest although they made known to them that they were Gen Preston's daughters. The Misses Prestons were very much incensed as it was really a great loss to them. Nothing the Rebels could do would be so apt to turn them against the Confederate cause as destroying their valuables.

The most prudent role for women to play in this civil war among military men was to remain virtually invisible—out of sight playing the hospitable, submissive role of woman. Mag Preston was still living in her father's house, the Old Duke of Fayette County's Glendower, with her family (six children of her own as well as a son of an

English aristocrat under her guardianship) with several of her slaves, when she received the following notice:

> Office Post Commandant
> Lexington, Ky. May 19th 1863
> Madam:
>   In accordance with "General Orders No 66 Dept of the Ohio" Yourself and family will prepare to remove beyond and South of our lines by the 1st day of June next.
>   Should you wish to select and furnish your own transportation, or feel disposed to take the Oath of Allegiance, you will please make the same known at this Office at your earliest convenience.
> By order of
> Col. J.K. Sigfried

When the State of Kentucky formally accused General Preston of treason on July 7, 1862, his wife and family became vulnerable to confiscation of property and exile. Nevertheless, except for apparently random burglaries, the family continued the lifestyle they had enjoyed in peacetime. Among the Preston family papers in the University of Kentucky Special Collections and Archives was found the following statement (not written in her handwriting):

> I Margaret W. Preston do pledge my word of honor as a lady to do no act, and abstain from uttering any expression, calculated or by me intended to give aid assistance information or comfort to the Southern Confederacy or its supporters while I remain within the military lines of the Federal Government or to injure embarrass or weaken the United States Government or loyal citizens in their effort to restore the authority of the Government over the Confederate States and reestablish the Union. This pledge is given with the sincere purpose of faithfully complying with its terms in their full meaning & spirit.
> Lexington May 23d 1863.

It is not clear whether she actually took the oath—her later letters intimate that she did not—nevertheless she was not exiled, nor was her property confiscated. In Lexington, it is likely that many of her peers were in the same condition. By the end of 1863, out of 1,558 men who entered military service from Fayette County, only 380 went to the Union Army—and over one-fourth of those were officers. Almost 90 percent were cavalrymen who furnished their own horses and thus left Kentucky well mounted.

The fact that Mag Preston, the well-known daughter and heir of the Old Duke of Fayette County, Robert Wickliffe, was able to retain most of her "valuables" is astounding considering the amount of time that Lexington was under military occupation. In particular, she very ably maintained control over most of the slaves in her possession, both at Glendower and on her several outlying farms. Abraham Lincoln had halted the enlistment of blacks in Kentucky until 1865, but the local military forces could impress black labor whenever they were bold enough to do so. In fact by October 1863, General Boyle forced all unmarried free black men between the ages of sixteen and fifty as well as those having slave women for wives to work on the military railroads in Kentucky. White Kentuckians, never having much love for their native son Abraham Lincoln and his party anyway, became even more hostile. Rumors of the impending recruitment of African-American soldiers infuriated the local guards and nearly created rebellion in the Union soldiers' ranks. Colonel Frank Wolford of the First Kentucky Cavalry spoke out virulently against the Lincoln administration right after receiving a commendation for his work with the First Kentucky Cavalry against the Confederate forces. General Burbridge arrested him for treason, but Lincoln ordered his release.

The Union forces gave the Old Duke's daughter wide latitude in the continued property rights in human bondage. They found and imprisoned "the boy Anderson" who had escaped from one of her farms and they paid her for the hire of her slaves at Camp Nelson in Jessamine County. Nevertheless, she was clearly vulnerable to remote local authorities who might not immediately recognize her or her slaves. Her black slave overseer, the man her children called "Uncle Green," went to one of her outlying farms and there met up with local military forces. "The faithful Green has just escaped from Prison at Mount Sterling, where they arrested him as a rebel spy, and Green says every truth he told, they proved a lie immediately." Upon seeing Green's pass signed by a Confederate general's wife, the Union forces at Mount Sterling who were angry at the successful guerilla warfare and banditry there refused to acknowledge Green's liberty. Several white men had to vouch in person for his identity before he was allowed to return to Lexington.

Mag had to show publicly that even though her husband was in the Confederate Army, she had her own identity and would participate still in elite Lexington society. She paid $20 for Saxton's Quadrille Band to play at her forty-fifth birthday party on February 16, 1864, and everyone knew that Henry Saxton was a staunch Unionist who had refused to play for Kirby Smith's troops when they occupied Lexington. Her girls wrote to their father that they felt cooped up in the house, reading in French aloud to each other and schooling the younger children. The eldest daughter, by then twenty-three years old, described their relations with the Union occupying troops: "We rarely went anywhere but to church—were never presented to any officer but where by chance brought into contact with them always treated them civilly—Hating them most cordially." Mag did not hesitate to remind important Union men that she was still her father's daughter: she signed her name "M Wickliffe Preston" on the letter to Union General Fry for request

Continued on page 113

Identified originally as an "Old Indian Fort," this photograph depicts a prehistoric earthwork, but not a fort in the sense we think of it. There are several such "sacred circles" in Fayette County including the Mt. Horeb circle that is now owned by the University of Kentucky. There are many theories as to what these sacred circles were for—one idea is that they were used for celestial observation to track the seasons. (Art Work of the Blue Grass Region of Kentucky, Special Collections and Archives, University of Kentucky.)

Old Ryman Mill, South Elkhorn Creek, Fayette County. The many creeks and springs in this area made it easy for entrepreneurs of all nations to see the value of the land; when the Anglo-American settlers came to live here, they took advantage of the water sources to build all sorts of mills and this area became—as in the past for Native Americans—a commercial, cultural, and transportation hub for local producers. (Art Work of the Blue Grass Region of Kentucky, Special Collections and Archives, University of Kentucky.)

Front page of the earliest known issue of the Kentucke Gazette, the first newspaper published west of the Alleghenies, commissioned by statehood convention delegates to help convince the early settlers to separate from Virginia. The first issue (August 11, 1787) has not survived the ages. (Lexington Public Library Kentucky Room.)

Lexington Light Infantry
LEXINGTON, KY. 1789

The dashing costumes of the Lexington Light Infantry made it the first uniformed militia company west of the Alleghenies when it formed in 1789; the militiamen elected the popular James Wilkinson their first captain. (Kentucky Historical Society.)

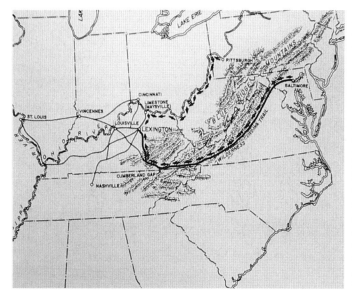

Major Routes to Frontier Lexington (1775–1815): northwest on the Wilderness Trail from Cumberland Gap and south on Maysville Road from Limestone (Maysville) on the Ohio River. Limestone Street in Lexington is part of the old Maysville Road. (The Historical Development of Lexington and Fayette County, Ky. *Lexington Community Development Plans, Research Report #2. James B. Griffin, Planner I. City-County Planning Commission of Lexington and Fayette County, 1963.)

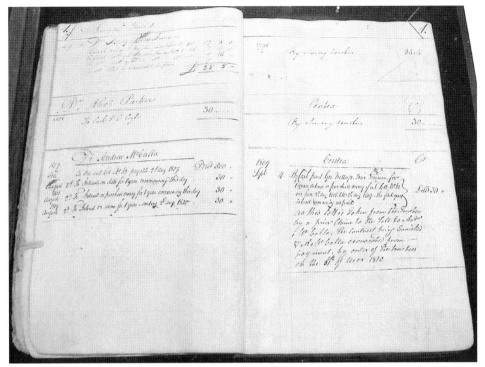

A page from the Lexington Town Ledger Book (1791–1821) shows the use of both pounds and shillings as well as dollars and cents in early Lexington. (Records Management, Lexington-Fayette Urban County Government, Lexington.)

This modern recreation of an antebellum hemp field shows how many of the different components of a Fayette County farm and community contributed to this industry. (Kentucky Historical Society.)

Rose Hill on Limestone Street, built c. 1820 as a one-story adaptation of the Classic Revival design by John Brand, whose profitable hemp bagging factories powered by slave labor helped bring large fortunes to early Lexington.

YOURSELF and family are invited to attend the funeral of CHARLES WICK-LIFFE, from the residence of his father, to Howard's Grove, this morning at 10 o'clock.

SATURDAY, OCTOBER 10, 1829.

1829 funeral notice for Charles Wickliffe, who published an article in the Kentucky Gazette under the name "Coriolanus" in which he defended the virtues of his father, the Old Duke of Fayette County, and denounced Thomas R. Benning, the editor. He was finally killed for this attitude in a duel with his friend George Trotter. (Special Collections and Archives, University of Kentucky Libraries.)

Reproductions of the first engine and coach used in 1835 on the Lexington and Ohio Railroad, and the strap rails used on the road, which then terminated at "Villa Grove," a summer resort six miles west of Lexington. (C. Frank Dunn Photographs Collection, Library Special Collections and Archives, Kentucky Historical Society.)

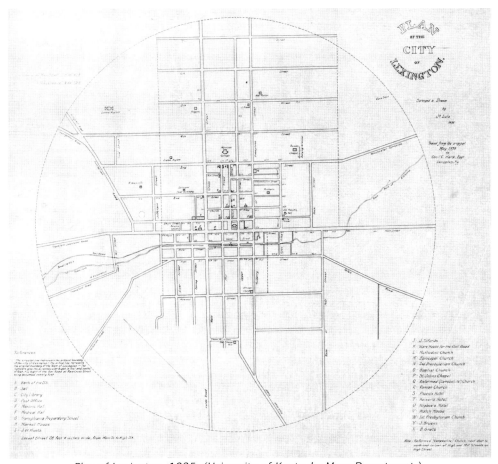

Plan of Lexington, 1835. (University of Kentucky Maps Department.)

Robert J. Breckinridge, preacher and abolitionist whose fiery speeches and political maneuverings often clashed with the Lexington elite. His kin Robert Wickliffe, the Old Duke of Fayette County who was a strong pro-slavery advocate and the first president of the Kentucky Colonization Society, called him "Judas" in a great war of privately published pamphlets in the 1840s. (Kentucky Historical Society.)

The funeral procession of Henry Clay lasted for ten days as it traveled toward Lexington in July 1852; his body was reinterred from Ashland to the monument in the Lexington Cemetery in 1864 after the death of his wife Lucretia Hart Clay. (Nollau Nitrate Photo, courtesy of University Archives and Records Program, Special Collections and Archives, University of Kentucky Libraries.)

Lexington at Main and Limestone Streets in 1859, just before the series of occupations by U.S. and C.S.A. armies. (Nollau High Bridge Photographic Collection, Special Collections and Archives, University of Kentucky.)

Asylum for the Insane, now Eastern State Hospital, the second oldest state-funded institution for mental health services in the United States. (Art Work of the Blue Grass Region of Kentucky, Special Collections and Archives, University of Kentucky.)

Sayre Female Institute as it looked in the 1890s. The school was founded in 1854 as the Transylvania Female Institute; this girls' boarding school was the prototype for Matthew Vassar when he visited Lexington. Suffragist Laura Clay was a graduate.

Central Christian Church, modern-day legacy of the combined New Light churches of Alexander Campbell and Barton Stone emerging from the revivals in the early 1800s, the second "Great Awakening" movement in U.S. history. (Art Work of the Blue Grass Region of Kentucky, Special Collections and Archives, University of Kentucky.)

Lexington troops on parade at Transylvania University c. 1860. This might have been the pro-secessionist Lexington Rifles since they drilled in the "little college lot" in front of Transylvania while the Lexington Old Infantry and Chasseurs drilled at Cheapside. (Kentucky Historical Society.)

Notice the date for a slave sale in this Lexington newspaper advertisement. Many schoolchildren still recite the myth that Kentucky-born Abraham Lincoln freed the slaves, but Kentucky's slaveowners were exempted from the dictates of the Emancipation Proclamation. Even those who were pro-Union and anti-slavery held on to their federally-sanctioned right to own human beings as long as they could profit from them—and maintain a sense of prestige from being of the elite. (Lexington Public Library Kentucky Room, Lexington, Kentucky.)

AS Trustees of Neal McCann, the undersigned will sell, at his residence on the Todd's road to Winchester, nine miles from Lexington,

On Wednesday, 26th Feb., 1862,

The following valuable Property:

200 ACRES OF LAND!

A lot of likely young

Negroes!

Men, Women and Children;

Young Cattle; Mule Colts, Brood Mares; Young Horse Stock;

100 good Sheep—Southdown and Cotswold;

Corn; Oats; 3½ stacks of Hay, &c. &c.

For the purpose of paying the balance of an execution in favor of Richard Higgins, the above property will be sold *for cash.*

WM. E. McCANN,
R. C. ROGERS,
Trustees of Neal McCann.

Fayette co., Feb 15   90

John Breckinridge Castleman (1841–1918), captain of Company D of the 2nd Kentucky Confederate Cavalry, distributed to his men the beautiful Saddlebred horses from his mother's farm when he joined up under General John Hunt Morgan's command in 1862. (Kentucky Historical Society.)

The movement behind the Kentucky Non-Importation Act of 1833 developed from a combination of politicians seeking a compromise on slavery. Though identified primarily with the cause for gradual abolition, the act also served as a way to keep non–Kentucky born slaves from entering the thriving slave trade in Lexington and thus boosting the prices for Kentucky slaves. This handbill from a scrapbook kept by abolitionist Casius Clay explains the anti-slavery sentiment of some local slaveowners such as Henry Clay and Robert J. Breckinridge. (Kentucky Historical Society.)

TO PEOPLE,
Who wish to do Right!

There are thousands of persons in Kentucky who conscientiously believe, that

Slavery is injurious to the prosperity of our beloved State:
Inconsistent with the fundamental principles of free government:
Contrary to the natural rights of mankind:
Adverse to a pure state of morals:
A great hindrance to the establishment of Free Schools:
That it depresses the energies of the laboring white man:
And in many other ways, is

A CURSE TO THE COUNTRY.

Many of the persons who so believe, have formed themselves into a party,

OPPOSED TO THE PERPETUATION OF SLAVERY IN KENTUCKY,

Composed of such men as Henry Clay and Dr. R. J. Breckinridge, of Fayette; Judge Nicholas, Wm. L. Breckinridge and Hon. Wm. P. Thomasson, of Louisville; C. M. Clay, of Madison; Judge Monroe, of Franklin; Dr. J. C. Young, of Boyle; J. McClung, of Mason; Judge Ballinger, of Mercer; J. R. Thornton, of Bourbon, and thousands of other persons of both parties; hard-working, honest, industrious, virtuous Mechanics, Manufacturers, Laborers, Farmers and Slaveholders of the Commonwealth, who for *Talent, Education, Virtue, Uprightness of Character* and *Intelligence*, can't be beat in any State in the Union!

These men object to the Perpetuation of Slavery by the Constitution of the State, and so ought every other GOOD REPUBLICAN who loves the prosperity of his home. The *way* and the *time* to do this, belongs to the CONVENTION TO CHANGE THE CONSTITUTION, which will assemble in Frankfort in October.

This party has adopted and published a PLATFORM OF THEIR PRINCIPLES, so that every body may see that their *design is a good one*, and the manner in which they wish to do this, is a **Peaceable, Quiet and Lawful one.** For which purpose, they are going to run candidates in the various counties in the State, favorable to the two following objects, and no matter how their *enemies may misrepresent them,* this is

THEIR PLATFORM.

1st. "The absolute prohibition of the importation of any more slaves into Kentucky."
2d. "The complete power in the People of Kentucky to enforce and perfect *in* or *under* the new Constitution, a system of gradual prospective Emancipation of Slaves."

We believe that a majority of the people of this State, *are in favor of the principles* laid down in this Platform; and that if left alone to vote their *real sentiments,* uninfluenced by Democratic and Whig *party demagogues,* they will give a tremendous vote in their favor. But cunning, long-headed demagogues, wire-workers and politicians of both political parties, will try to convince you that we are Abolitionists. If a man tells you so, set him down forthwith as a person *who is trying to mislead and deceive you.*

We are *opposed to any more Slaves* being brought into Kentucky, and wish TO RESERVE THE RIGHT AND POWER TO THE PEOPLE, *whenever they please,* if it is tomorrow, or next week, or next year, or within five years, or ten years, or fifty years, or for *any unusual length of time, and at all times,* when they shall find that SLAVERY IS NOT A BLESSING, but the reverse, to say so; and that the *Constitution shall be left open for THE PEOPLE to say so.*

What more do you want? Are we not right?
Lay your hands on your hearts, and you will answer **YES!**
You will no doubt, find some persons who will curse and damn this party; but are *you* willing to curse and damn them, because these men tell you to do so; and before you have heard the arguments? As sensible and good men, we know you ought not, you will not.

If you are willing *to do what is right;* if you are willing to be *guided* by TRUTH and JUSTICE; if you are willing to listen to *Reason and Argument;* if you are *not* willing to be bound up in the horrid shackles and fetters of PARTY *names* and PARTY *preferences,* come

Next Saturday, the 12th of May,

At 3 o'clock in the afternoon, to the COURT-HOUSE in Lexington, and listen to Mr. CLAY, Dr. BRECKINRIDGE, Mr. SHY, and others who may address you on that occasion.
Come with your aprons on! Come any way! Drop your work for one afternoon, and bring all your hands, and you will hear splendid speeches.

FULL OF TRUTH AND ARGUMENT.

Whilst "the whole world is vocal with the shouts of men made free," add your voice; lend your shout; pour out your loudest *hosanna* in unison with the HYMN OF LIBERTY which has just commenced to be sung throughout the length and breadth of *this great, this beautiful, this noble State,* and remember

"Where the SPIRIT of the LORD is, THERE IS LIBERTY."

James E. Pepper & Co. Distillers, built on a Lexington spring in 1879 by the grandson of an early Kentucky distiller, Elijah Pepper. James used the slogan "Born With The Republic" and the trademark "Old 1776" to emphasize his family's long history in bourbon-making. Today, James E. Pepper bourbon is sold only outside the United States. (Art Work of the Blue Grass Region of Kentucky, Special Collections and Archives, University of Kentucky.)

Louisville and Cincinnati had their steamboats' port of entries, and Lexington had her stagecoach stops. Lexington's hotels, taverns, boardinghouses, livery stables, road paving contractors, tollgate keepers, and carrier pigeon and postal systems flourished in the 1800s in support of the lucrative stagecoach businesses. This 1881 photo shows one of the last stagecoaches and future Lexington historian Charles Staple, the boy with the rifle. (Elmer L. Foote Lantern Slide Collection, Kentucky Room, Lexington Public Library.)

INAUGURATION AND DISPLAY
OF THE
Lexington Water Works!
Friday, January 30th, 1885.

PROGRAMME OF FIRE STREAMS.

10:30 A. M., SIX SIMULTANEOUS STREAMS

From Hydrants at the corners of Winchester and Race, Limestone and Seventh, Georgetown and Third, Broadway and Bolivar, Maxwell and Rose and Court House.
Run thirty minutes.
After a test at Limestone and Seventh, a change of stream will be made to Hamilton College.

1:20 P. M., TEN ONE-INCH STREAMS

On Main street, bet. Dewees and Spring streets.
Run twenty minutes.

2:10 P. M., TWO ONE-INCH STREAMS
Through
500 feet and 1000 feet of hose,
On Main street, near Court House.
Run twenty minutes.

2:30 P. M., ONE TWO-INCH STREAM
Through
Siamese Attachment
At Court House.
Run thirty minutes.

C. G. HILDRETH,
President, Lexington H. & M. Co.

M. KAUFMAN,
Chairman, Water Works Committee.

The Transcript Print.

Lexington Water Works Inauguration, 1885. The Lexington City Council contracted with a local private company to build a new public water system; Italian immigrant labor laid the new pipelines through the streets of the city, and the influx of non-English-speaking laborers inflamed public opinion against the project. Another scandal involved the 600 to 700 convicts hired to dig the water works reservoir. The contractors were accused of beating two convicts to death and attempting to secretly bury them in a blacks-only graveyard. (Special Collections and Archives, University of Kentucky Libraries.)

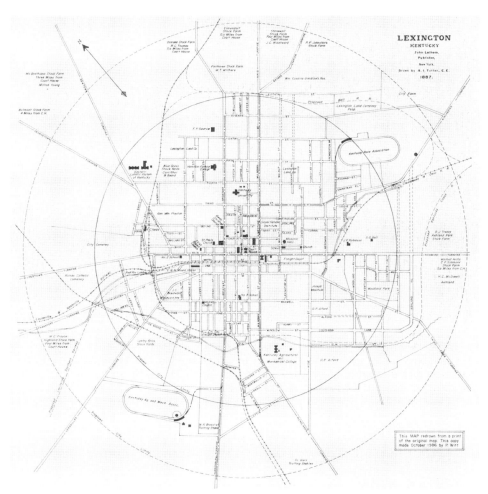

1887 Map of Lexington with Horse Farms. (University of Kentucky Maps Department.)

John C. Breckinridge (1821–1875) in his mid-forties had already fought in the Mexican War, served in the state and federal legislatures, and as vice president of the United States. His first defeat came in the presidential election of 1860 and his second during his role as Confederate secretary of war.

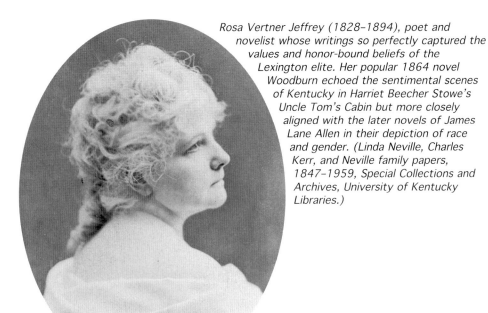

Rosa Vertner Jeffrey (1828–1894), poet and novelist whose writings so perfectly captured the values and honor-bound beliefs of the Lexington elite. Her popular 1864 novel Woodburn echoed the sentimental scenes of Kentucky in Harriet Beecher Stowe's Uncle Tom's Cabin but more closely aligned with the later novels of James Lane Allen in their depiction of race and gender. (Linda Neville, Charles Kerr, and Neville family papers, 1847–1959, Special Collections and Archives, University of Kentucky Libraries.)

The first electric streetcar in Lexington, in front of the Phoenix Hotel, spring 1890. (Bullock Photograph Collection, Special Collections, Transylvania University.)

W.C.P. Breckinridge (1837–1904) ran his last campaign for Congress in 1894. He had served as a U.S. Representative since 1885 but in 1894 a former mistress successfully sued him for breach of promise and the scandal ended his political career. The banner is strung across Main Street in front of Union Station. At left: wholesale grocery of Bryan-Hunt, Capt. C.C. Calhoun's business college, Tracy and Wilson's livery stable, and the Phoenix Hotel. (C. Frank Dunn Photographs Collection, Library Special Collections and Archives, Kentucky Historical Society.)

Even after the Civil War many black families in the Bluegrass continued to live in cabins on the edge of large farms such as in this picture taken in the late 1800s on part of James Ben Ali Haggin's new horse farm Elmendorf. (Elmendorf Farm Photographic Collection, Special Collections and Archives, University of Kentucky.)

"Woman Triumphant," a popular statuary group by local artist Joel T. Hart, purchased from Tiffany's by the "Women of the Bluegrass" who placed it in the foyer of the Fayette County Courthouse. The statue was destroyed on May 14, 1897, when the courthouse burned and the cupola crushed it. (C. Frank Dunn Photographs Collection, Library Special Collections and Archives, Kentucky Historical Society.)

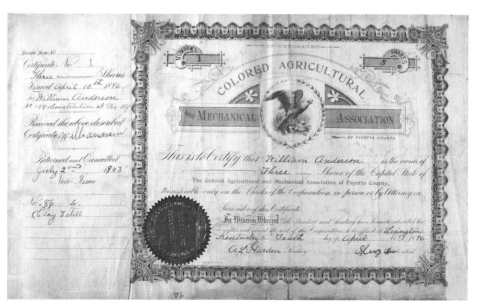

An 1896 stock certificate for the Colored Agricultural and Mechanical Association of Fayette County, which sponsored the Lexington Colored Fair every year. (Dr. T.T. Wendell Collection, 1894–1947, Kentucky Historical Society, Frankfort.)

Ashland, at the site of the original home of Henry and Lucretia Hart Clay. Built by their son in 1857 on the same foundations as the original Ashland and photgraphed in 1898 when the McDowells (Ann Clay McDowell was their granddaughter) lived there. From 1866 to 1878 the house served as the residence of the University of Kentucky's regent, John Bowman, while it was part of campus. Today it serves as a centerpiece of Lexington community and tourist activities. (Art Work of the Blue Grass Region of Kentucky, Special Collections and Archives, University of Kentucky.)

Mary Belle Brezing (1860–1940), a powerful madam whose house of prostitution was well known throughout the United States. She insisted that her employees dress formally and behave with genteel manners. (Special Collections and Archives, University of Kentucky Libraries.)

Lexington, bred by Dr. Elisha Warfield, "Father of the Kentucky Turf," charter member of the Lexington Jockey Club, and leased to freedman Harry Burbridge, one of the great trainers of the day. This great horse raced often in four-mile heats and set a world record of 7:19, but the thoroughbred industry followed the English customs of breeding for speed over stamina, and Lexington excelled at this task until he was retired due to blindness at age five. He led the sire list longer than any other with his famous progeny of champions who helped create the great American thoroughbred industry the Bluegrass enjoys today. (Art Work of the Blue Grass Region of Kentucky, Special Collections and Archives, University of Kentucky.)

Dr. Thomas T. Wendell (1836–1930), a Lexington physician, in his office on Short Street c. 1900. (Kentucky Historical Society.)

A typical side road near Lexington, probably sometime around 1900. (C. Frank Dunn Photographs Collection, Library Special Collections and Archives, Kentucky Historical Society.)

Class of 1909

ANN MARIE SIMPSON
MARY ELIZABETH BROOKS
†ELGETHA ILYLENE SMITH
DORA ESTHER WHITE
HATTIE ROBINSON
GEORGE BERNARD BUCKNER
*BENJAMIN WESLY PATTERSON ALLEN

*First Honor
†Second Honor

Programme

Chorus—Jubilate Deo	School
Prayer	Rev. M. W. Alexander
Chorus—The Blue Waltz	School
Oration—Universal Peace	Hattie Robinson
Instrumental Solo	Jane Lee
Oration—Prometheus Rock-bound	Dora White
Chorus—Out on the Deep When the Sun is low	School
Oration—The Triumph of Liberty	George B. Buckner
Vocal Solo—Villa	Cora Lee Boulder
Oration—America at Hodgenville	Mary E. Brooks
Chorus—On to the Sea	School
Oration—Woman Triumphant	Elgetha I. Smith
Duet—Waltz Dream	Cora Boulder and Lucille Combs
Oration—A New Issue	Benjamin W. Allen
Chorus	School
Presentation of Diplomas	Principal G. P. Russell
Chorus	School
Benediction	Rev. M. W. Alexander

Mrs. Hattie B. Baker, Pianist

Russell High School graduation program, 1909. Elite groups of blacks such as these who graduated from high school during the tumultuous times at the turn of the century bolstered the professional class of black Lexingtonians. (Fayette County Public School, Records Warehouse, Lexington.)

Madeleine McDowell Breckinridge (1872–1920), probably around the time she founded the Associated Charities and the Lexington Civic League, implementing the casework method of social work that her sister-in-law Sophonisba Breckinridge introduced at the University of Chicago. (Kentucky Historical Society.)

Leslie Combs II, son of the esteemed lawyer-politician-soldier of the same name and Margaret Trotter, and heir to the general's great breeding stock, became chairman of the Transylvania University Board of Trustees during the heyday of Transy's medical and law schools. (C. Frank Dunn Photographs Collection, Library Special Collections and Archives, Kentucky Historical Society.)

Laura Clay (1849–1941), born to antislavery activist Cassius Clay and woman suffragist Mary Jane Warfield Clay, Laura Clay rose to prominence in the Kentucky Equal Rights Association and then in the national woman's rights movement. A staunch states rights advocate, she opposed both the 18th and the 19th Amendments with equal vigor. (Special Collections and Archives, University of Kentucky Libraries.)

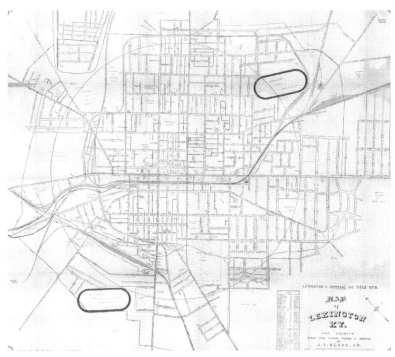

This 1912 Map of Lexington clearly shows the two racetracks: the 1828 Ky. Association track for thoroughbreds in the northeast and the 1875 trotting track in the southwest. (University of Kentucky Maps Department.)

World War I recruits at Union Train Station coming in for training May 7, 1918. (Nollau F. photograph courtesy of University Archives and Records Program, Special Collections and Archives, University of Kentucky Libraries.)

Yearlings being shown near the barns at the Kentucky Association track, probably for the yearling judging contest that continued into the post–World War II era at Keeneland. (Bullock Photograph Collection, Special Collections, Transylvania University.)

An unidentified black neighborhood in Lexington in 1930, perhaps Pralltown, Goodlowtown, or Kinkeadtown. (Comprehensive Plan for Lexington and Its Environs, Prepared by L. Segoe, Consulting Engineer and City Planner. City Planning and Zoning Commission, Lexington, 1931.)

Looking north on Georgetown Street (U.S. 25) in 1930. On the right is the new Booker T. Washington Grade School; in 1935 Lucy Hart Smith became the principal and served until her retirement in 1955. Smith developed the Kentucky curriculum for black history and was the only woman to serve as president of the Kentucky Negro Education Association. (Comprehensive Plan for Lexington and Its Environs, Prepared by L. Segoe, Consulting Engineer and City Planner. City Planning and Zoning Commission, Lexington,1931.)

Looking north on Limestone Street (the entryway to the old Maysville Road—U.S. 27—then known as Dixie Highway) in 1930. City planners complained that the streets had become too congested and redevelopment of the downtown needed to take place. (Comprehensive Plan for Lexington and Its Environs, Prepared by L. Segoe, Consulting Engineer and City Planner. City Planning and Zoning Commission, Lexington,1931.)

Will Harbut, famous groom and storyteller, with Man O'War at Faraway Farm in 1937. Harbut died October 1946 and his beloved horse died less than a month later. (J.C. Skeets Meadors Photo, Keeneland Association Library.)

Harness Races at Trotting Track c. 1935. The KY Trotting Horse Breeders Association opened the track under the leadership of Robert Alexander of Woodburn in 1875. It is currently the oldest running track in Lexington.

An aerial view of Keeneland just before it opened in 1934. (Louis A. Beard scrapbook, Keeneland, 1935–1940. Keeneland Association Library.)

*Elizabeth Daingerfield, daughter of the great trainer Fauxhall Daingerfield, owned Haylands Farm, leased Hinata Farm, and also managed Faraway for Sam Riddle. (*The Story of Man O'War, *reprinted from* The Blood-Horse, *1947; Keeneland Association Library)*

*James "Soup" Perkins was born in Lexington in 1880 and at the age of eighteen was in high demand as a jockey. (*The American Turf: An Historical Account of Racing in the United States, *Keeneland Association Library.)*

Hal Price Headley, first president of Keeneland Association, 1934. (Louis A. Beard scrapbook, Keeneland, 1935–1940. Keeneland Association Library.)

*John Madden, "Wizard of the Turf," courted and won Lexington society with his winning ways at Hamburg Place. (*The American Turf: An Historical Account of Racing in the United States, *Keeneland Association Library.)*

Lexington's tobacco industry almost overwhelmed the city landscape in the early twentieth century.

Iroquois Hunt and Polo Club pony polo teams (Red and White), July 25, 1931; the Herald-Leader *announced a crowd of 1,500 watched the match at Woodland Park.*

American Tobacco Warehouses in December 1931, looking south on South Broadway.

Stop Over Station at 109 Esplanade, April 1944. Opened February 28, 1942 and closed January 31, 1946. It provided lodging, meals, and entertainment for free to military passing through—unlike Brezing's establishment.

Blue Grass Troubadours, October 1947. Local bluegrass musicians made it big in the 1970s in Lexington.

An eastern Kentucky Listening Center. Elmo "Bromo" Selzer was director of UK Radio and won a Foster Peabody Award for establishing listening centers in Kentucky after World War II. (UK Radio Photographic Collection, Special Collections and Archives, University of Kentucky.)

A Lexington street scene in a predominantly black neighborhood in 1954.

Col. E.R. Bradley cleverly used modern means to advertise what his Idle Hour Farm's great stallions, Eternal Bull and Blue Swords, brought to Lexington's prosperity. (MacKaye, Kentucky Historical Society.)

1963 Report on Lexington's Map of Lexington Urban Service Area marking the horse farm crescent that would define Lexington's Green Belt and the "crazy quilt" of service areas that helped spawn public acceptance of city-county merger. (Griffin, University of Kentucky Maps.)

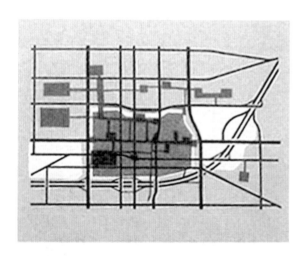

1964 Downtown Development Plan: the AIA Downtown Design Study Group launched the process for changing the downtown scene and using federal funds for urban renewal, although not all of its original plan was actually implemented. (Image courtesy of Helm Roberts.)

A campaign card in 1965 when the city council races depended on organized "tickets" supported by prominent local businessmen such as Fred Wachs.

ELECT THE GREATER LEXINGTON GROUP

KELLER • IRVIN • UNDERWOOD • WYLIE
For City Commissioners
City Primary September 18, 1965

"FOR CONTINUED PROGRESS AND A GREATER LEXINGTON"

Guy Mendes, UK's student president in 1968, taking the lead during a campus protest. He and his compatriots don't look as scary as Governor Nunn made them out to be when the National Guard was sent in May 1970. (Photograph courtesy of University Archives and Records Program, Special Collections and Archives, University of Kentucky Libraries.)

Pam Miller ran for the Urban County Council in 1973 and became the first woman to serve in that capacity. She then went on to serve as Lexington's first woman mayor in 1993. Serving two terms, she was an ardent supporter of planned growth. (Records Management, Lexington-Fayette Urban County Government, Lexington.)

Tree-planting ceremony to celebrate the new wing at Russell Elementary School in the late 1970s—do you recognize the young curly-haired teacher at the far right? That's former Tates Creek Elementary school principal, Stanton Simandle, in his first teaching job. (Fayette County Public School, Records Warehouse.)

Steel, concrete, granite, and quartz sculpture of Duality in the University of Kentucky Chandler Medical Center courtyard designed by Amerigo J. Brioschi (1908–1997) of St. Paul, Minnesota. According to Brioschi, the rising boomerang is the "epitome or heights man has reached" and the downward form is "man's mediocrity, his failures and disappointments." (Photo by the author.)

In the early 1990s Isabel Yates (Lexington's vice mayor from 1999–2003) led the campaign to clean up Lexington's founding site, McConnell Springs, which is now a 26-acre historical and environmental education center close to downtown. In 2000 she launched the Town Branch Greenway, which offers a hiking trail along the banks of the city's original water source. (Records Management, Lexington-Fayette Urban County Government, Lexington.)

Woodland Skatepark opened in September 1999 thanks to the leadership provided by the Triangle Foundation and the Aylesford Neighborhood Association. (Photo by the author.)

"Circus Horse" by Judy Anderson. In 2000 Lexington hosted a public art campaign, Horse Mania, in collaboration between the Kentucky Thoroughbred Association and the Lexington Arts and Cultural Council that produced 79 fiberglass horses auctioned off for a public art fund. (Photo by the author.)

John Hunt Morgan (1825–1864), Alabama-born veteran of the Mexican War and captain of the Lexington Rifles, whose success as leader of the Kentucky mounted raiders during the Civil War got him promoted to general and larger-than-life mythic status in Kentucky. The "Lost Cause" sentiment of early twentieth-century Lexingtonians funded this equestrian statue still standing outside the old Fayette County Courthouse, which is now the site of the Lexington History Museum. (Photo by the author.)

Civil War, Military Occupation, and "Readjustment"

Continued from page 80

for payment for her slaves' hire at Camp Nelson and again on a promissory note for $1,000 to David A. Sayre, a prominent banker who supported Union recruitment efforts.

The turning point for Mag personally, and for most of Lexington in general, came in June of 1864. Morgan had routed Generals Burbridge and Hobson's infantry at Mt. Sterling, and moved toward Lexington, which was protected only by the First Ohio Heavy Artillery who had retreated to Fort Clay. Morgan's men and southern sympathizers began setting fires in the city: the brewery of Wolf and Walker, the large government corral on East 3rd Street, and two large stables owned by James A. Grinstead at the Association racetrack. Hundreds of cords of wood at the Kentucky Central Railroad building near the Lunatic Asylum were set on fire. Morgan's men broke into the local stores and stole what they could. They stole $10,000 from the Northern Branch Bank of Kentucky where Madison C. Johnson was president, and the finest horses from the livery stable of Frank Hord—John M. Clay lost about $25,000 worth of horses, including his famous Thoroughbred mare Skedaddle. The Union Army began shelling the town, terrorizing the citizens, and skirmishing with Morgan's men. By noon Morgan rode north to Georgetown where he met up with Burbridge's troops and barely escaped with his life.

Mag Preston wrote to her husband, "Life is most unpleasant—After John Morgan's raid, searched, insulted, & hated, & I dread things growing much worse in stead of better." She must have been re-thinking her husband's idea that she join his cousin John S. Preston and his family in South Carolina, but knew too well the cost of becoming a refugee family dependent on the mercy of others. Her eldest daughter bemoaned the prospect of leaving Lexington: "I am sorry Mama is discontented for we are so comfortably established and all things considered leading such a quiet easy life that I dread a change, besides it would take such a lot of money, so much more than we have, for a family of our size to live anywhere, except just here. Moreover everyone says the house would be seized by the soldiers either for a hospital or Hdqtrs and Mama has gone to such expense in fitting it up."

By refurbishing Glendower during the Civil War Mag knew that she was making an important statement to her community that she belonged there. She was, in her own way, reconstructing her household in a very public manner, stating her class and status in an unequivocal way. She ordered crimson velvet and gold ceiling and wall decorations from Stewarts in New York; she bought 300 fruit trees from a Jefferson County nursery; and she paid local merchants for repairing and varnishing her expensive rosewood furniture, painting the house, hanging chandeliers and curtains, and repairing the indoor plumbing and expensive water closets. Elizabeth Simpson, a local historian, described the house as it looked in its finished state: "Double doors open into the broad hall that traverses the house from front to back, with a glassed in gallery that runs across the main structure in the rear. A door at the end of the hall opened to the patio." The hall carpet was dark red velvet, and between the parlor doors on the right, on a pier table, the bust of Robert Wickliffe by Joel Hart was prominently displayed. Another bust, one of Robert Wickliffe Jr. by Hiram Powers, stood on a marble pedestal in the parlor. Heavy molded cornices and solid silver hardware such as knobs and hinges bespoke a socio-economic prominence. "The front room on the right, which was known in the manner of the English as 'the morning parlour,' opened by double doors at the back into a room of similar proportions known as the back parlour." From the morning parlour a visitor who was close to the family could enter the book-lined library where the Prestons received informally. The drawing room on the left side of the front hall was larger and extended to the rear of the house, opening onto the back gallery. Here "a large Canton bowl filled with punch was placed on the grand piano . . . Mrs. Preston called it 'son-in-law punch,' declaring that none who drank it were the worse for having imbibed." She held many parties for the officers of the occupying forces and this symbolic effort was probably more effective than any oath of allegiance she might have taken.

Morgan's high-profile guerilla raid in early June 1864 caused a series of military decisions, two of which wreaked havoc on Lexington and raised the level of anger and violence in the city. The Federal government began enlisting all able-bodied blacks and offered bounties and protection for all who volunteered. Thousands of African-American volunteers crowded into Lexington from surrounding counties, and one large group of recruits from Mercer County marched through the streets of Lexington shouting hurrahs for the Union and President Lincoln. Polly Preston wrote to her father on June 5:

> You should see the wild confusion, in the domestic arrangements of Lex. caused by the enlisting of negroes. The "disloyal" take it very composedly, having forseen it ever since the Proclamation but the "Loyal" are "agast" and not so ardent in their Unionism as they once were. . . . Mama has lost 7 or 8 and will doubtless lose more. Carriage drivers were in great demand, as well as cooks, so people are taking it afoot and dining less well. Mama never ceases to congratulate herself that she sent Watson with you.

The staunch Unionist Rev. Robert J. Breckinridge refused to allow his slaves' families to join their men recently recruited. Though committed to public support for the Union and President Lincoln, the reverend continued personally to enforce his role as a slave owner. In July 1864 he went to the Federal headquarters at Camp Nelson, Kentucky, and demanded Gen. Speed Fry return to him seventeen women and children who had run away from his farm to join their male relatives stationed there. The Enlistment Act of 1863 provided that any slave who enlisted received his freedom and that of his wife and children. But when the newly enlisted blacks returned home to claim freedom for their wives and children, the slaveowners often refused to recognize the federal law and claimed the federal government had no right to confiscate the "property" of loyal citizens under the 5th Amendment. The Emancipation Proclamation never legally affected Kentucky, but over 23,000 black Kentuckians earned their freedom by joining the Union forces—57 percent of Kentucky black males aged eighteen to forty-five. This was the second largest number of black Union troops enlisting from the slave states.

On July 16 General Burbridge issued General Order #59, which ordered the arrest, confiscation of property, and deportment of rebel sympathizers living within five miles of any guerrilla activity. By this time lawlessness in the countryside was rampant and banditry by deserters as well as squads of Federal soldiers self-styled "Home Guards" had become the usual. Horses in particular were often targeted since the Federal government would pay $2,000 per mount. Burbridge ordered four guerilla prisoners shot for every loyal citizen or soldier harmed in any way. Military executions became frequent; Confederate prisoners were often mistaken for outlaws. All it took was a few words of criticism, a reported rumor of a Confederate soldier visiting a local relative, or the refusal to take the oath of allegiance upon command for citizens to suffer confiscation, arrest, imprisonment, or exile.

Pooggie, Mag's favorite daughter, became extremely ill during this time, or perhaps she was the best actress to create a screen for the family. At any rate, her illness gave Mag several days' grace from immediate deportment. She wrote to her husband from a New York hotel:

> Genl Burbridge sent me word by Col Hunt that I must leave Kentucky the succeeding day or I would be sent South—I said I could not leave that my daughter was in extreme danger & I asked Col Hunt & John Brown [the Union hero in halting Morgan's raid, and later Mary's husband] to get Genl Burbridge to suspend the order a few days until Pooggie had passed the crisis of her fever—Through their influence Genl Burbridge permitted me to remain from Friday till Monday. . . . I left Mary & Carrie with Mrs. Eyrand to nurse her.

Perhaps Mag was rejecting the ignominious fate of being forced to leave Kentucky and left on her own volition. At any rate, both the Federal and local authorities left her estate alone while she was gone.

Her eldest daughter wrote from Montreal to her father about this critical decision her mother made, emphasizing Mag's control over the situation:

> . . . a number of Southern people were arrested and sent off but Mama got information of the proposed wholesale banishment and left before she received any order. Pooggie was desperately ill at the time, and Carrie and I remained to nurse her and pack away the furniture. Aunt Sue stayed with us, and finally brought us on to Mama [in New York].

She went on to describe how others did not fare as well as the Preston family:

> We left Ky in a dreadful state—People were being taken up by hundreds
> and sent off without money or clothes—Mr. McCaws family was sent away
> with but 20 minutes notice—Mr Grinstead was permitted on account of a
> petition signed by a number of radicals to make NY his place of exile.
> Ephraim Sayre, Mr. Dudley Judge Buckner and a good many of the old
> Union party, barely saved themselves by flight and even the most ultra were
> quaking with fear.

That summer Kentucky's Union Democratic Party had split, and Lexington's own Rev. Robert J. Breckinridge led those who were "Unconditional Unionists." He stumped across the state openly opposing such Conservative Union Democrats as Governor Bramlette, Lieutenant-governor Richard Jacob, and Louisville *Journal* editor George Prentice. Unconditional Unionist delegates chose Breckinridge to represent them at the 1864 Baltimore convention where he served as temporary chairman. The Kentucky delegation then called upon the President they had just renominated and, with Breckinridge as their spokesperson, protested against the draft in Kentucky for home defense and especially against the military power of Governor Thomas Bramlette. Ironically, between July 20–25, 1864, the Unconditional Unionists gave names of their political competitors to the military to be arrested for treason and thereby secured their own election. In Lexington on July 27, while a grand ball was taking place in the old Phoenix Hotel, eight Confederate prisoners were taken out of the jail on Water Street and shot. R.G. Wooten and Wilbain Woods were taken to Georgetown and shot in retaliation for the supposed disappearance of a Union man named Robinson, who later turned up unharmed. On November 15, Walter Ferguson and another Confederate soldier named McGee were taken from the jail on Water Street and ordered by General Burbridge to be hung at the trotting track.

In early October of 1864, Reverend Breckinridge fell from his horse and while convalescing met with elite groups of Unionists including General Burbridge. These meetings became widely known, and Breckinridge was labeled as the leader of a "Secret Inquisition" that pointed out to the military authorities who should be targeted for arrest, imprisonment, or deportation. By the fall of 1864, most men in the Bluegrass area were either in the Army or in prison. Slaves had run away, farms left neglected, and many houses deserted.

Polly reassured her father of her mother's political astuteness, and described how the Federals perceived Mag:

> I believe we came away with the ill will of no one. [General Ambrose E.]
> Burnside said, when he commanded the Dept that "Mrs Preston's family
> had behaved with such singular discretion and good taste that they were

> not to be molested" and when Mrs. Humphreys (Sarah Gibson) went to see
> what could be done, she asked if we would not be ordered off. He said "by
> no means. Mrs. Preston left Ky of her own free will and consent and her
> daughters will do the same.

Finally, Polly wrote that their status as self-exiled refugees was not particularly an improvement from their life at Glendower. In fact, she implied, they had come down in the world: "We have lived so long under oppression that I almost feel afraid even here to write this. . . . Canada is filled with refugees a class of persons, by the way, that I don't, as a general thing admire."

On January 31, 1865, the Republican U.S. Congress completed passage of the proposed 13th Amendment freeing the slaves, and Kentucky's Governor Bramlette recommended that the Kentucky ratification be contingent upon receipt of $34 million (the value of Kentucky's slaves in 1864). Both houses of the Kentucky General Assembly rejected ratification of the 13th Amendment and in fact, Kentucky did not ratify it until 1976 under the leadership of the two African-American legislators Senator Georgia Powers and Representative Mae Street Kidd.

In February of 1865 Major Gen. John M. Palmer became commander of the military district of Kentucky and announced that he would use black enlistment as a means to free as many slaves as possible. Black women took their freedom into their own hands. Even though Kentucky law did not recognize slave marriages, if a couple could convince a slaveowner that they were married, that might be enough. Certainly the women in the Lexington area took advantage of the fact that their husbands were at Camp Nelson only a few miles away. Reverend Pratt described how Lucinda, a slave in his home, had learned from a letter from her husband Henry that she was free. She confronted Pratt and he offered her $2 to continue working three days a week. It took her only two weeks to realize that this was not a good enough deal: Pratt awoke one morning to find "the Kitchen cleaned up, the bread . . . ready for baking & kindling at hand to start a fire," but Lucinda gone.

On April 9, 1865, Lee surrendered to Grant at Appomattox, and the Unionists of Lexington greeted the news with cheers, tolling of bells, and salutes from Fort Clay. Gen. S.S. Fry, Dr. Robert J. Breckinridge, and other Unionists spoke to a crowd at Cheapside, parades and exhibitions were held throughout the day, and fireworks and bonfires lit. Southern sympathizers remained off the streets and in their homes. It is hard to imagine now, but the 65,000 remaining slaves in Kentucky were still not free.

Two days later, the news that President Lincoln had been assassinated came to Lexington. Like most in the nation, Lexingtonians grieved. Reverend Pratt wrote in his diary, "Never was my moral sense so shocked nor did greater gloom fill my mind. Lizzie, only 10 years old went out by herself & cried as if her heart was broke." The Lexington *Observer & Reporter* stated: "Differing as we did from the deceased

President, we yet do not hesitate to say that in our judgment he was a man of remarkable mental endowments and possessed many excellencies of character."

Kentucky observed April 19, 1865, the day of Lincoln's funeral in Washington, as a day of humiliation and prayer, and in Lexington, by order of Col. S.W. Price, the flags of the city flew at half-mast and twenty-one guns were fired from Fort Clay. All the churches held special services, businesses were closed, and many were draped in mourning—though not all. Reverend Parsons gave a eulogy in the historic Morrison Chapel at Transylvania and all attending sang the "Star Spangled Banner." During that spring and summer, General Palmer issued free passes to black Kentuckians. "Palmer Passes" allowed many to leave the state, move to the cities to look for jobs, hike through the countryside looking for relatives, and crowd into federal military camps hoping for food and protection from vigilantism. Many homes in Lexington, barely large enough to hold a few people, were filled with multiple families searching for a new life of freedom. Living conditions in the city became abysmal, disease and crime ran rampant.

On October 12 President Johnson lifted martial law in Kentucky. Most Kentuckians felt angry and disgusted with the Federal government they had helped to maintain. On December 15 the Kentucky Court of Appeals upheld a lower court decision declaring illegal the federal law that emancipated the wives and children of black troops. This vengeful stance was overturned three days later, when on December 18, 1865, the U.S. Secretary of State announced that two-thirds of the states had ratified the 13th Amendment and it became a national law. Slavery had remained legal longer in Kentucky than in any other state except for Delaware. By April 1866, when the last of the black troops in the state were demobilized, some 29,000 had been enlisted from Kentucky. This number equaled more than 10 percent of the African-American population of the day (as compared to 7 percent of Kentucky's white population)—and this percentage is even more astonishing since 95 percent of Kentucky's black population were slaves. Lexington's Emancipation Day celebration on January 1, 1866 included a military parade of blacks in full uniform followed by black businessmen and then several hundred children, ending with several hours of political speeches at the Lexington Fairgrounds.

Kentucky in 1860 had produced the most hemp of all the states in the nation and was second in the production of tobacco and mules, third in flax, fourth in hogs, and fifth in rye. The farmers in Kentucky were generally well off for their time and few resembled the stereotypical poverty-stricken images of the twentieth century. Lexington sat in the center of one of the most agriculturally rich areas of the state. Even though the early promise of a bustling manufacturing future had not panned out, Lexington's business and industry was not insignificant. Following the heritage of Henry Clay, her political leaders were strong advocates of internal improvements and differed from the attitudes often associated with southern anti-tariff and laissez-faire politics. However, state rights feelings also came strong in the heritage of the city's leaders, especially from the Breckinridges, from John Breckinridge Sr. who helped write the early Kentucky constitutions to John Breckinridge Jr. That very family, however, epitomized the split in Lexington's approach to slavery: Robert J. Breckinridge not only protected his right to own slaves, but also met with Abraham Lincoln to further the cause of colonization of freedmen outside the United States.

By 1870 approximately 4,600 freedmen migrated into Lexington, causing the black population to triple and making the whole town's population nearly one-half black. Even those Lexingtonians who had supported the Union cause felt threatened by the prospect of the former slaves gaining basic citizenship rights. The first decade after the Civil War witnessed scenes of racial violence that clearly aimed to protect the antebellum status quo. For many elite Lexingtonians, this era also emphasized the class differences among white citizens as their worst fears of African-American lawlessness were displaced by the ever-present realities of white bandits and vigilantism. The Money Kings found themselves in the curious position of serving as allies for the Kentucky blacks whom they knew personally or whose credentials linked them with someone the white person knew. The old pass system, where the African-American businessperson or laborer needed to have a white patron vouch for their legitimacy in an economic transaction or movement beyond racial boundaries, still flourished.

Violence in Lexington most often happened when a black person attempted to walk along public pathways near a hostile white person or when a black family attempted to make a living in the vicinity of a jobless or landless white male. Kentucky's refusal to enforce the federal Civil Rights Acts of 1866 and 1875 emboldened many whites to terrorize blacks and any whites who tried to support or protect them. After the Civil War, agriculture and manufacturing productivity was badly crippled and Lexington's fortunes suffered from the huge displacement of people and property. Nevertheless, Lexington's elite organized two new banks in the spring of 1865: the First National Bank of Lexington and the City National Bank. They also helped create new railroad lines: the Central Kentucky line and the Lexington & Big Sandy Railroad—much to the consternation of the stockholders and owners of the Louisville & Nashville road, which had a strong hold on the transportation options in the state.

The thriving African-American business community found avenues for a well-connected entrepreneur in their midst. By 1880 blacks owned eight shoe shops in Lexington, and Ferdinand Robinson owned a successful mattress factory. According to historian Marion Lucas, Moses Spencer, a secondhand furniture dealer, was Lexington's most successful black businessman, owning property worth about $20,000 by the 1870s. Downtown Lexington boasted many black-owned barber shops, bakeries, restaurants, catering businesses, and boarding houses. The Lexington Colored Agricultural and Mechanical Association, formed in 1869 under the leadership of black community leaders such as Henry King, Henry Scroggins, and James Turner, was a financial success. Black churches, always a locus of socio-

Lexington

economic power for black Lexingtonians—free or enslaved—became even more important in terms of education, business connections, and political strategy-building.

Lexington hosted two of the first Black Conventions where black leaders and white civil rights activists met to protest the restrictions on black rights. The first assembled on March 22, 1866, and called for a state central committee to organize future meetings. Over ninety people from all over the state attended the second conference in November 1867, the largest mass assembly of Kentucky's black leaders ever. Delegates debated how to gain full civil rights for blacks, including the right to vote and the right to testify in court against whites. The president, W.F. Butler, asserted in his opening speech that black soldiers had earned the rights of U.S. citizenship for all blacks: "We had the cartridge box. Now we want the ballot box, and soon we'll get the jury box." Former Union soldiers bonded together in Loyal Leagues, para-military groups not unlike the vigilance committees of antebellum times that protected refugees seeking relief in the personal liberty laws of abolitionist New England states. Lexington had many different menial jobs for unskilled laborers who did not want to return to the fields after emancipation. There were small properties for sale or lease where former field slaves could settle into their own homes and work their own land. In Lexington, black entrepreneurs dominated some key businesses like Edward Alexander, who gained a fortune as a drayman hauling materials by horse and wagon. Though most blacks did not earn enough money to own property, the benefits of living in or near Lexington, despite the low wages and even among fearful and hostile whites, far outweighed the risks.

Many of the urban black communities of Lexington that began in the late 1860s continue to survive into the present day. Though before the war the black population—both enslaved and free—was scattered throughout the city, after the war migrants mainly from the six rural counties surrounding Lexington came to live in cheap housing on the outskirts of town. "Pralltown" was developed from land near a railroad track southwest of the city subdivided in 1868 by a lawyer named John Prall. Landowners W.W. Bruce and George B. Kinkead sold land to form settlements named after them: Brucetown and Kinkeadtown. Brucetown developed in the area where the Union army had stabled hundreds of mules, and with poor waste disposal and a high population density, disease quickly spread through the "shot gun" shacks. Davis Bottom, also near a railroad, was a poorly drained bottomland that already had an antebellum African-American community and it became densely populated in this period. Other shantytowns sprang up: Goodlowtown and Adamstown were also near railroads, though others like Taylortown and Smithtown grew up from acreage that was once part of a larger plot associated with an elite white family. Taylortown came from the back acres of the large plot on which sat General Preston's mansion, Glendower. By the 1880s Goodlowtown became the largest of the black communities. Virtually all of the small antebellum black areas close to the expanding central business center of Lexington vanished as the land values began to climb, vagrancy laws grew more rigid, and racial violence escalated.

Civil War, Military Occupation, and "Readjustment"

After the Civil War, housing was at a premium, and black Kentuckians were eager to establish their own households. General Preston, concerned about the fluctuating nature of his once enslaved labor force, facilitated the process for African Americans to gain adequate housing. Preston installed valued former slave Peter Thompson and his family in the house they called the "Mentelle place," the former boarding school of Charlotte Mentelle. In 1871 the Ku Klux Klan exhibited its anger at the new citizen status of African Americans by killing Peter Thompson simply for being a black freedman and living in a house. According to the notice served to William Preston after the murder, the murderers were angry that Thompson and his large family had access to housing when poor whites did not. The *Kentucky Gazette* published an account of this "Midnight Assassination" on January 11, 1871. The editors of the *Gazette* were quite sure that the "most foul assassination" of "a negro by the name of Peter Thompson, who lived at the old Mentel place, opposite the gate at Ashland" was not the work of the "regular Ku-klux" but that of some "drunken men who pretended to be Ku-klux." Indeed, the *Gazette* asserted that "we not only defend the Ku-klux from this most foul assassination, but if they indeed by the regulators which we have thought them, they will signally punish those who have counterfeited their awful name and bedaubed it in debauchery and innocent blood." Peter Thompson was not the only African American to rent a piece of the 1,600-acre farm from the Prestons. According to General Preston's account ledgers, Garrison Jones, Brisly Miller, Sam Giles, Susan Green, and Major Irvine also worked at the Ellerslie farm "on the shares . . . giving me one half the crop."

While the deep south's former slave states underwent Radical Reconstruction, Kentucky experienced what historians have called "readjustment." President Andrew Johnson did not end martial law in Kentucky until October 12, 1865, yet the violence of whites who called themselves Regulators, Bull Pups, Skaggs Men, or the Ku Klux Klan continued. Major Gen. Oliver O. Howard took it upon his own authority to extend the jurisdiction of the Bureau of Refugees, Freedmen, and Abandoned Lands beyond the Tennessee border, establishing a branch headquarters in Lexington. Each of the four directors found out in turn that, as they subsequently tried to carry out the Bureau's implementation of fair contracts for blacks and the rights to personal safety and schooling, their agents were in great physical danger. Too few troops were assigned to protect the Freedman Bureau agents and those they tried to serve. In addition, contracts often resulted in disputes when the employer would accuse a worker of disobedience or laziness and refuse to make final payments. Apprenticeships, long a feature of Kentucky labor laws and used regularly in Lexington for children of both races, became a source of power for former white masters who could apprentice black children without the consent of parents or relatives. The courts often ruled for white supremacy status quo. The arrest and conviction of any white for crimes against black Lexingtonians rarely occurred.

Lexington

The continued rejections of federal Civil Rights legislation and constitutional amendments combined with the failed efforts at the state level for basic human rights. For example, Kentucky's marriage law in February 1866 allowed cohabiting blacks and mulattos to pay a 50¢ fee for the legalization of slave marriages and declared their children legitimate. At the same time the law disallowed for the first time in Kentucky the marriages between blacks and whites. Bills that would allow for black testimony in courts failed to garner enough votes in the Kentucky legislature until 1872. Black leaders working toward ratification of the 14th amendment organized a barbecue in Lexington on July 4, 1867, which included many white speakers in favor of black suffrage. The editor of the Kentucky *Statesman*, William Cassius Goodloe, a staunch Radical Republican, admitted he was skeptical that Kentucky blacks would be able to vote in his lifetime. Blacks finally voted in the Kentucky governor's race for the first time in 1871, but with the coming to power in the state legislature of what were called "New Departure Democrats" promoting white economic and political progress in combination with the traditional Kentucky conservatives, led to the rise of Lexington's "polite" segregation. The police aggressively enforced the new, broadly defined vagrancy laws. Land transfers often included exclusion clauses that disallowed black ownership along with the sale of alcohol. The city charter was amended in 1871 to delegate power to the City Council to elect not only the mayor but all the city officials, thus negating the anticipated power of the black vote gained by the upcoming ratification of the 15th amendment. The revised charter also imposed a poll tax on voting that effectively restrained black voter participation. By the 1880s and 1890s, Lexington's own Jim Crow laws were in full force.

At the same time, black churches and black-owned businesses began actively asserting their separateness and formed myriad black organizations and benevolent societies. Even before the war ended, the black communities of Lexington discussed the future of a public school system for their children. Little or no state public funds were available until 1874 for black children's education; however, by the fall of 1865 there were five grade schools with 300 tuition-paying students. E. Belle Mitchell, a black woman from Danville who had spent only three tumultuous weeks teaching school at the American Missionary Society's school at Camp Nelson, came to teach at the First Baptist Church for $20 a month plus board. A group of Lexington's black women organized a fundraising campaign for a free school for poor children. The Howard School opened in September 1866 in a brick building on Church Street with three black teachers and 500 students, though only one class had desks. The Freedman's Bureau and numerous benevolent societies established local schools by working through the black communities in army camps and churches to find teachers and school-age students. In 1867 the black First Baptist church hosted the State Convention of Colored Baptists, and in 1869, reorganized as the General Association of Colored Baptists—which established a State Sunday School Board—planned a church newspaper and committed to the founding of a college for the education of black ministers. This institution was eventually founded in Louisville as State University. The Methodist Episcopal Church, South, had two districts in Kentucky, one headquartered in Lexington at Asbury Church. In 1869 the Methodist Church created a separate organization with the "Lexington Conference" led by a black bishop, Rev. Edward Thomson.

While the rest of Kentucky, mostly rural and relying on agriculture, suffered from out-migrations, business depression, and regional infighting over the control of tobacco and coal markets, Lexington slowly adjusted to her new urban identity. The elderly mayors elected in the two decades following the war did little to lead the city toward improving its water supply, sewage system, public buildings, or streets. The dramatic changes in the size of the city with the rise of the urban black communities and the impoverished nature of the majority of her inhabitants combined poorly with the white population's continued mistrust of the federal government. Vigilantism by rural whites targeting the new black urban population and the strict regulations on black labor kept Lexington from growing into the type of city with a diverse population, thriving commerce, and social services such as in Louisville, Covington, and Newport.

Chapter Five

MODERNIZATION IN A NEW NATION: QUEEN OF THE BLUEGRASS

The modernization of Lexington came early in its history. As an urban center too far from the steamboat trade, it could not rely on modernity coming down the river from the East. But the city's leaders were determined to stay at the forefront of modern America with a concerted effort to support their own infrastructure and cultural accoutrements, with or without support from the national government. Lexington was the first city in Kentucky to have street lights, an early deployment of police, and regulations against hogs in the streets. Early on, the city paved the urban sewers and walkways. The city had a diverse though transient population; this promoted an openness to the new and different, a truly modern climate of thought.

At the same time, the agrarian culture still dominated. An example is the "time change war" of the early 1890s. The farmers and grocers in the city halted an attempt by the mayor to change all the city clocks to the standard time used by the railroad companies and most other cities since 1883. It took a lecture by Mrs. Mary Dudley Short of the Women's Club of Central Kentucky to convince city council members that the traditional solar time (or "God's Time") was also man-made, and that the city clocks, the clock at St. Paul's Church, and the tower bells at the fire station should all be turned back twenty-two minutes to conform with the rest of modern America. The County Courthouse clock overlooking Main Street continued on solar time for three months until a tie-breaker vote in the Fayette County Fiscal Court caused it too to be set to standard time.

Some disagreed with the New South rhetoric of Kentucky promoters like Henry Watterson of the Louisville *Courier-Journal* and William Campbell Preston (W.C.P.) Breckinridge of the Lexington *Observer and Reporter*. Those who dreaded the end of slavery also feared that Yankee modernization would be forced upon the city, changing it forever. However, long-time Lexingtonians like former Confederate Colonel Breckinridge knew that the violence engendered by groups like the Ku Klux Klan would destroy Lexington and encouraged a "New Departure" faction in the Democratic Party. While Kentucky was gaining a national reputation as one of the most violent places in the country, and the Appalachian mountain-man stereotype gained prominence in the national imagination, Lexington's promoters clamored against the trend toward vigilantism. The New Departure Democrats supported the post-bellum federal amendments and wanted to take advantage of the new economy centered once again on a national government. This was nothing new for Lexington:

the city had grown to national prominence on the coattails of the founder of the American System, Henry Clay. What in fact happened is that the continuity of Lexington's culture from antebellum days far outweighed the changes in the modern world around her. Lexington's traits—the centrality of her mercantile, financial, and transportation professions; the service-oriented labor market undergirded by a black community with a strong identity of its own; the epicenter of socio-political clubs and assemblies for the Bluegrass agrarian interests—all came from before the Civil War and lifted Lexington into the twentieth century. The tight-knit synergy of these traits led to her rising status by the 1920s and 1930s as the horse capitol of the world.

By the 1880s, Lexington promised her citizens she would be a thriving city in the New South: a system of street railways, telephone lines, a new public waterworks, and an ice factory marked a continued emphasis on city infrastructure necessary for expansion and financial stability in her role as a mercantile and transportation center. Lexington was still an "Athens of the West" with ten newspapers, twenty-five schools (including a university and four colleges, one of which was the new State College), eighteen churches, four bookstores, an agricultural and mechanical association, a racing association with the fastest course in the United States, a new Opera House, two quadrille bands, a musical society, and a theater. Lexington also served her population with a Chautauqua Association that offered weeks of cultural and educational programs, four public halls, a public park, a public library, public health officers and mandatory smallpox vaccinations, asylums for orphans and the insane, a workhouse for the impoverished, a Roman-style bath house, three railroads, and an omnibus line.

Her principal trade was in groceries, dry goods, whiskey, livestock, and hemp manufacturing—soon to be replaced by tobacco. Her importance as a nexus for several railroads, including the Cincinnati Southern Railroad and the Lexington & Big Sandy Railroad, reinforced the age-old Lexington-Louisville competition for an interstate transportation industry. Mostly, Lexington served as the center for the lucrative industries surrounding the rise of the Kentucky blood-horse and tobacco. Nearly every farmer around Lexington was a breeder, and horses reigned supreme with such thoroughbreds as Lexington, bred by Dr. Elisha Warfield, and standardbred trotters such as Mambrino Bertie, bred by Dr. L. Herr. In 1883 President Chester Arthur visited Lexington, and former Confederate Gen. William Preston officially greeted him on behalf of the town. President Arthur ate lunch at the old Ashland estate, then owned by H.C. McDowell, then toured the Ashland Park Stock Farm across the street to see the two race tracks and elegant stables filled with some of the greatest Kentucky horses.

Despite the ravages of war and military occupation, Lexington retained its role as the agricultural and manufacturing keystone for surrounding farms. The new Chamber of Commerce, founded November 2, 1881, highlighted this role when it coined the city "Queen of the Bluegrass." The campaigns to end the toll-gate system and establish "free roads" maintained by public taxes reflected this growing concern for the needs of the outlying farmers relying on the city markets, financial institutions, and transportation hubs. The toll-gate system in the Bluegrass was extensive—travelers encountered a toll-gate every five miles from the city limits and tolls were often assigned differently and not in keeping with the condition of the road. An editorial in the Lexington *Daily Transcript* on February 24, 1882, complained: "Such absurd restrictions as the toll-roads are utterly too medieval for a rejuvenated Kentucky." Many of the toll-gate keepers were Irish-American, and during this post-bellum era they were often the victim of a horsewhipping, vandalism, or worse from "turnpike regulators." The vigilantism heated up in the 1890s during a time when, according to Duane Bolin's book *Bossism and Reform in a Southern City*, Lexington had the highest murder rate per capita in the nation. By the end of the decade, the principal turnpike companies sold their roads. Fayette County bought 8.19 miles of one of the most prominent turnpikes, the Lexington and Maysville Road, for $15,555 in 1897. The building of roads using local, state, and federal monies by this time had became more of an important strategy for political patronage and influence than an expression of the needs of rural Kentuckians.

The business boom of the 1880s allowed Lexingtonians to flirt with the idea of local government reform, and the city charter was amended in 1886 to put legislative power in the hands of a general council made up of a board of councilmen and a board of aldermen (also known as the "Upper Lords"). This move crushed the political patronage ring of Dennis Mulligan, an Irish political boss who commanded the Lexington ward system through his payments for poll taxes, whiskey, and political paybacks for black and Irish small business owners, railroad workers, and the fire and police departments. Lexington's local politics had been the personal realm of Mulligan and his machine, but by the 1880s Henry T. Duncan, the editor of the Lexington *Daily Press*, moved Lexington into the Progressive Era.

One of the most controversial newspapers in the United States started in Lexington at this time. Charles Chilton Moore founded the *Bluegrass Blade* in 1884 and championed not only women's suffrage and temperance, but also agnosticism and eugenics. The *Daily Press*, which had started in October 1870 with Henry T. Duncan, Jr. and Hart Gibson as the city's first daily newspaper (and the first one here printed by steam), was viewed as the organ of the Mulligan machine, according to Bolin. By 1895 it merged with the *Morning Transcript*, which had been founded in 1876 and edited by the son of Dennis Mulligan, Judge James H. Mulligan. The resulting *Morning Herald* became the most powerful voice in the state for progressive reform. Desha Breckinridge, son of W.C.P. Breckinridge, took strong positions on controversial issues of the day such as women's suffrage, Purity Leagues, child labor laws, and prison reform. He roared in protest against his Republican-oriented local competitor, the *Kentucky Herald*, an afternoon paper. Even after Breckinridge died in 1935 and John G. Stoll merged the two papers in 1937, the morning and afternoon editions continued their separate political stances.

In 1899 Lexington's young Democrats, led by the reform-minded Moses Kaufman, helped Billy Klair, the son of a German immigrant, to beat "Colonel" Roger Williams, a steeplechase horseman who founded the prestigious Iroquois Hunt Club, in a race for representative to the state legislature. Klair's campaign efforts reflected his political base, the poor white populations of German and Irish descent in Lexington. His constituency could always reach him somewhere in the twenty-five to thirty saloons crowded into one square block between North Broadway, Main, and Mill Streets. In a 1983 interview with historian Duane Bolin, former Governor A.B. "Happy" Chandler described Klair as a master at personal politics and noted that he "absolutely controlled Lexington." He was head of the local Democratic Party, a bank director, the vice president of the Lexington Union Station Company, vice president of the Yellow Cab & Transfer Company, director for the Phoenix Amusement Company, and his textbook publishing company held the lucrative monopoly for Kentucky schools.

Spearheaded by Klair in the state legislature, the State University in Lexington gained the motto, "Athens of the West" as part of its legal name, and the institution continued to grow under increasing state support. In exchange, the president James K. Patterson gave the Klair & Scott Insurance Company the full contract without having put it out for bids. Klair & Scott also wrote insurance for most of the state and later, in 1936, for the Keeneland Racetrack as well. In time, Klair became a central part of what Henry T. Duncan Jr. called Lexington's "Big Six:" Fayette County Judge Frank Bullock, road contractors Louis des Cognets and Ernest Ellis, Mayors Thomas Combs and John Skain, and hotel owner Joseph Skain. Under the watchful eye of Klair and Mayor John Skain, the city charter was amended in 1911 to remove the mayor, eight aldermen, and twelve councilmen (elected from six wards) and replace them with a more centralized form of government popular then in Progressive Era cities: a commission of five who represented the city at-large.

Despite the efforts of progressive Lexingtonians the city fell in rank among U.S. cities: from 110th largest city in 1880 to 153rd in 1900. In general, Kentucky began its long fall in all sorts of national rankings. At the same time Lexington's boundaries began to change, and the growth of a well-oiled mass transit system allowed for the majority of Lexington's white population to find suitable housing in outlying subdivisions. But, her growth as an urban transit center was outpaced by more cosmopolitan areas. Lexington's black population census numbers were more like Nashville and Birmingham than Louisville or Covington. The number of foreign-born citizens, as high as 49 percent in Cincinnati or 38 percent in Louisville, was barely 12 percent in Lexington—more like Montgomery or Chattanooga. Even when, during World War I, Lexington once again became a mobilization site for Kentucky troops and Camp Stanley was established on the north side of Versailles Road (west of Hamilton Park), the only foreign element that came to Lexington to stay was an addiction to cigarette smoking.

Lexington's white population held the upper hand in the city even though at least half of her population was black: African Americans held less than one tenth of the city's wealth. The 1870s, 1880s, and 1890s in Kentucky were rife with cultural conflict. The insistence on white superiority over black civil and human rights was exacerbated by the unsettling prospect of women taking more active political roles in public. Lexington, in the center of the Bluegrass area of hemp and bloodstock breeding, had always had a clear sense of boundaries between the races, but the city did not geographically divide along racial lines until after the Civil War. The spatial areas bounded by race were not large: a working-class neighborhood in Lexington's north side suburbs had white residents on one side of the street and blacks on the other side and sat only one block from turn-of-the-century city mansions owned by the white professional class. Lexingtonians had a long history of clarifying who was non-white and skin color did not always matter: white-skinned people had stood at the auction block at Cheapside to be sold because their mothers were enslaved. After the Civil War white Kentuckians reluctantly removed the shackles of their black workers, but they continued to restrict black liberty. Many whites angrily refused when black citizens claimed basic rights. Brave efforts to open black schools, allow black testimony in court, and provide equal access to private property ownership and the vote were met with indignities and violence. The violence was frightening to all and contributed to a general feeling of chaos and disorder under all the new rhetoric trumpeted by the Chamber of Commerce.

One of the ways that many post–Civil War communities chose to create order out of the socio-economic chaos was with monumental public art. Art for morality's sake (as opposed to art for art's sake) reached new heights in the Reconstruction Era. Through public art, city elites could dictate social redemption in the face of the new national identity—and white Lexingtonians, crafting the mythic Lost Cause, commissioned art that would instruct their community in this new order. A group of elite women, calling themselves the "Women of the Bluegrass," worked for several years to purchase and display Kentuckian Joel T. Hart's white marble statue grouping, "Woman Triumphant." Hart thought of his statue as "modern," and art critics of the day agreed with him. He asserted that, unlike the nude statues of antiquity, his idealized woman's brow was "with light, and truth, and love imbued," which had vanquished lust and unreasoned earthly passions.

In the early 1880s the historian Robert Peter chronicled how the grouping was perceived by contemporaries who viewed it in Hart's studio:

> Cupid, fully armed and equipped, is ignominiously defeated in an attack upon a virgin just arrived at perfect womanhood. . . . It is a group of two figures only—a perfect woman and charming Cupid. Love in the shape of a bewitching Cupid has assailed the fair one, has shot arrow after arrow, all of which are broken and have fallen at her feet. His quiver is exhausted, his last shaft has failed of the mark, and this splendid woman has caught the barbed arrow, and with her left hand has raised it above his head out of reach of the villainous little tempter, who struggles vainly on tiptoe to regain it. The composition tells its own story. Virtue is assailed; reason is brought to bear and all attacks are harmless.

At the same time, the Women of the Bluegrass commissioned another Kentuckian, Rosa Vertner Jeffrey, to craft a poem to be read during the ceremonial unveiling of the statue and printed in the accompanying pamphlet and in the newspapers that covered the event. The ceremony and unveiling of the statue took place on April 15, 1884, and the fifty-page pamphlet describing the purpose of the statue was published in advance. Jeffrey, a Lexington poet/novelist, waxed eloquent over this intellectually sensuous image of womanhood. In her poem written for the Lexington *Observer and Reporter*, Jeffrey agreed that the nude woman was symbol of "the soul's high triumph over earthly passion." His statue was "homage" to the women of his native home. More importantly, "No purer women live, and none are fairer / Than those he has immortalized in stone." As an idea, the statue did not belong in a domestic environment or even in an exhibition hall, but in the county courthouse belonging to the public.

Thomas W. Boyd of Pittsburg designed the new courthouse in Lexington but a local contractor, William E. Bush, revised the plans and built it. The cornerstone was not laid until July 4, 1884. Clearly the building was meant to be built around the statue, which was placed in a glass-enclosed rotunda, prominently displayed on a dais for all to see after they climbed up the stairs to the main door. Her powerful nudity, not hidden away in a domestic setting, gained special significance in its architectural context. In contrast, E.V. Valentine's bronze statue of native son, vice-president, and Confederate Gen. John C. Breckinridge was placed in 1887 outside and to the left of the courthouse in the center of the street market area. "Woman Triumphant" remained in the open foyer of the Fayette County Courthouse in the center of Lexington until it was destroyed along with the courthouse in a fire in the spring of 1897.

We can only imagine what the majority of observers saw when they stared at her nude body on their way to settle a fine or watch a court case. Surely very few Kentuckians saw Hart's statue in the same realm of meaning that the elites like Jeffrey did: Victorian portrayals of nude women titillated and excited the viewers by their very existence. Lexington's men had plenty of opportunities outside their own homes to view living naked women. Only two years before "Woman Triumphant" was placed in the Fayette County Courthouse, Belle Brezing, an infamous prostitute, had earned a pardon from Governor Luke P. Blackburn for keeping a bawdy house only one block away. Brezing was financially successful even though she was indicted more times than any other citizen in Lexington. Research after Margaret Mitchell's death confirmed that Brezing was the inspiration for Belle Watling, the generous-hearted, well-connected madam in *Gone with the Wind*. Her early sexual activity was not unusual for the urban working-class population from which she came, but her ability to become a successful entrepreneur was indeed unusual. Brezing's creative and interesting mind is evident in this little scrap of a poem written around 1874 when she was a teenager:

> "Kisses"
> Sitting to night in my chamber, a school girl figure
> and lonely, I kiss the end of my finger, that and that only.
>
> Reveries rises from the smokey mouth. Memories linger surround
> me. Boys that are married or single. Gather around me. School boys
> in pantalets romping, Boys that now are growing to be young lads,
> Boys that liked to be Kissed; and like to give kisses.
>
> Kisses. I remember them: Those in the corner were fleetest:
> Sweet were those won the Sly in the Dark were the sweetest.
> Girls are tender and gentle. To woo was allmost to win them.
> They lips are good as ripe peaches, and cream for finger.
> Girls are sometimes flirts, and coquettish; Now catch and Kiss if
> you can sin: could I catch both—ah, wasent I a happy Girl.
>
> Boys is pretty and blooming sweetly, yea sweetness over their rest!
> Them I loved dearly and truely. Last and the best.

The Lexington *Daily Press* on January 13, 1889, carried a "Petition of Citizens" on the front page that urged the closing of three "houses of ill fame" on North Upper Street. But Brezing's connections with influential men of the Lexington area and beyond were too strong. With the help of William M. Singerly, a multimillionaire from Philadelphia, she bought another house on the corner of Wilson and Megowan Street. This brick house included twenty-five acres with an orchard of nearly 400 peach trees and one of the largest gardens in town. There she and her girls, sometimes as many as twenty-five of them, entertained men with great flair until 1917. Tremendously popular with men of all political backgrounds, Brezing's entrepreneurial spirit kept her business secure and financially sound even into a late age. In the late 1930s, U.K. professor Dr. Thomas Clark, Samuel M. Wilson, and history buffs William Townsend and J. Winston Coleman Jr. visited her to see what books they might want from her collection. Townsend tucked into his pocket one of her account books for her business activities in 1882–1883. Belle Brezing, heavily addicted to morphine, died of uterine cancer at the age of eighty in 1940. Her household effects were sold at public auction and the house converted to apartments. It burned in 1973 and soon thereafter the building was razed.

Lexington was home to many strong and creative women, and the publishing market of the nineteenth century allowed for more and better documentation of their efforts. Like most other places, however, the press was of two minds about women's roles in the post-bellum era. In the Lexington *Daily Press* of February 3, 1874, a small editorial was borrowed from the *Rural New Yorker* and printed under the banner "Love, Honor and Obey." It serves as a testimony of how some—and perhaps most—in Lexington perceived women's role.

> On the whole, married women, that is, real women, prefer to be ruled than ruling. It is scarcely in her nature to go speechlessly on doing what she has to do without aid or counsel. Almost say one of our sex is happier if she can "talk things over" with some man upon whose discretion she relies; and in married life most wives do, even in the smallest things, what "he" likes, and fancy that they like it themselves. Since independence has become the fashion, and strong-minded women have sneered at the more gentle sisters, there is great affectation of despising the opinion of men, but it is all sheer pretence. Almost every wife chooses her gloves and her ribbons of the tint that her husband admires, and the man she loves inevitably gives her her political opinions, and biases even her religious views. Her speech, her dress, her manners change under his influence. What he desires her to do she does in nine cases out of ten. The tenth case we find in the divorce courts. You may rule your wife as you please, good married reader, if you only love and pet her enough. Haughtiness and fault-finding alone will make her restive. And you, dear girl, remember that it will be well to choose a husband good and noble and upright, so that you may obey him to your heart's content without losing your own self-respect; for you will obey him if you love him; and if he be low and mean you will sink to the level slowly but surely in the course of years.

Lexington women, however, often had a different view of the world than most other urban women of the nineteenth-century south. Sophonisba Breckinridge, daughter of the ex-Confederate Colonel W.C.P. Breckinridge, was the first woman to pass the Kentucky bar exam, though it wasn't until 1928 that a woman was appointed to sit as a judge in Kentucky: Kathleen Mulligan, daughter of Judge James H. Mulligan. Mary Desha, granddaughter of Governor Joseph Desha, organized the Daughters of the American Revolution as part of a protest against the Sons, who seemed to think they did it all. Mary E. Britton, an African-American school teacher, went on to earn her M.D. and was the first woman physician licensed to practice medicine in Lexington. Since 1838—ten years before the famous Seneca Falls Convention and almost ninety years before women could vote in national elections—some women in Kentucky had the right to vote in school board elections: property-owning widows or unmarried women over twenty-one who paid taxes in a district. Though Louisville had been the site of the first women's rights convention south of the Ohio River when Lucy Stone's American Women's Suffrage Association met there in October 1881, the Fayette County Equal Rights Association came on strong. It was organized in Lexington in the parlors of such women as Mary Jane Warfield Clay, whose divorce from the philandering Cassius M. Clay showed that Lexington's elite women could make it on their own. Two of her daughters, Mary and Laura, went on to national prominence in the many different women's movements of this era.

Organized women's political power made great gains during this time. In 1894 the Kentucky Equal Rights Association succeeded with its petitions from Lexington, Covington, and Newport to the legislature for a school suffrage law with a broader scope, though its final wording limited the franchise to all women in the areas that had petitioned for it. Lexington women had gained the right to vote on issues regarding public schools and could serve on school boards. During the Lexington school board elections of 1901 there was a swell of political activity by black women who were supporting the Republican Party. In fact, more black women registered to vote than white women. In the very next legislative session, the Kentucky General Assembly repealed all women's rights to vote in school elections, even defeating a compromise effort by white suffragist leaders who suggested adding a literacy test to voter applications. Even though the Democrats won that local election in Lexington, the male legislators' fear of organized women's political power caused the unprecedented repeal of women's suffrage in 1902.

After the Civil War and during Reconstruction (or what in Kentucky has been called "Readjustment" since there was no official Reconstruction in this state), Americans worked to rebuild a nation. When the survivors of the war began planning the one hundredth anniversary of the adoption of the Declaration of Independence, patriotic organizations became popular. The Centennial celebrations spawned a great variety of fraternal and benevolent societies that united the descendants of Revolutionary heroes and patriots. The Society of the Cincinnati (founded in 1783 by officers and first born sons in the original thirteen states) gave these organizations a model based on pedigree and ribboned ritual. The first came in San Francisco in 1875 at a conference where the men in attendance coined themselves the Sons of Revolutionary Sires. This grew into the Sons of the Revolution, General Society by February 1876. By 1890 there were at least thirty-five such patriotic hereditary societies, and by 1900 there were over seventy. A national conference of the Sons of the American Revolution (founded April 20, 1889) met in Louisville in April 1890. Even though women were already admitted in the local organizations in some eastern states, the national conference voted down a proposal to admit women. This led to the beginning of the Daughters of the American Revolution.

Mary S. Lockwood, an ardent suffragist and business owner in Washington, D.C., wrote a letter to the editor of *The Washington Post* complaining about the insult done to patriotic American women by the SAR at the Louisville conference. At this time two key Kentuckians were living in Washington. Mary Desha of Lexington came to the capital with her brother-in-law, W.C.P Breckinridge, a Kentucky senator. She was working as a clerk in the Pension Bureau and responded privately to Lockwood's letter. Her childhood friend Ellen Hardin Walworth was a widow who lived also in Saratoga Springs, where she was the first woman elected to a local board of education in New York. Another friend, Eugenia Washington, a direct descendant of Colonel Samuel Washington, was employed at the U.S. Postal Department. These three met in July 1890 at Walworth's apartment in the Langham Hotel to re-write the SAR constitution. They determined that Mrs. Benjamin Harrison, the wife of the president, should be president general.

Mary Desha merged her previously organized club Wimodaughsis, then led by the suffragist Anna Howard Shaw, into the new club. Of the nine members of the board of management, four were Kentuckians: Desha, Walworth, Sophanisba Breckinridge (W.C.P.'s sister and the founder of the discipline of Social Work at the University of Chicago), and Virginia Grigsby. The club was incorporated in the District in 1891 and chartered by the federal government in 1896. Women not less than eighteen who proved lineal descent from a loyal soldier, sailor, or civil officer—and who were "acceptable to the society"—were eligible members. The objects of the society were:

> 1. To perpetuate the memory and spirit of the men and women who achieved American independence;
> 2. To promote, as an object of primary importance institutions for the general diffusion of knowledge, thus developing an enlightened public opinion;
> 3. To cherish, maintain and extend institutions of American freedom, and to foster true patriotism and love of country.

The club was charged with reporting annually to the Smithsonian Institute and to Congress. In 1896, the Lexington chapter of the DAR claimed it had made history by erecting the first memorial ever built by women in honor of women. They erected and dedicated a stone wall around a historic spring at Bryan's Station in tribute to pioneer women who carried water from the spring to the fort during a Native American siege in 1782. The story in the pamphlet created for the occasion made clear the heroism of the white pioneers and their loyal black slaves in the face of non-white savagery. By 1911 the DAR proudly outnumbered the Sons by a substantial margin: 80,000 to 18,000.

The DAR clearly strove to create a new nation based on racial and social "purity." They were strongly anti-suffragist and anti-immigration, and by the 1920s they were anti-communist as well. Surely, its most infamous act was in 1939 when the DAR prevented Marian Anderson from performing in Constitution Hall because she was black. By the 1950s they were leaders in the demands for loyalty oaths and censorship, and in the 1960s they were determined to put their version of God in public schools.

Lexington

Yet their work in the memorialization of American patriots (and the flag) and in the restoration of historic landmarks cannot be understated.

Lexington women like Sallie McDowell Preston, president of the Woman's Club of Central Kentucky, most often used oblique strategies to craft public policy. For example, Preston formed a "Good Citizenship League," which presented research to the male decision-makers on how other cities solved problems similar to those in Lexington. The carefully worded announcement in the sympathetic Lexington *Sunday Leader* on January 22, 1899, described: "In other words, the object of the League will be merely to present facts and then Councilmen and local politicians can form their own conclusions." But many believed it to be the women of Kentucky who helped to defeat W.C.P. Breckinridge when he ran for reelection to the U.S. House of Representatives in 1894. He had recently lost a scandalous court case in which his mistress Madeline Pollard accused him of breach of promise when he married his third wife Louise Scott Wing instead of her. The streets of Lexington thronged with a parade of indignant women urging the male community of voters to reject the "Silver-tongued Orator."

Usually propriety ruled, and women very carefully lobbied male leaders who would act on their behalf. In fact, the Woman's Club of Central Kentucky passed a resolution in 1894 that if a new recruit were pregnant, she could not be accepted as a member because her presence would be too indecorous and her controversial actions—attending club meetings while becoming a mother—might taint the respectability of the club. This same club protested a highly politicized effort in 1899 to remove Dr. Louise Bergman-Healy who headed the white women's ward at the Lunatic Asylum (now Eastern State Hospital). However, on their petition to the governor, they chose to sign their husbands' names.

Overall, Lexington clubwomen were a powerful force in their own right. The Kentucky Federation of Women's Clubs (KFWC) was founded in July 1894 under the leadership of Lexington's Mary Gratz Morton. The KFWC led a campaign for school reform, which led to a revamping of the school system in 1908; their projects related to conservation, the arts, home life, international affairs, public affairs, and health issues. Well into the twentieth century, women continued to couch their public activities in politically correct terms. Since 1923 the University of Kentucky's County Extension Office had used Home Demonstration Agents to organize Kentucky women into working and learning groups. By 1934, the Kentucky Federation of Homemakers, formed at the University of Kentucky during a Farm and Home Week, assured their male counterparts that their role was not to take women out of their prescribed roles but to help women "learn how to raise future citizens with integrity and moral character."

In 1924 the women in Lexington's Volunteer Service League successfully founded the Lexington chapter of the Association of Junior Leagues. Dr. Caroline Scott remembered in a 1983 interview with University of Kentucky archivist Bill Marshall that her work for the Volunteer Service League included trips to Ashland to collect donated milk from the granddaughter of Henry Clay, Mrs. McDowell, and then Scott would drive over to the impoverished section of Lexington, right across Richmond Road, and hand it out in cupfuls to mothers standing in line for the free fresh milk. Scott remembered that the reason she had become part of the League was because she "had nothing else to do"—being the daughter of a prominent doctor, she could not take on a wage-earning job without reflecting poorly on his status in Lexington society—and that she was bored with the endless string of parties. She admitted that the organization was not very well organized, and that the transition to the Junior League meant a greater prestige and professionalism to this group of clubwomen.

Historian Rebecca Hanley researched the backgrounds of the ten founding members of the Lexington Junior League: Virginia Bell Finnell, Harriet Gay, Margaret Kirk, Mabel Bundy Marks, Frances Jewell McVey, Ruth Rodes, Ethel Rounsavall, Mary Stewart, Laura Kinkead Walton, and Estelle des Cognets Yancey. Walton was the founding member of the Lexington Planned Parenthood Association. Both Marks and McVey were Vassar College graduates and brought with them the Progressive ideas and activism fostered at that women's school. McVey had taught in the university's English department and was dean of women before she married the university president, Frank McVey. She led many other organizations as well: the International Club, the YWCA, the Lexington chapter of the American Association of University Women, and the University of Kentucky Women's Club, and served on the boards of the Lexington School, Vassar College, and the Frontier Nursing Service. McVey's prominent contribution to the Junior League was the creation of the training course for new provisional members. The novitiate attended the training classes, kept a journal of her observation of the conditions in Lexington, and wrote a long essay on a particular social issue such as health, housing, education, or recreation. The League required active members to then undertake one hundred hours of volunteer work per year.

The women of the Lexington Junior League founded a Temporary Baby Home in 1927 that became a Day Nursery in 1931 complete with modern kindergarten equipment and Mothers Clubs. Only three years later, when the Depression years hit Lexington homes hard and women lost what few wage-earning jobs they had, the Nursery was shut down and the League started a Child Guidance Clinic. This work, under the consultation of University of Kentucky psychologist Dr. Graham Dimmick, entailed the League members taking on as professional social workers the cases of "mal-adjusted" mothers, making recommendations and referrals until 1944. The League also served as founding partners of the Baby Health Services in 1938, providing health care for the children of uninsured working families, and the Lexington Children's Theater in 1939.

African-American women in Lexington spearheaded a separate club movement that was equally based in a cult of respectability. The establishment of the Colored

Lexington

Orphan and Industrial Home, founded in 1892 in Lexington by Eliza Belle Jackson from Boyle County and other elite African-American women, is a good example. This home offered shelter and care for orphans and destitute elderly women while supporting itself through cottage industries such as shoemaking. However, the children were isolated from the rest of the black community in the hopes of inculcating a different worldview, and they were taught self-help principles promoted by the national leader, Booker T. Washington. The building now houses the Robert H. Williams Cultural Center.

One of the most respected women leaders of the Lexington black community was Elizabeth "Lizzie" Cooke Fouse. Born in 1875, she became the first president of the Kentucky Federation of Colored Women and established a scholarship loan fund for black students. She networked with local and national club women to promote racial equality, increase access to public assistance, and improve the cultural opportunities for blacks. Her club's motto was: "Lift as We Climb." Fouse founded the Phyllis Wheatley branch of the YWCA in 1920. She led the City Federation of Colored Women's Clubs, including the Acme Art and Culture Club, the Women's Improvement Club and Day Nursery (volunteers who staffed a nursery for black children of working women), and the women's auxiliary of the Emancipation League. She also worked for the National Association of Colored Women (NACW), traveling across the country and serving as an expert on child welfare issues. She coordinated the NACW's Better Homes Movement, a project dedicated to helping women and their families become more self-sufficient and exhibit respectable behavior despite the violence and degradation of segregation.

There were many smaller organizations that black women of Lexington contributed their time, money, and organizational skills to foster. For example, in 1934 several women met at the Dunbar High School annex building, which once had served as an orphans' home for white children whose parents died in the cholera plagues of the nineteenth century. Carolyn Blanton founded a local chapter of Kappa Alpha Kappa, Beta Gamma Omega, along with Alberta Robinson (a high school English teacher), Ollie Davis Miller (a social worker), Myrtle Hummons Jones (an elementary school teacher at Booker T. Washington School), Irene Hawkins, and Zelma Fuller Weaver (both teachers at Russell School). Under their leadership Marva Louis, Joe Louis's first wife, participated in a style show at the Lyric Theater, located on the corner of Deweese and Third Streets.

More documents are available on two well-connected white women of Lexington: Madeline "Madge" McDowell Breckinridge and Laura Clay. Both were great orators who gave popular lectures for women's rights and both were descendants of influential Kentucky politicians. Breckinridge was the great-granddaughter of Henry Clay and those who heard her speeches often compared her to the Great Compromiser. Her education included some time at Kentucky State College (now the University of

Kentucky), and though she had tuberculosis of the bone leading to the amputation of a portion of one leg, she was very active in local, state, and national organizations. She joined the elite women's organization called the Fortnightly Club in the 1890s where she continued to educate herself by studying science, literature, and philosophy. She wrote book reviews for the Lexington *Herald* and after she married the newspaper's editor Desha Breckinridge in 1898, she wrote a weekly women's page.

Breckinridge disparaged "small change charity" efforts, such as holiday dinner baskets handed out by the local political machines of Lexington's ward bosses or soup kitchens of the local police or Salvation Army. Instead she promoted "scientific charity," which sought "a basis for its actions not in sentimentality but in reason." With the help of her sister-in-law, Dr. Sophonisba Breckinridge, founder of the Graduate School of Social Services Administration at the University of Chicago, she began using the "casework" method. In 1899, inspired by Jane Addams's Hull House in Chicago, she directed the women's group the Gleaners of Christ Church Episcopal, in establishing a settlement house in Proctor, near Beattyville in eastern Kentucky. The winter of 1900 was long and hard and in response to the lack of emergency relief from the city, she helped found the Associated Charities, which would coordinate relief activities and better distribute donations for whites. Black applicants for poor relief were directed to Professor Green Russell, who organized donations for African Americans.

Also in 1900, on April 17, the Lexington Civic League formed out of a mass meeting called by the Lexington Woman's Club and Women's Christian Temperance Union in response to several murders. Led by male officers, the League was unusual in its affiliation with women's clubs and in its primary concern, to initiate programs in Lexington for political education of its mostly illiterate citizens. Under Breckinridge's committee leadership however, the League sponsored civic improvement in more material ways such as building parks, playgrounds for white children (the first one was in Irishtown, one of the poorest sections of the city where the pollution from the Tarr Distillery overwhelmed the shantytown), public kindergartens, and vocational training in public schools. The League's women-led committees also lobbied for laws on compulsory school attendance and child labor. Breckinridge used the League's connections to create a combined school and social settlement in Irishtown called the Abraham Lincoln School and Social Center. In 1906 the League worked with legislators to establish a juvenile court system, the first in the south. There were many other Civic Leagues in Kentucky towns as a result of the fame of Lexington's efforts. Together with the Civic League, the Associated Charities led the fight against tuberculosis, establishing a sanatorium in Lexington and eventually helping to establish a state tuberculosis commission.

Most important, however, was Breckinridge's belief that only through the extension of voting rights to women would true social reform take place. She insisted to her conservative community that she was forced into the suffrage movement by the indifference of politicians to women's pleas for social reform. A prime indicator of socio-economic progress is the status of women and children, and the legal and economic status of Kentucky women was one of the lowest in the nation. Women could not sign a contract, keep their own wages, serve as guardians of their own children, or vote in state or national elections. The "age of consent" to be married for girls was twelve. By the time Breckinridge successfully lobbied the General Assembly to regain school suffrage for women in 1912—that right which had been revoked by the Lexington political machine boss Billy Klair ten years earlier—many of the key indicators for women's rights had been reached.

Lexington's Henrietta B. Chenault, along with Laura Clay and her sister Mary Barr Clay, had organized the Kentucky Equal Rights Association (KERA) in November 1888 with suffragists from Fayette and Kenton Counties. The Kentucky Woman Suffrage Association was organized earlier in 1881 under Lucy Stone's leadership with Laura Clay as president and local affiliates in Louisville, Lexington, and Richmond, but it had fallen apart. Besides the suffrage, the KERA was also interested in winning legal, educational, and industrial rights for women. By 1894, married women gained the right to make a will and own property. A wife's claim to her own earnings was protected by law in 1900, and the age of consent had been raised from twelve to sixteen years of age by 1910. In that same year the co-guardianship law recognized a mother's claim to her own children. Laura Clay laid the foundation for these milestones. She graduated from Sayre Female Academy in 1865 and spent one year at school in New York City. She came back to Kentucky and spent some time learning to be a successful farmer like her mother Mary Jane had been while her father, Cassius M. Clay, went to war and pursued a life of politics. She continued her education at the University of Michigan and Kentucky State College in Lexington.

The women's rights movement had a long history in Kentucky even though the self-styled national organizations ignored the south. In 1853 the great orator Lucy Stone spent three days in Louisville giving lectures on women's status in American society. By 1867 the Glendale Association was established in Hardin County though it was disbanded by the time that Elizabeth Cady Stanton visited Kentucky in 1872. In 1879 Mary Barr Clay got Susan B. Anthony to speak at Richmond on the need for the vote for economic protection for women, which led to the founding of the Madison County Equal Rights Association, the state's first permanent women's rights association. Mary B. Clay, who was a vice president of both Stanton's National Woman Suffrage Association as well as of Stone's American Woman Suffrage Association, also invited Lucy Stone to stay at Mary Jane Clay's house while she toured Louisville and Lexington, and the Fayette County Equal Suffrage Association was created. It later was reorganized into the Fayette County Equal Rights

Modernization in a New Nation: Queen of the Bluegrass

Association by Laura Clay in 1888 with committees on Hygiene and Dress Reform, Industrial Training for Women, Bible Study, and Work among Young People.

The popularity of the Women's Christian Temperance Union (WCTU) in Kentucky far outstripped even this local organization with such expanded goals. Lucy Stone was credited for having said that the temperance movement that had such a hold on Lexington's socially conscious men and women was so popular because "it is so much easier to see a drunkard than it is to see a principle." But with the determined efforts of the Clay sisters, Josephine Henry, Mary C. Roark, Ellen B. Dietrick, and Eugenia Farmer, the suffragist arguments swayed many of the WCTU members who began wearing yellow ribbons, the woman's rights color, along with the white ribbon of the WCTU. By 1892 Frances Beauchamp, leader of the Women's Christian Temperance Union in Lexington, decided to support the vote in order to fight in the polls against the alcoholic wife-beater; often the WCTU speaker would begin a public lecture and then a suffragist would finish it. Clay's conservative plea of "taxation without representation is tyranny" worked well for southern audiences who might otherwise have been put off by her emphasis on white women's exact equality before the law.

In 1916 Laura Clay became the vice-president of the Southern States Woman Suffrage Association, an organization founded to win the right to vote through state enactment. The goal of gaining women's voting rights should, Clay and other southern suffragists asserted, come through state legislators and not be mandated by the federal government. When the combined woman's rights organization National American Woman Suffrage Association (NAWSA), asked all the suffragists in 1919 to halt state campaigns in order to support federal amendment, Laura Clay split off and formed the Citizens Committee for a State Suffrage Amendment. She didn't openly oppose the 19th Amendment until then, pleading the cause of states rights. In a biography of her sister-in-law Madge Breckinridge, Sophonisba claimed that Clay was also concerned about the NAWSA's emphasis on including black voters in the constitutional amendment—a stand that she, like most southern suffragists, abhorred. Clay, a WCTU member, also condemned Prohibition and served as the chair of the ratifying convention in Frankfort when Kentucky voted for its repeal in 1933.

It was Clay's distant cousin Madge Breckinridge who won the Kentucky legislature over to full suffrage for women. In 1919 Breckinridge became president of the KERA after her work as vice-president of the NAWSA and worked tirelessly to inform the legislators of what was happening nationally to support the federal amendment. On January 6, 1920, the Kentucky General Assembly ratified what became the 19th Amendment, but it also granted presidential suffrage for Kentucky women so they could vote in the next election in case the amendment was not ratified in time. The federal amendment finally passed on June 4, 1919, and though Madge Breckinridge was ill, she attended the "Jubilee" convention in Chicago the following spring with the other state suffrage association presidents. There, according to her biographer sister-in-law, she recited to rave reviews a parody on the sentimental "My Old Kentucky Home:"

> The sun shines bright on my old Kentucky home,
> 'Tis winter, the ladies are gay,
> The corn top's gone, prohibition's in the swing,
> The colonel's in eclipse and the women in the ring.
> We'll get all our rights with the help of Uncle Sam,
> For the way that they come, we don't give a _____.
> Weep no more, my lady, Oh, weep no more today,
> For we'll vote one vote for the old Kentucky home,
> The old Kentucky home, far away.

Breckinridge came back to Kentucky to vote in the presidential election, but she did not rest on her laurels. After attending the International Women's Suffrage Alliance in Geneva, Switzerland, she toured several states on behalf of the Democratic Party and lobbied for the formation of the League of Nations. Increasingly ill, she worked to convert the KERA into the League of Women Voters of Kentucky, but died before the final meeting took place. Most Lexington women continued to work for their community from "behind the scenes," however, and it was not until the 1930s that a woman from Lexington gained an elective office: Florence Shelby Cantrill, well-known as a descendent of Kentucky's first governor, first won a seat in the state legislature in 1933 then became Lexington's first woman city commissioner in 1936. She ran on Billy Klair's "Home Town Ticket" again a second time and served as mayor pro-tem. Her standing in the Democratic Party did not, however, influence her service to the Woman's Club of Central Kentucky. According to the Woman's Club's history, "Regal in bearing and aristocratic in manner, Mrs. Cantrill lent stature to the Woman's Club through her presence. During her later years she filled a matriarchical [sic] role within the Club and provided a living link to its earlier days."

Lexington's women, however, did not hold a monopoly on expressions of ethics and morality. The popular novelist James Lane Allen was first a Ketucky schoolteacher and short story writer in the 1880s. When his hugely successful novel *The Choir Invisible* was published in 1897, it set frontier Lexington in the minds of his international reading public—and the noble Kentucky hero whose duty and honor forced him to leave behind his forbidden love, a married woman. In *Reign of Law* Allen took up the controversy over evolution that shook the world of religion and education in the 1920s. It was another Lexingtonian, Baptist minister John W. Porter, who in 1920 sought to purge the teaching of evolution from local schools. Porter wrote *Evolution: A Menace* while his church's Board of Missions resolved to enact laws to stop teaching such a "false and degrading theory." William Jennings Bryan spoke in the state that year, and in 1922 he addressed a joint legislative session on the topic. The next day bills were introduced in both houses to prohibit the teaching of "Darwinism, Atheism, Agnosticism, or the Theory of Evolution." Kentucky was the first state where fundamentalists had enough power to propose anti-evolution bills. They failed, along with those presented in 1926 and 1928, due in large part to the sustained efforts of the University of Kentucky's president, Dr. Frank L. McVey, who called for tolerance for the diversity of religious and scientific thought. Meanwhile, yet another Lexingtonian (nephew of the Confederate Gen. John Hunt Morgan) and graduate of the University of Kentucky, Thomas Hunt Morgan, was busy working on his fruit fly experiments that would provide great insights into genetic theory and garner him the Nobel Prize in 1933.

The rise of intolerance included a clear sense of who could sit, stand, or walk in certain public areas, especially since the 1891 Separate Coach Law. Even earlier, however, the Kentucky legislature had been working to implement Jim Crow laws: in 1876 the state endorsed the racial segregation of mental asylums and the world changed for those patients being served at the Lexington asylum, one of the oldest in the nation. By the 1880s most African Americans in Lexington worked in unskilled or semi-skilled jobs and owned little property. Over 90 percent of those who registered to vote indicated their loyalty to the party of Lincoln, the Great Emancipator. In fact, by 1904, 76 percent of Lexington's registered Republicans were black. Local politics, run by the Klair machine, centered around the Democratic Party. The differences between Germans, Irish, Scots, and British—rich or poor, landowner or wage-earner—coalesced into a common culture of whiteness within the Democratic Party. In September 1893 the Lexington Colored Fair reported its largest attendance: 12,000. The event had been supported by whites as well as the black communities as a way to promote the new separateness.

Much like during the military occupation of the Civil War, armed mobs during and after World War I committed acts of violence fueled by racism. Most happened under the cover of dark, and some were probably inspired by D.W. Griffith's 1915 movie *The Birth of a Nation*, which played in Lexington with great fanfare. But the city did not tolerate the activities of the second version of the Ku Klux Klan that reigned in the midwest during this time. However, the Klan's belief that only white Protestant Anglo-Saxons should determine the future of the citizenry was widely accepted and implemented by white Lexingtonians.

The respect for the "Lost Cause" of the Confederacy was an important part of the city's public art. The Ladies' Confederate Memorial was erected by the Ladies Memorial and Monument Association of Lexington in 1874, and the 1893 Confederate Soldier Monument overlooks the 160 Confederate dead in the Lexington Cemetery. A memorial to U.S. Vice-president and Confederate Gen. John C.

Lexington

Breckinridge was placed on the Fayette County Courthouse west lawn in the center of Lexington from funds from the Kentucky legislature in 1887. The United Daughters of the Confederacy received financial support from the state legislature to erect a monument to the heroic southern cavalier of Civil War memoirs, and in 1911 Lexington's streets filled with over 10,000 cheering spectators when they unveiled the sedate equestrian statue of Confederate Gen. John Hunt Morgan, "Thunderbolt of the Confederacy." Most public ceremonies in Lexington included the "Gray" along with the "Blue." When the Grand Army of the Republic conducted its 15th annual encampment on May 10 and 11, 1897 at the courthouse and at Woodland Park, the ceremonies included speeches by members of the Confederate Veteran Association of Kentucky and rousing versions of the song "Dixie."

In 1895 Lexington hosted the thirty-fifth Annual Kentucky Sunday School Union Convention. For three days sessions took place in the newly constructed Central Christian Church (out of the 447 delegates only 214 were men), and many of the elite white women of Lexington served as hostesses to the women from out of town. Rev. A.L. Phillips D.D. of Tuscaloosa, Alabama, delivered one of the most popular talks: "Opportunity and Necessity for Work Among our Colored People." The convention requested that Phillips speak at a mass meeting "for colored people" on the last evening held in the Asbury M.E. Church. The International Committee expressed the racism that undergirded the age of European colonization as well as Lexington segregation laws:

> Resolved, That we recognize that God has placed us in peculiar relations to the negro race, involving the greatest responsibility for their religious training, from which, as His children, we dare not turn away, and has given us rare privileges in bringing Christ to them individually.
> Second—That their ignorance, poverty and docility, combined with our affection for them, strongly urge us to immediate action . . .

They then asked the national organization for money for a "colored Field Organizer" who would answer to a sub-committee of five members, of whom at least three would come "from some southern point." The sentiment clearly indicated race as a definer: whites, whether nostalgic for a southern antebellum world or not, were to remain separate from blacks.

The city's white population began to expand into the outlying farm areas, avoiding the African-American communities that had sprung up in the 1870s in the rural areas around Lexington. One example is the dispensation of the Lexington area farms of the Preston descendents of Robert and Mary Owen Todd Wickliffe. One of the farms that the Wickliffe-Preston families owned was the 1,600-acre Ellerslie farm, which lay between Winchester Road and the old east-bound Boonesborough Road, now Richmond Road. In 1909 Robert Wickliffe "Wick" Preston and his wife Sallie

McDowell Preston incorporated the Wickliffe Land Company and began to partition the farm. The local newspapers reported on the sale of the subdivided property, providing free advertising in the process. The thrust of the appeal for purchasing one of the 170 lots was that it was "just outside of the city limits," easily accessible by a seven-minute trolley ride via the "McDowell Speedway," and more importantly for those loyal to Lexington's heritage, the property was located "in front of the old home of Henry Clay." The clincher was the "fact that business men have felt that such an addition would be a successful enterprise" and it was "only one of the many evidences of the rapid strides" of Lexington's growth. Another article on the Wickliffe Land Company's sale put the idea of progress more succinctly: "Lexington cannot go 'backward,' Northward, Southward, or Westward, but is bound to grow EASTWARD. This addition is just outside of the corporate limits and escapes CITY TAXES. And is the only suburban property that can get CITY WATER."

The auction of the Ellerslie property claimed the front page of the May 12, 1909 Lexington *Herald* and more than 1,000 people attended. Almost half the lots were sold that day, perhaps due to the restrictions placed on the sales: "No lot is to be subdivided, no liquor may be sold in the subdivision, and no lot can be sold to colored people, [and] on McDowell Speedway residences are to cost not less than $2,500." The *Herald* report went on to disparage the fact that the Wickliffe Land Co. had refused to allow any alleys in the subdivision. For a working class neighborhood alleys were an important part of social life, but from a professional man's perspective they attracted trash and unsafe conditions. The 1900 advertisement brochure for the adjacent Mentelle Park lots reflected similar concerns:

> There is just one broad, open street, with no short streets or cross streets or alleys. Every lot fronts on the park and they are all of the same high class, thus assuring desirable residents. Every building erected must cost no less than three times the cost of the lot, thus assuring nothing but high-class residences. No Negroes can ever own property or live in the park. No business house can be erected within in its limits. No adjacent or near-by Negro settlements. No nearby steam railroads.

When a Wickliffe granddaughter, Caroline Preston Thornton, sold two acres of the original Old Pond tract to E.J. Stanhope, the deed stipulated that the property would "never be leased occupied by or sold to any negro, no vinous spirits or malt liquors shall ever be sold therein said property shall never be used for any unlawful purpose nor be used in any manner so that by reason of said use the same shall become and constitute a nuisance." Even as late as 1932, when Wick's son William Preston sold seventy-six acres to be subdivided by the Fairway Lands Company, he stipulated that the land never be used by a business and that it not be sold or leased to blacks. The segregation of suburban Lexington bloomed.

Lexington

Throughout the 1920s the Wickliffe-Preston descendents sold and subdivided the bulk of the farm. Caroline Preston Thornton, the second eldest child, sold the property near the C&O railroad track to manufacturing interests, and so, behind the row of elegant houses on the east-west "McDowell Speedway," the streets going north soon delineated the rows of small cottages of poor white working-class families. Carrie sold parts of the northern end of Ellerslie to the Lexington Brick Company and to the Hemp Company of America. The intriguing mix of wealthier professional and poor working-class families is still evident in this area today. Evelyn Rice Ewan Robertson, the daughter of educator and principal Julia Rice Ewan, said in a 1998 interview that she came with her mother to the Kenwick Elementary School in 1924 when it was located in a rented house at 193 Sherman Avenue. She entered first grade and her mother taught math and served as principal. Because the children were so poor, Mrs. Ewan decided that they should have a hot, nutritious, and cheap meal at school during the day, so she started a hot-soup kitchen in the coal shed behind the school. She also organized the parents to grow vegetables for the children in the school garden. Kenwick was the first school in the state to serve "penny lunches."

With the animosity between blacks and whites so apparent, it is surprising that Lexington's newspapers made a point of stating that it was outsiders, not Lexingtonians, who made up much of the unruly mob that tried to lynch Will Lockett and put the town under martial law in 1920. Lexington police had used bloodhounds to quickly apprehend a black World War I veteran, Will Lockett, charged with the rape and murder of Geneva Hardman, a ten-year-old white girl. Though the story captured the notice of national newspapers, there is little known about Lockett except for his arrest on February 5, his confession (without benefit of counsel) the next day, his forty-minute trial three days later, and finally his electrocution at the state penitentiary in Eddyville. Sergeant H.H. Fuson of Company D of the Kentucky State Guards called the event the "Second Battle of Lexington" when he wrote up a summary for the March 1920 issue of *National Guard Magazine*. The state militia officer described the actions of his Captain, L.V. Crockett, and the seventy-five troopers against hundreds of rioters who tried to rush the courthouse while Circuit Judge Charles Kerr presided over the short trial.

According to the militiaman, the mob rushed the front of the courthouse just as the trial was starting and the troops fired into the crowd. Six people were killed and a dozen more wounded, though other accounts estimate that up to fifty people in the crowd were injured. Fuson wrote that the trial and death sentence "proved to the entire country that there was no excuse for a mob to try to take the law into its own hands. These acts of lawlessness caused Lexington, the pride of the Bluegrass, to bow her head in shame; but at the same trial a body of courageous court officials from the judge on the bench to the Deputy Sheriff who led Lockett out of his cell, were dealing out swift justice to the criminal." From 9:40 a.m. to 3:45 p.m. that day, 5,000 rioters threatened the militia with a constant noise. They threw a "tirade of epithets" as well as eggs, but the soldiers did not retaliate. Professional soldiers (the 1st Division) soon arrived at 3:45 p.m., and martial law was declared in effect in Fayette County by Brigadier Gen. F.C. Marshall. Troops marched up streets with drawn bayonets and cleared out the mob; more units arrived that night to a total of 800. Congratulations were sent to the State Guard for their work; Fuson was proud to relate that the veteran governor Edwin P. Morrow wrote, "You did not defend on yesterday the murderer. What you defended was the supreme law of this state and the good name of Kentucky."

Lexington's black community did not remain silent in the face of obvious attempts to keep the black population in its "place." The first great Black Convention was held in Lexington in 1866, and many social organizations such as the Colored Union Benevolent Society and the Soldiers League of Lexington had long worked to educate its members of national events and to lobby for black political rights. The conventioners' affiliations split between the Republican and Democratic parties: neither party's white leaders offered much in terms of political patronage after an election, but both would hand out treats in exchange for votes. Under the three-decade rule by Billy Klair, Lexington's political boss behind the scenes, black neighborhoods were gerrymandered out of the city electorate and those who did vote their conscience were intimidated or even murdered. This threat did not stop many brave Lexingtonians. Robert Charles O'Hara Benjamin, born 1855 in the West Indies, was a lawyer and journalist. He served as an editor of one of Lexington's earliest African-American newspapers, the Lexington *Standard*. He was killed on October 2, 1900, while working to register black voters. Kentucky's railroads were strictly segregated by the late 1880s, but in 1891 the legislature began to explore the possibility of establishing separate "coaches" or railcars for blacks. A separate-coach convention was held in Lexington June 22, 1892, and though the organized effort to stop the passage of a bill in the legislature failed, the work to have it struck down in court was successful.

A key aspect of Lexington's past is the fact that her black population was once central to the formation and maintenance of three of the city's defining economic features: hemp, tobacco, and the blood-horse. As discussed in previous chapters, Kentucky African-American workers made Kentucky hemp a central part of the Great Compromiser's American System. Kentucky was a leading producer of the world's hemp supply, used for making rope and fiber products. Another leading crop was corn, the principal ingredient in Kentucky bourbon, an export that had captured the imagination of whiskey drinkers around the world as early as the 1790s. Black farm labor kept the supply high. Large-scale coal mining in Eastern Kentucky's mountains began in the early 1900s as the railroads advanced into previously isolated areas, bringing new ethnic identities to the hills and hollows of Appalachia. Louisville became one of the nation's major trading and industrial centers, while Lexingtonians jostled for control of the coal market in alliance with political leaders of Eastern Kentucky. Lexington's tobacco industry, including warehousing, processing, and transportation, began to re-shape the city. Though agriculture had always been the economic mainstay for the Bluegrass, after the Civil War tobacco became a primary cash crop for the small farmer. This was due not only to the decline in demand for Kentucky hemp, but also the development of burley tobacco.

Burley tobacco became more valuable on the market since it held the sweeteners that were popular in plug tobacco at the time. Finally, during World War I, blended cigarettes took plug tobacco's place in popularity. Spittoons became a relic of the past, though Lexington's laws against spitting in public, on public property, or on fellow pedestrians are still on the books. Fortunately for Kentucky's tobacco farmers, burley was an important ingredient in both plug tobacco and cigarettes, and even today, Kentucky farms produce much of the nation's burley.

Lexington's promoters and leading citizens were well aware of this shift from hemp (and its accompanying bonded labor system) to burley tobacco. Before the Civil War the Bluegrass had voted consistently with western Kentucky, but by the 1870s the two regions had become deadly political enemies because of rivalry in the tobacco market. The violent tobacco wars of western Kentucky in the early 1900s only made the Bluegrass stronger. Important innovations in the marketing of the tobacco industry made Lexington the center of the world's burley sales. The formation of the Burley Loose Tobacco Warehouse Company and the adoption of the looseleaf auctioning system, though utilized in Virginia for many years before, started Lexington's rise in 1905. The city's first tobacco redrying plant also opened that year under the direction of W.L Petty of North Carolina. In 1910 Lexington promoters boasted that the Queen of the Bluegrass served as the largest tobacco market in the world.

Tobacco sales houses sprang up all along South Broadway, and yet as with her history of slave sales, the Bluegrass did not allow the free market to reign in such an important industry. As with the industry of slave-buying and selling, Lexingtonians made sure that the state and federal government protected the tobacco industry. By 1921 Lexington became home for the Burley Tobacco Growers Cooperative Association. This pool provided a stable burley market for its producers, borrowing funds from the federal government to advance loans to burley growers. The Co-op's board of directors administers the tobacco prices support program. Members of the Burley Co-op were and still are "any producer entity (quota holder, landlord, grower, tenant, lessee, and spouse thereof) who is currently involved in the production and marketing of a Burley Tobacco Quota in Kentucky, Indiana, Ohio, Missouri, and West Virginia." This included black farmers—men, women, and children.

Hauling the tobacco crop to Lexington has been a Kentucky tradition for several generations, and the economic effect from the tobacco sales and the influx of the farmers' families has always had a great impact on Lexington's businesses. Today, approximately 50 percent of Kentucky's burley is used in the production of cigarettes that are consumed in the United States. Unfortunately this has cost Kentuckians in the long run. The beautiful stock farms that surrounded Lexington lost their diversity, and the small farmer family—once the backbone of Kentucky's agricultural base—became entwined in a monocrop tobacco culture, losing the remarkable self-sufficiency for which the Kentucky pioneer and antebellum landowner was so famous. Over 70 percent of the food consumed in Kentucky today is brought in from outside the state. The efforts to diversify the Kentucky farm have just begun, and Lexington will continue to adjust to find the entrepreneurial spirit she has always had. Thankfully, the former tobacco warehouses that clustered around the center of the old city have been either razed or turned into nightclubs, restaurants, recycling centers, and antique markets.

Chapter Six

HORSE CAPITAL OF THE WORLD

The centerpiece of Kentucky's international identity was and is the horse. Lexington was home to great horse breeding and racing from its founding years: early owners and breeders included Gen. Leslie Combs, the founder of five generations of Combs who even today prove themselves leaders in the U.S. thoroughbred industry. The wealth and prestige of the Kentucky Association's members during the early nineteenth century allowed them to completely renovate the local turf racetrack in 1832. The Association built an enclosed racetrack that had been "skinned"—the sod was removed from the traditional racing turf and the loamy soil harrowed. This was the second such track ever built in the United States: the first was Union Course in New York on Long Island.

"Thoroughbred" means a breed of horse whose ancestry can be traced back to three seventeenth-century foundation sires in England: the Darley Arabian, the Godolphin Arabian, and the Byerly Turk. The British aristocrats established a credible breeding process that proved its success in turf races. James Weatherby compiled the first records of thoroughbred pedigrees and published *An Introduction to a General Stud-book* in 1791. As racing proliferated in North America, the need for a pedigree registry of American-bred thoroughbreds, similar to the *General Stud Book*, became apparent. Colonel Sanders D. Bruce, a Lexingtonian, played an important role in the development of the blood-horse industry. Colonel Bruce, as captain of the State Guard company called the "Lexington Chasseurs," had recruited a portion of what became the U.S. 20th Kentucky Infantry and was placed in command of a brigade. Bruce had had the onerous task of serving in the military occupation forces in Kentucky during the greater part of his service. After the Civil War he moved to New York and founded the popular journal *Turf, Field, and Farm*. Bruce spent a lifetime researching the pedigrees of American thoroughbreds, and in 1873 he published the first volume of *The American Stud Book*. Bruce closely followed Weatherby's pattern, and published six volumes of the register until 1896, when the project was taken over by the American Jockey Club in New York.

Though horse breeding farms had flourished in the south during the 1700s and 1800s, especially in Alabama, Tennessee, Kentucky, Virginia, and Maryland, racing had been in the main a local sport for large landowners. The Civil War destroyed horse racing as it had been known. The great stallion Lexington was in his prime then, but most of his progeny went to war or were stolen. The best riders and trainers focused more on gaining their freedom than staying on the farm. Only in Kentucky did the southern racing culture survive. The great owners and breeders like the Combs and the Alexanders continued with their elegant farm-based yearling sales and myriad race meets with competitions that involved multiple heats to determine a particular purse winner. Some of the best black trainers were able to stay in Lexington, under military occupation, and focus on their trade and build up great stables at the Kentucky Association track.

In post-bellum New York, horse breeding and racing became a new type of sport-business for the newly wealthy of the Gilded Age. In 1863, Saratoga on Lake George near Albany featured a new racetrack in addition to its elegant spa. There the Travers Stakes started, which remains today the competition to prove champion horses—and Kentucky-bred thoroughbreds ruled. In 1866 Leonard Jerome built Jerome Park on Long Island and promoted the formation of an American Jockey Club. By 1870 Monmouth Park and Pimlico opened in New Jersey, then Sheepshead Bay and Aqueduct in New York. Instead of multiple heats to determine a winner, these new tracks offered the new English-style "dash" racing, six races with different horses every day. Race meets lasted longer than the traditional one week, and the purses grew past the traditional $300. Betting, once conducted orally between individuals, expanded with the rise of a new professional called a "book maker." Racing became a fad of the glitzy New York elite. August in Saratoga became the place to find the two-year-old sensations, as well as to mix with the most elegant society.

By the 1890s the gambling element dominated and the elegant race tracks of New York crumbled and faded from the scene. New York and New Jersey governments cracked down on racing as part of a general crackdown against vice. In response New York transportation magnate August Belmont II chaired the governor's newly created Racing Commission in 1893. In 1894 fifty horsemen organized the American Jockey Club, which wrote and promoted racing rules, issued licenses in New York, appointed judges, and regulated the timing of New York meets. This club represented to the anti-gambling faction a new respectability for racing, and promoted the formation of great races such as the Futurity with a $34,000 purse.

Meanwhile from the 1870s through the 1890s, the Kentucky Trotting Horse Breeding Association's new track on the south-west side of town and the old Kentucky Association track on the north-east side were going strong. Interstate betting via telegraph and bookmakers made the Lexington racing scene very exciting. Pari-mutuel betting did not take hold in Lexington until 1910 when five machines were put up at the Lexington Spring Meet offering $2 and $5 tickets.

By the 1870s Kentucky's anti-Klan laws helped provide a modicum of protection to an entrepreneurial African-American horseman, and even though there were regulations against blacks officially entering a horse in a race in Lexington, many owned, stabled, trained, and won races at the Lexington tracks. Lexingtonians Ansel Williamson, a great trainer; and jockey H. Price McGrath earned great wealth in their time. But the acclaim was mainly within the closed circle of the horse industry. When Oliver Lewis rode Williamson-trained Aristides to victory in the first Kentucky Derby in 1875, the newspapers that day were more interested in the death of another Lexingtonian: former U.S. vice-president and ex-Confederate John C. Breckinridge. Most famous today of that era's black jockeys is Isaac Murphy, the first to win three Kentucky Derbys. Murphy won 44 percent of all races he rode, a record that has not been approached by any other jockey since. The richest jockey in the United States, Murphy became a thoroughbred owner in 1888, a member of the Knights Templar, and a Mason. He died in 1895 perhaps from a lung infection due to "flipping," a violent form of weight control by vomiting. He was the first jockey inducted into the Jockey Hall of Fame at the National Museum of Racing in Saratoga in 1955. His unmarked grave was moved from a "blacks only" cemetery in Lexington to a place of honor at the Kentucky Horse Park.

The 1890s were the heyday for Kentucky born jockeys and trainers. The usual pattern was that a young farmhand would be apprenticed by a jockey-turned-trainer and taught the trade. Then when he was too old or too big he would become a trainer himself. A popular jockey at thirteen, black Lexingtonian "Soup" Perkins signed a contract for $4,000 per year (plus a percentage of the winnings) in 1893 to ride for Fleischmann Stables, and in 1895 won the Derby on Halina. Edward Dudley Brown, known as "Brown Dick," had been bought as a child by Woodburn farmowner Robert A. Alexander and apprenticed to Ansel Williamson to become one of the best jockeys in the United States by age sixteen He began his career as a trainer at age twenty-two, and by 1895 Brown Dick was one of the wealthiest African Americans in the nation. But by the 1920s and 1930s, new managers of the great Bluegrass horse farms began to avoid hiring blacks, and the "Irish lads" took over the stables. The great Calumet trainer, "Plain Ben" Jones, would not allow any blacks anywhere at Calumet, where the gleaming white fences stand today as a reminder to those who drive past on Versailles Road.

Between the Depression of 1897 and the shutdown of New York tracks by anti-gambling proponents a few years later, horse owners and breeders began selling both thoroughbred and standardbred horses to Europeans for steeplechase racing there. August Belmont established a breeding farm in France to start a thoroughbred racing string separate from his Kentucky-bred stables. The British protested that the "colonial half-breeds" destroyed their pedigrees when in 1899 Kentuckian James Ben Ali Haggin sold over one hundred yearlings at Tattersalls. Many other owners sold their best horses to South America and Texas for polo and Quarter horse breeding. By the early 1900s though, Colonel Matt Winn, public relations genius for the Kentucky Derby, worked with nine other track owners to form the American Turf Association and in 1906 the legislature approved the newly created Kentucky State Racing Commission. This quasi-governmental regulatory agency functioned much like the one in New York, and the Bluegrass farmers often dominated its membership.

Horse Capital of the World

In 1916 the Thoroughbred Horse Association formed in Lexington under the leadership of Hal Price Headley, and the secretary Tom Crowell edited a twenty-page monthly bulletin called *The Thoroughbred Horse* with a circulation of 690 members across all the racing states. The Association served as an advocacy group to protect racing interests against anti-gambling legislation and to put pressure on the railroad companies to run horse cars on schedule. By 1928 the Association had crumbled though Cromwell continued publishing the bulletin, renamed *The Blood-Horse*. Cromwell explained in the September 1928 issue that the old name was too much like *The Thoroughbred Record* and since *The Blood-Horse* was "merely another way of saying The Thoroughbred" it would not be that much of a change. In May 1929 Cromwell published his first weekly issue of *The Blood-Horse*, a twenty-eight page magazine, and soon thereafter brought on Joe Estes and Joe Palmer, who as *Turf* writers then, just as later *Blood-Horse* editors did, helped to make Lexington the horse capitol of the world in the minds of their readers. *The Blood-Horse* is today the oldest continually published North American Thoroughbred magazine. Now owned by the Thoroughbred Owners and Breeders Association, the magazine is famous for its advertising success as well as its independent editorial coverage of the industry.

Johnson Newlon Camden, chair of the new Kentucky Racing Commission, helped to form the Kentucky Jockey Club in 1918 along with Colonel Winn and Thomas A. Combs, a state senator and former Lexington mayor. The Jockey Club purchased four of the best Kentucky tracks: Churchill Downs in Louisville, the Kentucky Association track in Lexington, Latonia near Covington, and Dade Park in Henderson. The leaders of the Club assured their control with heavy support to legislators in Frankfort who were friendly to pari-mutuel betting, a contentious issue that had spawned local anti-gambling organizations. When evangelist Billy Sunday visited Louisville in 1923, he made sure to condemn the power of the racetrack owners.

The "Great War" to end all wars—ironically known now as World War I—came to Lexington in a burst of patriotic fervor. Desha Breckinridge, editor of the Lexington *Herald*, had joined "Marse Henry" Watterson of the Louisiville *Courier-Journal* in calling for an early entry into the conflict between France and Germany. Women worked in public campaigns to speed the advance of American democracy at home: both the struggle for women's suffrage and social purity movements (especially for temperance and Sunday Schools) gained great strides during this time. Camp Stanley not only helped local business owners and horse farms alike to profit from the influx of federal wartime funding, but also highlighted the effects of prostitution on the health and morals of Lexington society. After the war, many of Lexington's saloons and bawdy houses were gone. The influenza epidemic of 1918 hit Lexington hard and the return of the veterans was quite somber and without celebration.

The gubernatorial elections of 1927 focused on the combined powers of coal mine owners, the Jockey Club, and liquor interests. The Democratic incumbent governor

Lexington

J.C.W. Beckham, hoping to ride on the popularity of the anti-gambling, pro-temperance elements of conservative Kentucky, went down in defeat to the Republican Flem D. Sampson, who had remained neutral on the issues of taxing coal and breaking the monopoly of the racing world. Duane Bolin, in his monograph on bossism in Lexington, described this crucial political defeat as largely due to the work of Lexington's boss, Billy Klair, who turned against his party and took out full-page ads in the Lexington *Herald* and the Lexington *Leader* to endorse the Republican candidate. The ads claimed, "Beckham's election means the end of racing in Kentucky." The Democrats voted split tickets with the help of Billy Klair's machine, and as a consequence the Klair machine could not recover in time to halt the Republican sweep the next year when Kentucky supported the Presidential candidate Herbert Hoover over the "wet" candidate, Al Smith.

When the crash came in 1929, Lexington did not feel its immediate effects. Since the city did not experience many of the problems that the manufacturing centers did during the early days of the Depression, its newspapers marveled at its resiliency and crowed that Lexingtonians should "be glad that Lexington is Lexington." As the third largest city in the state—even with a population of over 45,000 the city was only one-sixth the size of Louisville—Lexington still had a substantial number of black citizens, and very few of the white population claimed to be foreign-born. The principal industries of tobacco and horse farming contributed heavily to the success of the city and allowed for continued growth in both public and private sectors. John Y. Brown introduced a bill in the state legislature in 1929 to change the city charter to a city manager format, hailed as a more efficient form of local government. A great variety of progressive reformers had joined together in 1928 to form the Charter League, including the League of Women Voters, the Board of Commerce, the Lexington *Leader*, and several men's clubs. The municipal elections on November 4, 1931, drew the largest number of voters in the city's history—more than 16,600 Lexingtonians voted and the Charter League's entire ticket won the majority in a landslide. W.T. Congleton, the new mayor, worked with his commission of four to appoint the new city manager. They selected the native Kentuckian Paul Morton, the city manager of Alexandria, Virginia, to be Lexington's first professional to run the municipal government.

Morton organized the departments of public welfare and public works for the first time and the Klair machine lost its power to appoint its friends to key positions in the government. This reorganization resulted in a cash surplus in the city coffers by 1933, even though the new Department of Public Welfare had a huge increase in activity as the economic downfall began to hit Lexington's workers. The federal New Deal programs found an efficient path for deployment in the new government structure, and with the federal money Lexington got new storm sewers, a sanitary sewage plant, two community centers and a public health center, finished up the new airport and began a new city jail, took over garbage collection, installed a police radio system, and even added $50,000 to appropriations for charities. In addition, due to this federal support, the new city manager was able to cut local taxes as well as lower operating expenses for the city government. Lexington's good fortunes were chronicled in many reform-minded journals and newspapers of the day.

At the same time, Lexington in 1931 had more homicides per capita than any other city in the United States. The political patronage activities of Billy Klair had been temporarily halted, but the city still belonged to the dog-eat-dog world of bossism. Morton gave up trying to gain control of the police and firemen and resigned in May 1935 to take a higher paid job in Trenton, New Jersey. Klair's "Home Town" ticket swept the polls in 1936. Around that same time, Governor Sampson took over the highway commission, a powerful monopoly that controlled half the state's expenditures by 1931. Lexington's construction companies had long benefited from the careful control of the legislature by Billy Klair. One of the visible manifestations of Klair's power in the city of Lexington was a public assembly on April 9, 1932, at the Fayette County Courthouse to choose the county representative for the state Democratic Party's central executive committee. The county meeting to select delegates to the state convention usually served the interests of a few active political workers and local bureaucrats, but the 1932 challenge from John Y. Brown against Klair for the post led to one of the largest gatherings on the streets of Lexington ever. Newspapers claimed that there were anywhere from 2,500 to 6,000 in the crowd with marching bands delineating the two sides of the candidates. Billy Klair's supporters arrived in truck loads, forming militia-like companies on Main Street and marching into the Cheapside Square, filling the south side of the area where the popular Court Day events had always taken place. The Brown supporters stood near the Short Street entrance to Cheapside, to the north, and soon saw that they were far outnumbered.

Meanwhile, the fall of James B. Brown's National Bank of Kentucky in the fall of 1930 had shaken the state's power base in Louisville. Klair's machine lost much of its control as Prohibition officially ended in 1933 and beer sales became legal in Lexington. Women's groups like the Central Kentucky Women's Club worked hard to get Lexington employers to sign National Recovery Administration agreements and to get every housewife to sign a consumer's agreement requiring trade with NRA stores only. The NRA Labor Day parade sponsored by the Man O'War Post of the American Legion saw more than 30,000 lining the streets to watch a two-mile procession and then hear Mary E. Hughes, a Lexingtonian, speak on the importance of a new economic spirit in the bleak era of Depression.

Also in 1933 the Kentucky Association went into bankruptcy and the racetrack in Lexington closed after the spring meeting. The stables, the wooden grandstand, and once famous track were in sad disrepair. Kinkeadtown, a black community of skilled and unskilled laborers, had begun to envelop the land around the racetrack, and the road to the track served as too visible a reminder of the socio-economic inequities in

Lexington

Lexington. The elite horsemen of the white community knew they would have to expand to survive, and in this era of intense segregation the black community was not where they wanted to be.

At the same time the growing number of government agencies at the federal level came to be seen by Lexingtonians as a positive force in moving toward regional prominence and loosening themselves from past dependencies on state political patronage. The Agricultural Adjustment Act was very popular for central Kentucky farmers, and according to Duane Bolin, the AAA's burley tobacco program served as a way to change Kentuckians' attitudes about federal government interference with private property. The University of Kentucky's College of Agriculture also gained an unprecedented stature when it took on the administration of AAA funds as the state extension office. Its direct cash payments to farmers who signed contracts limiting their production also wrenched much of the power from the hands of the Klair machine. The relief efforts of the Civilian Conservation Corps provided aid to 25 percent of Lexington families, half as much when compared to what the mining county of Harlan received, but over twice as much as was distributed in the river city of Louisville. The organization of the Civil Works Administration (CWA) uniquely met the needs of Lexington's city manager Paul Morton, since the funds from the Federal Emergency Relief Administration (FERA) went directly to the municipal governments without any flowing through state or county hands. The CWA road projects paid out good wages in a time when jobs were few. In addition to the cash paid directly to the workers, merchants benefited from the scrip that was issued to be spent specifically in certain stores.

Unfortunately for Morton, the CWA gravy train came at a cost: state and local governments had to provide 25 percent of the total relief funds in cash. Governor Ruby Laffoon had not been successful in getting a new sales tax to supplement the existing beer and whiskey taxes, and he held tightly to state revenues unless he had direct control over their distribution for relief efforts. In 1933 he had ordered the banks and the burley tobacco markets to be closed. When matching funds were not found, the CWA ended in Kentucky and was replaced with a state agency that distributed the FERA funds in the era's typical partisan manner. The Public Works Administration (PWA) served as another attempt at establishing close relationships between cities and the federal government, and even the conservative Lexington *Leader's* editor John G. Stoll proposed public projects in which the federal money could be used to benefit Lexington's continued growth. The resulting storm sewers and municipal buildings improved the local landscape, and the University of Kentucky benefited greatly with new buildings, recreational facilities, surveys, and studies. However, the families on direct or work relief continued to have difficulty finding adequate housing in Lexington. Women and blacks found little if any relief employment offered to them at all.

Lexington's women, who comprised more than half the population in the 1930s, received less than one-seventh the amount of jobs offered to men, and most of the federal money associated with women's work was used for setting up and then maintaining the equipment for sweatshops devoted to sewing piecework. It was not until later in the decade that Bluegrass Park and Aspendale Apartments, where the Kentucky Association's racetrack had been, became Lexington's first public housing projects. The black population that lived there had begun to shrink, and by the late 1930s Lexington's African-American population had shrunk from nearly half the city's population to one fourth. The prospects for a wage-earning job, a main reason for moving to Lexington after the Civil War, were bleak and so Kentucky's best went elsewhere. In 1935 the Family Welfare Society of Lexington had on its books over 600 Lexingtonians who lived in substandard housing or were starving. Even though the eleven local agencies that made up Lexington's Community Chest worked to gather private funds with a gala burgoo picnic, the "starvation fund" was woefully inadequate for the needs of Lexington's poor. Overall, Kentucky received the smallest allotment from the federal government of any state in the nation; it also ranked as one of the lowest in the nation for state and local contributions to families on relief.

There is some documentation of a few organized attempts in Lexington to gain advances in basic bread-and-butter issues like wages. In the 1930s, Lexington building contractors had imported Swedish skilled labor to supplement the local workers in order to construct the federal buildings for the Veterans Administration Hospital and the Narcotic Farm, both west of Lexington on the Leestown Road. Lexington had eleven building-craft guilds and any efforts to expand or strengthen its skilled-trade unity were easily and quickly squelched. The employers who made up the Lexington Building Trades Council made sure that their collaboration remained mainly in the task of organizing Labor Day parades and picnics. According to a 1987 interview by historian Glenna Graves with Jim McElroy of the Kentucky Workers Alliance, the Building Trades Council virtually closed its doors to any outsiders.

The Swedes were accustomed to an organized labor environment, and when they encountered the poor working conditions and wages in building the Spindletop mansion on the north side of Fayette County in the spring of 1936, they went on strike. Circuit Court Judge "King" Swope, in hopes of gaining the governorship, quickly called a grand jury investigation of the strike and accused the men of "banding and confederating." This anti-KKK law usually worked when established authority tried to break a labor strike or stop one from starting. In his interview, McElroy described the strike as a victory since the Swedish leaders won the court case and were free to go back to work—for higher wages.

The Kentucky Workers Alliance (KWA), affiliated with the socialist Workers Alliance of America, organized a mass demonstration the next summer to protest the WPA Administrative Order No. 44, which docked the wages of workers who lost time on the job, even through no fault of their own. Though it was a peaceful and orderly demonstration that ended up at the Dudley School building where the local WPA officer met them, the overweening fear of communists kept the KWA from doing much more than allowing unemployed or disgruntled workers a place to vent their frustrations in angry speeches. The KWA also sponsored a labor rally at the courthouse on June 7, 1938, where Lexington attorney John Y. Brown and the WPA district administrator Ernest Rowe joined the vice president of the national Workers Alliance on the stage to denounce Governor "Happy" Chandler's vain attempt to win over labor in the Democratic primary against Alban Barkley for U.S. senator. Though the Tammany-Hall-style ward boss system no longer held sway in Lexington (Billy Klair died in the fall of 1937), the types of programs and support structures that progressive reform movements in other parts of the country had brought to the urban labor communities did not come to Lexington. Wages stayed low and working conditions often were brutal.

A new project of building a racetrack, stables, clubhouse, and grandstand at J.O. "Jack" Keene's Keeneland Stud served as another important work site for Lexington labor in the early 1930s. Keene spent $400,000 on the project during a time when jobs and materials were hard to get, and his investment served Lexington well. In March 1935 an open meeting at the Lafayette Hotel in downtown Lexington attracted more than 200 horse owners and breeders, who chose an Organization Committee of Ten to negotiate with Keene to buy his property. Hal Price Headley, the son of a local horseman with two family-owned farms, Beaumont and La Belle Farm, led the negotiations along with Major Louis A. Beard. They succeeded in their purchase of nearly 150 acres, including the track, new buildings, and water system, for $130,000 in cash and $10,000 in preferred stock. The one-and-one-sixteenth-mile track, stretching 100 feet wide at the time, had cost Keene more than $40,000 to build. The clubhouse had been built in "Kentucky marble," a beautiful limestone, three stories high and nearly 260 feet long, and the whole estate landscaped beautifully with shade trees and shrubbery. The only improvements the new owners would need to undertake were to complete a quarter-mile indoor training track, build stables to accommodate hundreds of horses, and a grandstand for 5,000 spectators. In the fall of 1936, Keeneland held an open house and more than 15,000 people saw the new totalizator, the first to be installed in Kentucky. The totalizator took the power out of the hands of the bookmaker at the racetrack, implementing instead an automated system that recorded the betting tickets dispensed, calculated, and then displayed the resulting odds and finally the payoffs so the winnings would be publicly known. Winning bettors share the total amount bet, minus a percentage for the track, taxes, and any surcharges placed on the system.

The Keeneland Association took on the organizational role of scheduling the races, and today their Blue Grass Stakes serves as a final major preparation race for the

Kentucky Derby, and the Spinster Stakes in the fall exhibits the best fillies and mares in the United States. From its inception, Keeneland has emphasized the sporting aspect of thoroughbred racing, de-emphasizing wagering and serving as the pride of Kentucky's family farms. Just before Keeneland opened its 1937 spring meeting, Hal Price Headley explained, "We want a place where those who love horses can come and picnic with us and thrill to the sport of the Bluegrass. We are not running a race plant to hear the click of the mutuel machines. We don't care whether the people who come here bet or not. If they want to bet there is a place for them to do it. But we want them to come out here to enjoy God's sunshine, the fresh air, and to watch horses race." Keeneland, unlike so many other racetracks around the world, remains today a lovely park-like environment, with jockeys saddling up in a tree-filled paddock with an atmosphere that breathes of family and close friends.

The Lexington area's Bluegrass family farms had always been successful in breeding fine blooded stock, and the best in the horse industry knew that the limestone-rich soil was the best place to raise sucklings to hardy yearlings that won races. The Alexander's Woodburn Farm, home of the "Old Blind Hero," Lexington, had served many blood-horse owners as a nursery for champions. Before the Civil War the Alexander family had established a model of the modern commercial Thoroughbred operation in which the primary purpose of breeding fine horses was for the yearling sales. But it was probably Major Barak Thomas, former Confederate officer under Gen. Abe Buford, who was the first of the Lexington-based farmers to make breeding and racing a full-time occupation. Domino, his great champion and sire of many more thoroughbred champions, came from the beautiful horse farm Dixiana, a few miles north of Lexington.

By the 1870s easterners had begun to buy parcels of Bluegrass stock-breeding and pasturage farms and redesigning them for the sole purpose of raising yearlings, establishing stables of fine broodmares, and bringing champions to stand at stud. The first of these neo-plantation owners was Milton H. Sanford, founding member of the group that built Jerome Park in New York and formed the American Jockey Club. In 1872 he bought 544 acres of a former pioneer farm ten miles north of Lexington along Paris Pike, a turnpike that was part of one of the earliest modern highways west of the Alleghenies—the Maysville Road. John Howard and his wife Mary, the youngest sister of surveyor Colonel William Preston (1730–1783) of "Smithfield" moved there from Virginia in 1789, and under the management of their son Benjamin Howard (who later was the first territorial governor of Missouri) raised hemp and farmstock and produced everything necessary to sustain the large family and several black families that lived on the farm as slaves. Sanford bought the portion of Howard's Grove that had been sold in 1865 by the Howards's two eldest daughters, Elizabeth Payne and Mary Parker, to the Hughes family. He named his 544 acre farm Preakness Stud.

Lexington

In 1881 Daniel Swigert, a cousin of R.A. Alexander's wife and manager of Woodburn Farm, bought Sanford's farm and stabled twenty-six mares and four stallions, all progeny of the great sire Lexington. His horses won or sired winners in all major stakes races in the United States and Europe. This carefully crafted environment became the nucleus of one of the greatest of the modern thoroughbred horse farms, Elmendorf. Elmendorf was the name of Mrs. Swigert's grandmother. Swigert not only had the best horses of Lexington's pedigree, but also controlled the two best sires of the 1880s that had no Lexington blood: Glenelg and Virgil. This great horseman served as the model and key resource for the Lexington area newcomers such as the Belmonts, James R. Keene, John L. Madden, and H.P. Whitney, who all relied on "home" sires rather than outside breeders.

In 1885 the New York financier August Belmont I, one of the greatest in the modern thoroughbred industry, shifted his breeding operations from Long Island to the Bluegrass. He leased a farm on Georgetown Road just north of Lexington for his Nursery Stud where his English stallion St. Blaise stood at stud. When Belmont died in 1890 his estate held a dispersal sale, but his heir August "Augie" Belmont II with his wife Eleanor resurrected the "home" breeding operation with the great sire Fair Play. The Belmonts' stud farm by the turn of the century produced world-famous thoroughbred champions, including the great Man O'War. At that time, the manager was Mrs. Edward Kane, and the story is not clear on why the big chestnut colt had not been shown to previous potential buyers who had visited the famous yearling barns in Kentucky. At any rate, the Kentucky-bred yearling was up for auction at Saratoga Springs in August 1918, and though he went on the block late in the day, it was Sam Riddle's wife, the Cleveland heiress Elizabeth Dodson Riddle, who insisted he stay and buy the "big red." Riddle handed over that day most of the $5,000 in ready cash from his wife's purse. The average price for yearlings that summer at Saratoga was around $1,000, though other horses sold for over $10,000 that month. This yearling went on to be the greatest money-winning thoroughbred ever, and upon retirement from racing to stand at stud in Kentucky, he captured even more attention alongside his groom, Will Harbut. Harbut was a Lexington native who knew how to tell a story well, and it was as much due to his public relations skills that a visit to Man O'War was a main tourist attraction in Lexington. Man O'War was a Lexington hero from the 1920s to 1947 when he died at the age of thirty, only a month after the death of his beloved groom Will Harbut.

One of the greatest farm managers, Major Fauxhall Daingerfield, came to Lexington in 1892 to scout for a large farm for his brother-in-law James R. Keene, a Wall Street financier and co-founder of the American Jockey Club. Keene leased the 1,072-acre Castleton Farm, formerly the Breckinridge farm Cabell's Dale and then Castleton's home of the American Standardbred. One of Daingerfield's innovations that accommodated the Bluegrass landscape and climate was to allow the pastures to grow up in weeds to protect the grasses and clover during midsummer months, allowing the young horses to get at the fresh sprouts they needed. Between 1893 and 1912, Castleton mares foaled 113 stakes winners and champions, and many leading sires including Domino stood at stud there. Both Keene and Daingerfield died in 1913 and Keene's widow sold all the horses and left Kentucky. The farm reverted to a Standardbred operation again, becoming highly successful under the ownership of Frances Dodge Johnson Van Lennep. A saddlebred enthusiast, Van Lennep made her farm a showpiece for twenty-five years, especially noted for the great stallion Wing Commander. Daingerfield's daughter Elizabeth continued on very successfully as thoroughbred farm manager for other prominent breeding operations around Lexington.

John E. Madden, the "Wizard of the Turf," went from breeding and training Standardbred trotters to become one of the most successful breeders and trainers in the thoroughbred industry. His careful management of raising two-year-olds for sale, modeling his efforts after the Belmonts but extending his training efforts with a unique professional style, made him one of the greatest. He would start the year with about fifty-four two-year olds in his training stable, each of them identified only by number, training them so as to emphasize soundness and hardiness. He was the first to use large "open" three-sided sheds with feeding troughs down the center. Madden, himself a hardy runner who used to wow observers by successfully completing the steeplechase course at Sheepshead Bay in New York without benefit of a horse, built the Hamburg Place's pastures as large open fields to allow the young horses to roam and run. One field alone was two hundred acres, and his grandson Preston Madden continued this successful strategy when he revived Hamburg Place in 1961. The Hamburg Place horses might be skinnier than most other horses at auction by the end of the year, but everyone knew the Madden-bred racing performances, and these yearlings would sell all or most at large profit. In 1920 and 1923 Madden-bred horses won more than 400 races. Hamburg Place was the first breeding operation to produce as many as five Derby winners. Madden also bred five Belmont Stakes winners, the first Triple Crown winner (Sir Barton), 182 stakes winners, and produced the two top money earners in the United States in 1892: Zev and Princess Doreen. One of his famous maxims still stands true for Lexingtonians today: "Horses make men. Men don't make horses."

The son of Irish immigrants, this athletic entrepreneur from the zinc works of western Pennsylvania came to Kentucky as a wealthy thirty-year-old looking for the best trotting horses. In 1898 he bought prime farmland on Winchester Pike, only a fifteen minute drive from the Phoenix Hotel in downtown Lexington where he conducted most of his business buying and selling yearlings. He told his friends the reason he wanted Hamburg Place close to Lexington: "I wanted a place near town so, if I had a customer, I could get him out there before he changed his mind." According to Kent Hollingsworth, editor of *The Blood-Horse* and Madden's biographer, 1908 was his best year not only in racing and selling but also in trading on Wall Street. When asked how he could possibly be so successful so often, his biographer reported his response: "There's no trick to selling horses, so long as you're selling good horses." His chief client was William C. Whitney of New York, former U.S. secretary of the navy and founder of the Naval War College in Newport.

In 1898 W.C. Whitney leased LaBelle Farm on the west side of Lexington off Old Frankfort Pike. A lawyer-politician, Whitney had inherited his millions from his uncle, Oliver Payne (a partner of the first John D. Rockefeller) and by consolidating street and railway lines in New York City. He was one of the organizers of the Metropolitan Street Railway Company. By 1906 the Whitney firm merged with the Interborough Rapid Transit Company owned by August Belmont II. Together they shared great wealth and prestige in American society, working to make Saratoga Springs one of the most important social spots in the thoroughbred industry's seasons. In 1901 Whitney won the English Derby with Volodyovski, leased by him from Lady Meux. His marriage to Flora Payne, a Cleveland heiress, made him part of the social scene under the command of Mrs. Astor, queen of the "400" in New York. William C. Whitney topped the thoroughbred owners list three times in the early 1900s, and left his horses to his son, Harry Payne Whitney, whose stable topped the owners list eight times in thirty-five years of successful racing. Harry Payne's breeding operations produced the first female Derby winner, Regret in 1915, and by the time of his death in 1930 he had produced 192 stakes winners—a record not surpassed until 1979.

H.P. Whitney married Helen Hay, daughter of John Milton Hay, President Theodore Roosevelt's secretary of state. She became known as the "First Lady of the Turf" while the owner of Greentree Stables and breeding farm on Paris Pike just north of Lexington. On May 16, 1931, with the exciting last-minute win by Twenty Grand, Mrs. Whitney became the first woman owner to win the Derby twice. When she died in 1944 her children, John Hay Whitney and Joan Whitney Payson, took over this successful operation. The Paysons lived in the beautiful mansion, Fairlawn, originally built in 1850 by Thomas Hughes who had bought the property from Benjamin Howard, Missouri territorial governor and son of the Lexington frontiersman John Howard.

The Whitneys' success resulted from the great leadership of their manager, Major Louie A. Beard. The Texas-born World War I veteran won notice in the horse world when he captained the U.S. Army's polo team, which in 1925 defeated the aristocratic British team in straight matches. H.P. Whitney convinced Beard to leave his position as commander of the Remount Depot at Fort Royal, Virginia, and come to manage his farm near Lexington. Major Beard two years later became the manager of Greentree Farm as well. His service to the racing world included helping to organize the American Thoroughbred Breeders Association in 1934 as well as the Grayson Foundation, which funded research on the diseases of horses. Beard refused to take the top executive positions in the organizations he created, even when he helped found America's first non-profit race track, Keeneland. He was a convincing spokesperson for the future of thoroughbred racing, and he encouraged the honorable members of the industry to become more open to the professional regulation of breeding and racing. In a guest of honor speech at the annual testimonial dinner of the Thoroughbred Club of America in Lexington, Major Beard spoke on the future of the turf industry and decried the rise of commercial promoters of racing. He warned that "so much get-rich-quick promoting of minor sport value can easily put us in the category in which the saloon era placed the reputable distiller." He went on to state, "Racing is like a very valuable plant—it must grow, but it must also be pruned so that it does not outgrow its own roots." The only exception to his reticence in taking the number-one position in a club came from his first passion—he agreed to be president of the Polo Pony Breeders Society he helped create. This organization was of great importance to Lexington, since it is likely that through polo later great thoroughbred owners such as the Polish Count Henryk de Kwiatkowski and oilman William S. Farish became interested in purchasing farms in the Lexington area. These men contributed much to Lexington's stature as the horse capital of the world today. Whitney had bought two parcels of land that were once part of Howard's Grove, including the family burial grounds. The Howard women had married interesting Lexington men, and the family members buried there were colorful figures of their day and their stories are worth telling.

One of the famous Lexingtonians buried there is the Old Duke of Fayette County, Robert Wickliffe, who had married the youngest of the Howard girls, Margaret or "Margaretta." Their son Charles Wickliffe, who was killed in a duel with James Trotter on October 9, 1829 at the age of twenty-one, is there as well. He was the "Coriolanus" in the *Kentucky Reporter* who wrote a challenge against the Clay supporters that ultimately led to the famous duel with his former best friend. Also buried there is Transylvania law professor and judge Aaron K. Woolley, who died in the 1849 cholera epidemic, and his wife, the eldest of the Wickliffe offspring. Sallie Howard Wickliffe Woolley had lived on the farm as plantation mistress since the 1820s as well as in town at her father's mansion at the corner of Second and Market Streets until her death in 1873. Robert Wickliffe's second wife's grave is there but her tombstone acknowledges neither her controversial Todd nor Russell relations: instead it simply names her "Mary O. Wickliffe." On either side of her are simple markers for her first husband, James Russell, and her mother Jane, widow of Lexington founding father Colonel John Todd. Next to her lies the only child of Mary Owen Todd Russell Wickliffe, John T. Russell. He was the alleged father of Alfred Russell, a slave sent to Liberia who later became president of that new nation.

Though the papers for this wealthy antebellum farm include many lists of the blacks who lived at Howard's Grove, their graves are not marked. We can only speculate where the burial site is for the people listed in the shaky handwriting of James Haney the overseer when he wrote the 1829 farm account: "Tany, Edmon, Kato, Lewis,

William, Jacob, Isaac, Mitton, Alec, Coalmon, Eleck, George, Tom, Maria and two children emly and henry, Alcy and four children Kitty Oliver Sam July An, Hanner and four children milly anderson horris and john, Harriot and two children melviny tildy, Betty and two children mandy elmily, Caty, Milly, Peggy, Nancy, Movetillar and three children robbert marshel and betty, Sally Jacobs child = whole number 41."

In 1934 the tract containing the Howard's Grove burial ground was given to Cornelius Vanderbilt Whitney, who created his own bit of Kentucky thoroughbred history with the resulting 1,000-acre horse farm. With Major Beard as manager of his farm, C.V. Whitney was at the top of the owners list for each of his first four years as an owner, and his stable was the second in history to win more than $1 million in a single season. In his thirty-nine years as a thoroughbred breeder and owner, Whitney bred an incredible 146 stakes winners. In 1966 John R. Gaines, son of Standardbred owners, bought half of the Whitney farm and built the successful Gainesway Farm, which in 1997 was bought by the South African family of Graham Beck. Despite the change of owners, the restrictions to the Howard-Wickliffe burial ground remained intact, and today the public still has access to this piece of evidence to an important part of Kentucky history.

Helen Whitney's children, John Hay or "Jock" Whitney (publisher of the New York *Herald Tribune*) and Joan Whitney Payson (an owner of the New York Mets baseball team) owned the Greentree Stables. In 1928, Jock Whitney, then in his early twenties, was the youngest member ever to be elected to the Jockey Club. Across Paris Pike, the death of James Ben Ali Haggin in 1914 led to the sale and dispersal of Elmendorf. By the 1920s Joseph E. Widener of Pennsylvania bought up 1,200 acres and built some of the most beautiful horse barns there, the great Normandy bar, and the circular barn now on Clovelly Farm. Like the Belmonts, Vanderbilts, and Whitneys, Widener didn't live here year-round. The farms were managed and carefully tended by local area families, and when the owners arrived for the spring or fall meets, they had wonderful parties to which the elite Lexingtonians were invited. The L&N Railroad cut right through the Greentree farm, and the Whitneys would ride down from their other Greentree mansion on Long Island in a private car to their Kentucky farm once or maybe twice a year. The Lexingtonians who attended the raucous polo games and picnics, elegant luncheons and charity events, fancy balls and concerts, remained behind after the season was over and formed their own exclusive social circles.

Not all of the new Bluegrass horse farm owners were from the northeast. Nancy Tucker Clay of Paris married the heir to the famous Ellerslie horse farm in Virginia, Arthur Hancock. Their farm, Claiborne in Bourbon County, was at first an extension of the Virginia dynasty, but when their son "Bull" Hancock took up managing the Kentucky stables after World War II, Claiborne led the racing world with its high quality yearlings that went on to be stakes winners and champions. James Ben Ali Haggin, a self-made mogul born in Mercer County, Kentucky who built a mining empire in California, met Margaret Voorhies of Woodford County and came home to build a new empire near Lexington in 1897. He and Margaret bought Elmendorf, the horse farm built up by the great trainer Dan Swigert. Over the course of fifteen years he bought 8,000 acres along Paris Road, built the extravagant Georgian mansion "Green Hills," and implemented modern farming techniques for his horse stables and dairy. Lexington's interurban trolley ran each day out to the Haggin farm to drop off and pick up the hundreds of workers employed there. When Haggin died in 1914 it took his heirs ten years to disperse all his holdings, most of which went to other wealthy landowners who continued the tradition of thoroughbred breeding.

The rich parvenue helped to carve the beautifully sculpted horse farms out of pioneer stock farms, pouring money into the Lexington economy with plenty of jobs related to the horse industry and demands for the best feed, the best farm supplies, and good transportation. The extravagant parties gave rise to a new class of black wage-earners—butlers, cooks, and caterers. Lexington had always had very good caterers for its men's "stag" parties where political strategizing or literary reviews gave way to a evening of long-winded toasts, and restaurants abound still in Lexington with a strong tradition of good food and drink.

Some of the wealthy newcomers lived on their farms and became impressive leaders in the Lexington social scene and businesses. Col. E.R. Bradley, a professional gambler and colorful figure, bought 1,480 acres flanking the scenic Old Frankfort Pike west of Lexington. Bradley patterned his Idle Hour Farm after Keene, breeding and raising horses that dominated the racing scene in the 1920s and 1930s, including four Derby winners. He was a generous philanthropist to the Catholic Church, giving money regularly to support orphanages. He also helped organize in 1924 the private golfing club Idle Hour Country Club out of a piece of the original 1,600-acre stockfarm Ellerslie. All of Bradley's horses' names began with a B, but the successors to his farmlands did not think this too strange: the owners of the great King Ranch of Texas bought one part of his farm and the other half became home for the great racing silks of Mare Haven, Danada, and Darby Dan. Darby Dan Farm was created by John W. Galbreath, an Ohio entrepreneur who succeeded in the horse industry by purchasing or leasing the world's greatest stallions to stand at stud here. His grandson John W. Phillips gave up a law career in Columbus to come to Kentucky as managing partner of this flourishing venture.

Idle Hour Farm's success was surpassed only by Calumet, a farm that was not only a nursery for champions but also a winner in its own famous devil red and blue racing silks. William Monroe Wright, founder of the Calumet Baking Powder Company, was an Illinois Standardbred horseman who came to Lexington to construct this 850-acre farm out of old Kentucky stockfarms owned by Payne and Clay descendants. He built the distinctive white barns with red trim and ornate cupolas for his racing pacers and trotters, including the 1931 Hambletonian winner Calumet Butler. His son Warren

Wright Sr. converted the farm for thoroughbred racing and dominated the industry from the 1940s on. Upon his death in 1961, his wife Lucille Wright Markey owned Calumet as well as properties in New York and Florida, but she lived mostly in the lovely house at Calumet and is responsible for four of the farm's record nine Kentucky Derby winners; eight of them were foaled in the same barn. Calumet owners have raced seven Horse of the Year champions, and two Triple Crown winners: Whirlaway (1941) and Citation (1948).

When Markey died in 1982, the farm's fortunes plummeted under the management of her son-in-law J.T. Lundy, even while the great stallion Alydar continued making the Calumet name famous throughout the world. In 1992, Henryk de Kwiatkowski, a sportsman and entrepreneur from Poland, rescued Calumet to the great delight of Lexingtonians and the horse industry. Though he rarely lived on the farm, he and his wife desired that it remain the way it had been in its heyday during the 1940s. He spoke lovingly of his farm: ". . . the elegance, the quality, the way it was received worldwide gave great credit to the Bluegrass region and to Kentucky as a superior place for racing and breeding. Calumet personified all of this. They say that racing is a sport of kings. Well, this must be where one of the kings lived—without a doubt."

Not all rich transplants were welcomed with open arms, however. During the Depression Pansy Yount, a Texan who had gotten rich from one of the greatest oil strikes in U.S. history, bought a horse farm north of Lexington. She paid cash in 1935 for Shoshone Stud, previously owned by a W.R. Coe of New York, after her great oil find at Spindletop. Yount had signed oil leases to Gulf, Texaco, and Sun Oil and was wealthy beyond what any poor farm girl from Texas like herself could have imagined. By the time she decided to come to Kentucky and start a stock farm, she had already built Spindletop Stables in Texas, and had another mansion in Manitou near Colorado Springs. So, her plans for the beautiful mansion on Iron Works Pike and the elegant outbuildings were quickly implemented by a builder from Louisville. Her stock animals were of the very best breeds, and many neighboring farmers would bring their animals to her farm to be bred. She and her daughter Mildred worked to bring the American Saddle Horse to prominence in Kentucky again. She worked with many prominent Lexington women to create the Lexington Junior League Horse Show in 1937 as the League's sole fundraiser. Yount helped it serve as a key organization for the promotion of the high-stepping three- and five-gaited horses, and "winning at Lexington," which once was a prestigious goal for the Saddlebred community, has now come to be one of the Saddlebred industry's Triple Crown events. According to the fanciful biography of Pansy Yount by Linda Light, Mildred had a wonderful time dating one of the most elegant men in Lexington at that time, George Stanhope "Hope" Wiedemann. Nevertheless, Pansy Yount herself never fit in with the Lexington crowd, and she left Kentucky. Her friend Fred Wachs, editor of the Lexington *Leader*, and Dr. Frank Peterson of the University of Kentucky, made sure that she sold her farm and the mansion to the Kentucky Research Foundation for a pittance of its worth in 1959: only $850,000.

Lexington's boom in the 1920s, evidenced by the heavy growth in residential suburbs and new businesses downtown, slowed with the onslaught of the Depression years. Though the County Court Day activities in the Cheapside lot next to the courthouse ended in 1922 and the city market house closed, Lexington's downtown had to struggle to meet the demands of the new influx of consumers brought in by car and by the interurban electric railway. Lexington's new bus service, established in 1927, could not handle the traffic congestion around Main Street's hotels, Union Station, restaurants, theatres, and stores. By 1928 Lexington had a new City Hall with a beautiful front entrance of pillars reminiscent of the great municipal buildings of Philadelphia or old Richmond. New grade-school buildings sprang up all around the city, for blacks and for whites. By 1930 the city paid for a new water line to the Kentucky River; and city officials leased property on the Newtown Pike to build a new airport since Charles Lindbergh's visit to Lexingtonian Dr. Scott Breckinridge had proven the Halley Field on Leestown Pike was too small—the "Lone Eagle" barely missed the trees at the end of the runway.

In September 1939 Lexington heard of Hitler's invasion of Poland, and its citizens faced world war once again with patriotic fervor. Lafayette High School housed a national defense trade school by the summer of 1940 to get ready for the new jobs, and over 10,000 men from Fayette County registered for the first ever peacetime draft in U.S. history. In June 1941, a Civilian Defense Commission began to train volunteers to help firemen and police—and only two weeks after the Japanese attacked Pearl Harbor in December, Lexingtonians made plans for a practice blackout, appointing air raid wardens and installing air raid warning signals downtown. Clearly, Lexington was not a hot spot for enemy targets, however. In fact, Hubbell Company, an electrical equipment manufacturer, chose Lexington as a safe place to open a new plant in order to meet the nation's industries' new demands for electrical components and systems and to build electrical components for military use. The company considered the main plant in Bridgeport, Connecticut too vulnerable to air or sea attack.

Rationing, "victory" gardens, and war bonds became the norm. Lexington women gained access to wage-earning jobs to help sustain their families. The tobacco farmers and warehouse owners clamored to use German prisoners of war for cheap labor, and obligingly the Lexington officials gathered over 600 and housed them in the Kentucky militia armory on the Old Frankfort Pike to be sent out to the various surrounding farms for the 1944 and 1945 harvests. But nothing changed Lexington like the return of her veterans and the influx of money for higher education under the federal "G.I. Bill of Rights." This changed her landscape, her population, and her future completely.

Chapter Seven

EXPANSION

After World War II, life in Lexington changed completely. Nothing was the same. Or was it? Perhaps that's just what senior citizens tell us. Yet several events that took place in the late 1940s and 1950s support their claim. With the return of the war-seasoned veterans eager to spend their loans and grants from the "G.I. Bill," Lexington's schools and suburbs grew at unprecedented rates. The influx of new businesses and service industries to support them flooded the Lexington job market and attracted even more new families to the area. However, the case could be made that Lexington, while adjusting to the new economy and new socio-political demographics, kept her age-old identity. The horse and tobacco industries, Lexington's mainstays, blossomed in this post-war era. The black community, though growing increasingly smaller in proportion to the white population, kept its strong sense of heritage and continued in its strides toward equality. Lexington's ties with eastern Kentucky continued and the financial and mercantile interests worked together more effectively even though Lexington's role as a railroad nexus ended. The city's new shopping malls and basketball arenas served as even more effective reasons for Kentucky's highlanders to come to the Bluegrass. The promotion of education, the arts, and literature—long the basis of Lexington's boast of being the "Athens of the West"—gained from the new influx of wage-earners who could patronize and attend gala events. Though the landscape changed in the city of Lexington, as the Queen of the Bluegrass grew to accommodate these changes her basic character remained the same. Lexington's role as the service center for the rural areas around her continued, and her strong ties to heritage and age-old traditions did not unravel.

Even before 1940, Lexington businesses had begun to recover from the Depression years. New building projects funded by federal agencies as well as the wealthy members of the horse industry kept coming in all through the 1930s. By 1940 Lexington's population totaled 49,034—about 62 percent of Fayette County's 78,899; a decade later, Lexington's share of the county population rose to 75 percent with 55,534 people, even though the annexation of surrounding rural areas had often been stymied. As many urbanites moved further and further from the center of town, they crossed city boundaries and paid the lower county taxes rather than gamble on getting city services to their new communities. Some of the Lexington suburbs, which had been built a generation before with the promise of city water, sewer services, street lights, and interurban railway stops, still had not benefited from the high taxes their residents paid. Like many of the black communities that had formed along little country roads around Lexington during the 1880s, white Lexington residential areas sprang up along the major thoroughfares and developed their own associations to pave roads, build water systems, and provide electricity. There was little or no incentive to allow the growing city to annex their hamlets just to increase the city tax rolls.

Two major factors changed this situation: the growth of the University of Kentucky's teaching and research mission and the formation of the Lexington Industrial Foundation. Despite the paycuts in the 1930s, U.K. teaching services expanded during the 1940s with more late afternoon and evening classes, shortwave and then FM radio receivers for listening centers in the mountains, training centers and correspondence courses for soldiers, and downtown forums. Since the 1930s the state legislature tried to control the internal workings of the university, especially after Lexington city boss Bill Klair had shown how state finances could be readily handed over to key contractors such as insurance and construction companies to handle the university's needs. The attempt by the state to control university staff salaries in the early 1940s may have come from the public fear of free-thinking intellectuals during the restless times of worker alliances and tenant farmer unions. The university trustees, under the leadership of Governor Keen Johnson, had removed faculty governance to a "University Faculty" consisting only of deans and administrators to reassure local politicians. Herman Lee Donovan asserted in his monograph on the history of his presidency at U.K. that had he known this when he came from the presidency at Eastern Kentucky State Teacher's College in the summer of 1941 to U.K., he would not have accepted the position. However, he soon succeeded in empowering the faculty and raising U.K.'s prestige.

Wisely, Donovan turned to the horse industry for support. In 1939 Mrs. Margaret Voorhies Haggin donated a generous trust fund in memory of her husband, the great horseman James Ben Ali Haggin, for any purpose the U.K. Board of Trustees wanted, except for paying current expenses. In 1942 Donovan met with Hal Price Headley, president of the Keeneland Foundation, about the problem of faculty salaries. The Kentucky Court of Appeals had declared that the university faculty were "public officers" as defined in Section 246 of the Kentucky Constitution and so their salaries were capped at $5,000 just like all other state employees. Headley agreed that Keeneland would pay the difference between the cap and the faculty members' salaries, and they did until 1947 when the Court of Appeals reversed its decision. Donovan wrote that Keeneland "saved the University from educational bankruptcy."

During the 1940s, the need to accommodate the war veterans and their families led to the development of Cooperstown (built from surplus prefabricated houses brought in from Charlestown, Indiana and Willow Run, Michigan) and Shawneetown. Each village had its own major and council. The university also invested in paving the streets, and put in public lighting and sewer lines to handle the new housing. In 1946–1947 the university erected fifteen new buildings, twelve of which were temporary housing and classrooms. From 1948–1956 eighteen new buildings went up, eight of which were large dormitories. Memorial Coliseum, a general purpose auditorium that would be used for basketball, swimming, and department offices as well, opened in 1950 with great public acclaim since Lexingtonians had been planning for the construction of a large public arena since the turn of the century. The legislature provided 75 percent of the cost, and a newly formed Athletic Association was liable for the bonds sold to pay for the rest. The 1947–1948 basketball season with Coach Adolph Rupp's "Fabulous Five"—a team whose strength and talent was greatly enhanced by the addition of war veterans in their twenties—ended with both the Southeastern Conference and National Collegiate Athletic Association championships. Seven members went on to play on the 1948 Olympic championship team. The growing successes of the U.K. basketball and football teams soon became a bellwether of Lexington's community climate.

When Public Law 346, known as the G.I. Bill, went into effect in June 1944, the university had only 3,000 students. However, the succeeding five years saw the student population rise to 10,213 by 1950 and the faculty teaching staff doubled. When in 1950 the state legislature quietly passed a law that gave the state's Division of Personnel the power to set the pay scale for university and college employees, Donovan garnered support from prominent educators, alumni, and politicians to put the pressure on Frankfort to keep this authority with the institutions' governing boards. In 1952 the legislature under the new governor, Lawrence Wetherby, corrected the law. In addition, the university gained its freedom from direct control of the State Department of Education; however, the state colleges, then primarily teacher-training schools, remained within the department.

Another important facet to the changes in the university during the 1940s involved the enrollment of black students. Since the fall of 1931, the University Board of Trustees had allowed blacks to enroll for extension classes the same as white students, but they adhered to Kentucky's 1904 Jim Crow law on education (known as the Day Law) by sending the grades to be recorded at the Kentucky State College for Negroes in Frankfort. Violations of the Day Law carried a fine of $1,000 for any person or institution that violated it, and an additional fine of $100 a day if the violation continued after conviction. In 1941 Charles L. Eubanks applied for admission to study civil engineering at the university and upon denial he sued. The case never went to trial since both sides kept asking for continuances until federal judge H. Church Ford dismissed the case for want of prosecution.

In 1948 John Wesley Hatch applied to the U.K. College of Law. University officials carefully consulted with the state's attorney general before undertaking any action. Hatch was admitted to Kentucky State, given access to the law library at the Capitol, and attended tutorial sessions with part-time U.K. professors who drove from Lexington to teach him. By November of that year four Frankfort lawyers were hired to teach him, but Hatch complained that he had no peer interaction and he withdrew at the end of the semester. That same year Lyman T. Johnson, a teacher in Louisville with a masters degree from the University of Michigan, won his suit in Judge Ford's federal court against U.K. and was admitted to graduate school. Though his case did not overturn the state law, the point was made and after two contentious votes in the Board of Trustees, U.K. made no appeal to the decision. In the summer of 1949 Johnson and twenty-nine other black students registered and bravely attended classes despite later incidences of cross-burnings in front of the administration building. George H. Green, a doctoral student taking history classes that summer, recalled the cross-burnings in a *Herald-Leader* interview in 1999, saying that there was "a tension you could feel, but no one said anything. I remember telling somebody that I don't care if they burn all the crosses they want to, as long as they don't scorch me." Green remembered that he and two other black students sat in the back of the classroom. "I don't know if we did that on purpose or that's the way we were assigned."

According to President Donovan's memoir, the university's policy of integration was one of "gradualism"—a strategy long held dear by antebellum Kentucky abolitionists. As Donovan remembered it, the University Faculty agreed that the integration of black students should be taken on very carefully and with stringent control over the behavior of the black students. For example, Donovan remembered that the staff asked the black students to "sit together in the classroom rather than scatter over the room, that when they entered the cafeteria, they sit at a table with their fellow Negro students instead of each occupying a separate table." The staff further advised them "never to go to a table where white students were already seated, but that if white students on their own initiative came and sat with them, they should feel at ease." Some parts of campus were off-limits. Donovan said that his staff "asked the Negroes not to go to the Student Union for the first year of this experiment and to keep away from social programs." The black students had to find their own housing "and to work out their own social life with their own people." The black students behaved in an exemplary manner and the result, wrote Donovan, was that the whites "have for the most part ignored their presence; however, this is not to imply that they have been antagonistic or unkind." This careful policy of social segregation of the races within close physical environs had a long heritage in Lexington history.

Another factor in the expansion of the target audience for the university's education mission was the physical expansion of the correspondence offerings out of the U.K. Extension Office. In 1948, the U.K. Board of Trustees established the Northern Extension Center in Covington, on the Kentucky side of the river near Cincinnati. The goal was to offer an alternative way for students who lived at a distance from Lexington to start the first two years of college and then finish up their degrees on the university campus. This effort grew into what became the U.K. Community College System, offering associates degrees and easy transferability into capstone baccalaureate degrees. In 1997 the Kentucky legislature separated the Community College System from U.K., but the original goal to offer high need post-compulsory education opportunities close to home and to ease transferability of the resulting credits into a higher education degree program remains.

As the university grew in size, its faculty took on new roles in state and federal sponsored research projects. Traditionally those faculty associated with the Agricultural Experiment Station had been the most active in this arena, and the 1940s and 1950s saw even greater expansions in tobacco and animal research efforts. They were joined in the 1950s by the Bacteriology, Engineering, Chemistry, Sociology, and History departments in high-profile research projects, including rural and community-based sociology projects and the editing of the Henry Clay papers. By that time, the M.I. King Library, built in 1931 from the inheritance tax money collected by the state upon the death of Louisville magnate Robert Bingham's widow, had become the fifth largest library in the south. In addition to the growing library collections to accommodate the needs of scholarly research, U.K. faculty and students benefited from the founding of the University of Kentucky Press in 1943, maintained by an annual grant from the Haggin Fund. In 1952 the university library, benefiting from the continued support of distinguished professor Thomas D. Clark and the newly hired Special Collections librarian Jacqueline Bull, gained admittance to the elite Association of Research Libraries. The Kentucky Research Foundation incorporated in 1945 to "act as the agent of the University in the solicitation of and administration of funds" used especially for research, but also for public service activities, fellowships, or endowments of professorships. During the Cold War, U.K. spent much of its research time on national defense projects in chemistry, physics, and engineering.

From the direct support of the Kentucky Farm Bureau as well as the Kentucky Medical Foundation and the personal advocacy of Governor A.B. Chandler, the University of Kentucky Medical Center started up about this time. In the inaugural issue of the *University of Kentucky: Studies in Medical Service* (January 1931), U.K.'s student health physician Dr. John S. "Brick" Chambers and a political science graduate student, Harry R. Lynn, wrote up their findings for the number of Kentucky's physicians and Kentuckians' access to primary health care. Kentucky had 1 doctor for every 1,140 citizens—compared to the national ratio of 1 to 740 citizens. In 1954 the U.K. Board of Trustees officially established a Medical School to be funded by the state legislature and by private appropriations through the newly created Kentucky Medical Sciences Development Foundation. In the spring of 1956 the legislature appropriated $5 million to start the medical center, which would eventually cost $28 million and include a 500-bed hospital. Their investment paid off. By 1963 the federal government began a series of Health Professions Education Assistance Acts, which at first provided construction aid to medical schools in an effort to increase the number and variety of health practitioners across the nation, especially in underserved areas. U.K. started a rural health scholarship program to help educate physicians from eastern Kentucky who were expected afterwards to return to their eastern Kentucky region to practice—but this met with mixed success since many did not wish to return home. William R. Willard, the founding dean of the University of Kentucky School of Medicine and often called the father of the specialty of family medicine, believed that community medicine taught students the social organization and resources of a community, preparing them to become leaders in community health as well as clinicians.

At the same time, Lexington also took advantage of the new federal initiatives stimulating hospital construction at the end of the Second World War. A major health care industry grew up around the University of Kentucky Medical Center, the Veterans Administration Hospital, the Shriners Hospital for Crippled Children (built in 1955), and several other large hospital facilities. During the 1960s federal and state funding increased for community health centers and financed care for the poor and elderly through Medicare and Medicaid. The community health medical program set up by Dr. Kurt Deuschle, one of the world's experts on rural and community health, relied on U.K.'s Agricultural County Extension offices to introduce new physicians to their areas to build trust. However, this natural collaboration did not continue after Dr. Deuschle left Kentucky. Instead, U.K. opened the award-winning Center for Rural Health in 1990 in Hazard, a southeastern Kentucky town. This center provides educational programs as well as research in rural health policy analysis and community workforce needs.

According to an interview of Dr. Caroline Scott by Rick Smoot in 1983, the several Miners' Memorial Hospitals of the United Mine Workers of America relied on Lexington doctors, especially during the 1930s when union activity was literally a life-and-death situation in eastern Kentucky coalfields. These hospitals are now part of Appalachian Regional Healthcare, Inc., which today collaborates with the U.K. Medical Center to host the Area Health Education Center (AHEC). In the AHEC program, medical students and residents live and work in an underserved region of Kentucky as part of a rotation experience, learning a primary care focus from community-based faculty. The Hazard site, for example, serves as a training center for the U.K. Family Practice residency program. College of Medicine students and residents participated in over 300 rotations in AHEC sites during the 2002–2003 program year. In addition, the College of Medicine developed a telemedicine program, primarily for eastern Kentucky but now used statewide in the Kentucky Telehealth Network. Using compressed video and robotic devices, the state's two medical schools can collaborate with regional hospitals and clinics to solve complicated procedures that might not otherwise have been attempted.

One of Lexington's most flamboyant characters grew up in this health services environment. As a youth, James Herndon was abandoned by his family at Good Samaritan Hospital. Mary Ott, for whom the new wing for the building was about to be named, felt sorry for him and made the hospital administrator Lake Johnson give him a room at the hospital. There Herndon earned his own way and soon became head orderly, making enough money to buy a house in a black section of town called Pralltown near the U.K. campus. During the 1950s and 1960s, Herndon became a Lexington legend known as "Sweet Evening Breeze." Though he rarely dressed in full drag, he would accessorize his suits with a broach or scarf in excellent taste. He was a popular cheerleader for the Good Samaritan's annual basketball games pitting the male doctors against the female nurses. His—or as some said—her proud and self-conscious posture along with a prim sort of walk came to be well known in Lexington. Her legendary generosity included buying shoes for Pralltown children and putting one girl through college. When she died she gave her rather large estate to Pleasant Green Baptist Church. Her cooking skills were widely admired, and she hosted many parties for the Lexington homosexual community before the Gilded Cage, a bar frequented by gays, opened in 1963. When the eccentric painter Henry Faulkner came to Lexington in 1955 he lived in the basement of Sweet Evening Breeze until, with a growing success in his career, he leased his own house on Arlington Avenue in 1962. Some of Lexington's more upstanding citizens enjoyed her company, especially since she often brought along her famous coconut cake covered with Maraschino cherries. "Sweets" was as much a part of Lexington as the heterosexual community, and with the new populations of people coming to the city, even a gentle black gay man could find roots in the community.

Major manufacturing companies such as IBM, Square D, and Dixie Cup opened plants in the Lexington area during the "industrial revolution" of the 1950s. Trane Company opened its plant in 1963 to manufacture industrial strength central station air handlers. This influx of new jobs came easier due to the work of the nonprofit Lexington Industrial Foundation, founded in 1956 and led by Caruthers A. Coleman, Sr. The foundation purchased 139 acres on the northwest side of town between Georgetown and Leestown Roads and invested in sewers, water, and gas utilities as well as roads. The entrance of IBM on the Lexington scene came only after careful scrutiny of the local schools and the university, but the clincher came with Governor Chandler's offer of state land on the north side of town next to the Eastern State Hospital (formerly the Lunatic Asylum). The company brought in approximately 250 families from its Poughkeepsie, New York plant and began interviewing Lexingtonians for jobs. The huge draw for wage-earners pulled in thousands of people to Lexington and Fayette County, most of them from out of state. As a result,

Expansion

from the years 1954 to 1963 employment in Lexington rose 260 percent. The value of Lexington's manufacturing output rose nearly four times what it had been. Between 1960 and 1970, the city population rose to 108,137 with a 32 percent gain. This made Lexington the 14th fastest growing standard metropolitan statistical area in the nation. Housing, schools, and city services could barely meet the demand. By 1972, 85 percent of the non-white population of Fayette County lived in the city, and most of them lived on the north end of town.

With such a swift influx of new families, the city and county school systems could not keep up. The landmark decision of Brown v. Board of Education forced Lexingtonians to desegregate the old schools even as they tried to build schools in the new neighborhoods. The city officials vainly experimented with a free choice model to induce parents to take their children to schools outside their segregated neighborhoods. In 1964, under pressure from the federal Civil Rights Act, the city tried to close the high school for its only all-black public school, Douglas, and transform it into an integrated elementary school. This attempt was not successful either. Not much change took place, and by 1967 the Kentucky Court of Appeals mandated a merger of the county and city school systems to try to balance the racial composition of the whole system. Black students made up nearly half the city school population, while the county system was only 10 percent black. In another attempt at integration, the superintendent Dr. Guy Potts closed Dunbar Senior High School and assigned its black students to the four other high schools. This move outraged the black community around the school. Dunbar had been an important symbol for black Lexingtonians. In 1948, when the white community celebrated Coach Adolph Rupp's team of the "Fabulous Five," Dunbar's team, coached by S.T. Roach, defeated the Hopkinsville Attucks for the KHSAL title in a double-overtime game, one of the greatest high school games in Kentucky history.

In 1959 the Lexington chapter of the American Civil Liberties Union and several other concerned citizens formed a branch of CORE, the Congress of Racial Equality. This organization had its origins on the University of Chicago's campus in the 1940s and both black and white established organizations suspected CORE's membership of college students and their professors as revolutionaries bent on radical and immediate change. William O. Reichert, a political science professor at U.K. who knew of the difficulties encountered by his own students when they tried to find places off-campus to eat or use public facilities, agreed to head the local organization. Reichert described in a 1988 letter to historian George Wright (a copy is available in the U.K. Special Collections and Archives) his group's efforts to change the attitudes of downtown management to allow lunch counter service for black patrons. "Using non-violent means, we arranged visits by teams to each of the stores, one black person and two whites, all of the same sex, of course. The team would enter and sit down waiting to be served. The white persons were always served but the black person refused invariably." They kept up this nonviolent social action for several months to no avail. One busy Saturday noon hour, a large group of the Lexington CORE members entered one store and "the manager called the police, claiming a riot under way and of course the squad cars came from all directions with sirens shrieking, the manager hoping that we would become frightened and appear to be breaking the peace so that we could be arrested and brought to court."

A newspaper editorial called for U.K. president Frank Dickey to silence Professor Reichert, and that year Frank Peterson, the comptroller, made sure that Reichert had a lower than usual pay increase. Reichert soon left U.K. for a one-year appointment in Nebraska. Some assert that the activism of the Lexington CORE members led to the hiring of black drivers for city buses and as cashiers in local groceries; however, it is not clear what they did for the integration of downtown lunch counters. When the integrated professional basketball team the Boston Celtics came to play an exhibition game at Memorial Coliseum, they ate at the Phoenix Hotel's coffee shop. The servers refused to take the black team members' food orders and an enterprising newspaper reporter caught on film the ignominious scene of the players being thrown out of the hotel. The black athletes left Lexington on the next flight, leaving only the white players, including former U.K. star Frank Ramsey, to take on the St. Louis Hawks.

The Lexington newspapers, both the Democratic morning Lexington *Herald* and the Republican evening Lexington *Leader*, were managed by Fred Wachs, who refused to give much if any coverage of CORE or NAACP efforts to raise awareness of civil rights issues. The managing editor of the *Herald* explained to Reichert that they refused to publish CORE letters to the editor because, "we felt that they might have a tendency to intensify racial discord." The *Leader* took a more open stance by editorializing that CORE had instigated violence and "interfered with the peaceful conduct of private business." By 1963 the black community had had enough. Approximately 250 blacks and some whites marched from Pleasant Green and Greater Liberty Baptist churches, singing and picketing the newspapers. Upon hearing of the assassination of Martin Luther King, Jr. in Memphis on April 4, some in the Lexington black community took out their anger by setting fires and vandalizing local businesses. Lexington's first black city commissioner, Harry Sykes, walked through the black neighborhoods during that time working with other black Lexington leaders who counseled moderation. Also that year the city commissioners transformed the volunteer Committee on Religion and Human Rights into the Lexington Commission on Human Rights, and by the mid-1960s Lexington's downtown businesses had abolished most of their Jim Crow policies.

The black community had long relied on the strength of its churches, local business entrepreneurs, fraternal orders, and benevolent societies to craft and maintain a positive sense of identity. The children however lost this sense of community when they went to integrated schools, and black leaders founded the Mr. and Miss Black

Lexington Beauty Pageant in 1968 to help give children a sense of accomplishment and to develop self-esteem. One of the most effective organizations today is the Lexington chapter of the YMCA Black Achievers. Dr. Juanita Betz Peterson led the effort in 1985 to create this local connection to a national program, founded in 1971 at New York City's Harlem YMCA. The program's purpose is to help African-American youth (ages six and up) explore a positive sense of self and set high goals for themselves. African-American professionals donate their time to serve as role models and volunteer leaders for students in grades 7–12. Dr. Peterson organized activities such as career workshops and college tours, and established university scholarships and cash awards to youth.

Meanwhile, with the influx of white collar worker families to meet the needs of the new industry and the expansion of the university faculty, the Woman's Club of Central Kentucky grew in membership. In March 1961 it revived its pre–World War II luncheon Style Show as an annual fundraising event with great success. That same year the Lexington Symphony Women's League held its first charity ball. Ostensibly a fundraising event, the Blue Grass Ball has, since its origin, raised barely half a million dollars to be distributed among many different community organizations. Most clearly, this organization's driving force is to serve as a way for certain families to "present" their daughters as debutantes to Lexington's white society. The girls, whose parents had enough money to put them up as debutantes, attended parties nearly every single night in the summer, from the day that school ended until the day that school started up again. There were gatherings of some sort every day of the Christmas vacation, and the Bluegrass Charity Ball during the period between Christmas and New Year's Day was the crowning jewel. Sometimes the parents of the debutantes would host two or three balls during that time as well. By 1989 Lexington's black community responded with its own Roots and Heritage Foundation Charity Ball, minus the debutantes.

Wildcat mania found its first organized expression in the separately incorporated Athletic Association that could, under the direction of the U.K. president and a board of directors, get around Kentucky constitutional limits on salaries. President Donovan admitted that the state legislators, increasingly interested in U.K. athletics over academics, heralded this initiative; the U.K. presidency has ever since been obligated to attend to this statewide obsession. The Athletic Association's first major hire was football coach Paul "Bear" Bryant, who quickly turned around the sagging fortunes of the U.K. team. The 1950–1951 academic year was the best in U.K. athletics, but in October 1951 all of Lexington was shocked to find out that three members of the 1948–1949 basketball team had been arrested for accepting bribes. Then, three more from the 1949–1950 team. Five were convicted. The NCAA barred U.K. from playing basketball in the 1952–1953 year; meanwhile, the football team won the Cotton Bowl. The next year the basketball team was undefeated, but football coach Bryant left for Texas A&M.

Thus, the relationship between U.K. and Lexington at this time seemed to hinge mainly on athletic feats for entertainment. No one could yet see how the former agricultural and mechanics school might play such an important role in the development of the city. Looking at a map of the city political boundaries and the city service areas, one can see that Lexington's growth was a developer's dream. Many of the new white families wanted to live outside the city so as to take advantage of the lower taxes and avoid the inner city area. Lexington's nearly sixty precincts were becoming comparatively non-white and blue collar with an increasingly unpopular group of professors, students, and staff around the university and at Transylvania. Some of the developers offered private sewer plant systems at lower cost and higher efficiency than the older suburbs' septic tank systems. City leaders tried annexation of the crazy-quilt areas outside the city borders in order to increase the tax base, but rarely succeeded. The disparity in the property taxes and service surcharges seemed exorbitant to those in the county and very little benefit to their neighborhoods. For those neighborhoods where sewers were long overdue, especially in former black hamlets or Irish enclaves, the city was successful. A struggle over the city's power center ensued, with the concepts of annexation and merger at the crux of the matter.

Since 1937 Fred B. Wachs, the general manager of the Lexington *Leader*, the Republican Party's mouthpiece, had control also of the Democratic Lexington *Herald*. In 1959 he became president of the joint *Herald-Leader* and editor of the *Leader*. Even though the two papers maintained their separate party affiliations, Wachs was able to take a pivotal role in most city decisions. The politically-charged role of these city newspapers, not unlike that of Louisville's *Courier-Journal* of the time, cannot be underestimated. In an interview with oral historian Betsy Brinson in February 2000, former governor Ned Breathitt described "this little group that ran Lexington" in the late 1950s and early 1960s: Fred Wachs, Ed Dabney, Bob Watt, and Frank Peterson. Edward S. Dabney, president and director of Security Trust Company since 1940, became chairman of the board of First Security National Bank in 1961. This bank was the result of a consolidation of First National Bank and Trust Company and Security Trust, the largest and fourth largest of the six commercial banks in Fayette County. Dabney also served as one of the three directors of the *Herald-Leader* Company trust along with Wachs and Gayle A. Mohney, secretary of the Keeneland Association. Robert M. Watt went from being one of the first employees to president of Kentucky Utilities until 1957, when he became chairman of the board. Frank Peterson had served twenty-three years as comptroller at U.K. and vice-president for business affairs. During the Donovan and Dickey administrations he led the building program that ultimately redefined the university by the mid-1960s. The previously separate university community had begun to encroach more and more into downtown Lexington areas and city services, and Peterson was well aware of the advantages of a town-gown collaboration. Of these four men, Breathitt said he "always called it the oligarchy downtown that ran the town."

During the search for housing and new business service centers in the 1950s, downtown city lot owners found great profit in replacing older buildings with new construction. Crumbling and abandoned buildings lined the streets downtown and city leaders were sure that if they built bigger, newer buildings, higher leases could be sought. The need for more convenient and low-price parking lured many to build parking lots. Along Second Street the Thomas Hart House, where Lucretia Hart married Henry Clay, was torn down in 1955 and replaced with a small concrete lot despite the heroic efforts of the Blue Grass Trust for Historic Preservation. The Trust saved the Hunt-Morgan House, built in 1814 by John Wesley Hunt, the first millionaire west of the Alleghenies, whose famous descendents include Confederate Gen. John Hunt Morgan and Dr. Thomas Hunt Morgan, the first Kentuckian to win a Nobel Prize.

By the early 1960s Lexington's downtown was a diverse commercial area filled with lots of pedestrians. Unlike pre–Civil War Lexington, most of the mid-twentieth-century pedestrians were white locals who would dress up to go downtown to shop or do business. Though Union Station had been torn down in 1960, the railroad tracks that moved the passenger and freight trains through the city remained. Traffic jams resulted from the long waits for slow-moving trains cutting through the city at major intersections such as at Broadway, Limestone, and Midland Streets. Vine Street, one block away from and parallel to Main Street, retained its old Water Street identity from frontier Lexington days when it was lined with warehouses and industries using the Town Branch of the Elkhorn Creek. The Ben Ali Theatre closed and a parking lot was built in its place. The Opera House, once an important regional source of entertainment for Kentuckians in the Gay '90s, seemed destined for the wrecking ball. The State Theatre became The Downtown Cinema, an art house cinema. The Switow family, which owned both the all-white Kentucky Theatre and Downtown Cinema, switched to an X-rated format in The Downtown Cinema, which would support The Kentucky. The city cited Fred Mills, then the manager of The Downtown Cinema, The Kentucky, and The Strand, for indecency on several times to no avail. Meanwhile, "matchbox theatres" opened in the new malls such as Turfland on Harrodsburg Road on the south side of town.

A maze of billboard wall signs and sign "jungles" along the busy and congested main streets indicated the city's bustling new growth of services, but city leaders were determined to clean it up. Republican leader and financier Garvice D. Kincaid announced in 1963 that he would move the Kentucky Central Life Insurance Company from Louisville to downtown Lexington. At the time, Kincaid owned a radio station (WVLK), television station (WKYT), the popular hotels in town (the Campbell House, the Phoenix, and Lafayette), and the exciting entertainment area for whites, Joyland

Park. When he talked about urban renewal, people listened. The city had applied for the new federal urban renewal program grants, and the City Commission along with Mayor Fred Fugazzi began to implement a new downtown design.

The Kentucky chapter of the American Institute of Architects established a Downtown Design Group in 1964 to study how best to design a new downtown Lexington. It was primarily a volunteer effort by eleven architects and landscape architects, and the Lexington Planning Commission adopted the plan in 1965. Funding of the implementation of the plan came from a capital grant approved in 1966 by the Department of Housing and Urban Development (HUD). Basically, the plan centered on the Main Street retail area as the heart of the city. This core would be redesigned to include two public open spaces and a cultural hall with an auditorium surrounded by offices, agencies and institutions, and apartments. On the east end of the city, the plan would have zoned a "drive-in" secondary commercial area; on the west end, the slum residential areas would be replaced with more wholesaling and industrial service areas. Residential zones would be confined to the north and south of the central core area. A major interstate highway, I-64 (just before its interchange with I-75), would sweep through the Lexington downtown parallel to the east-west trajectory of a two-way Main Street. Second Street, also parallel to Main Street but further north, would become a wide boulevard parkway for local traffic. The railroad tracks would be taken up, and Vine Street converted to a minor one-way artery alongside Main Street to help move event traffic out from the cultural center.

By the summer of 1966, the Lexington Urban Renewal and Community Development Agency took on the responsibility for implementing the plan. There were almost 300 buildings under consideration, of which nearly half were to be razed. The plan included the demolition of older buildings on High Street, also parallel to Main Street but up the hill overlooking where the old Town Branch had once flowed. Prosperous whites lived there alongside well-to-do African Americans, even during slavery times, along with many artisans also living in the district. The Adam Rankin House, the oldest home in Lexington, still stands in this area. The South Hill Neighborhood Association worked to craft a West High Street Historic District and successfully listed fourteen of the buildings in the National Register of Historic Places in 1969. Around that time the Citizens Union Bank under the leadership of Republican lawyer William L. Wallace, a former corporation counsel of the City of Lexington, submitted a development proposal to the city commissioners to construct an office building on High Street. The city granted the bank a contract, and HUD approved the demolition of seven of the historic buildings.

The South Hill Neighborhood Association filed suit to halt the destruction of the buildings in vain. This author remembers being recruited as a member of the Young Historians Club while a junior high student at The Sayre School to write a compelling story about one of the historic buildings to raise public awareness of the buildings' worth to our city's heritage. It was something that seemed natural and honorable since meeting in or touring old buildings was something many Lexingtons grew up doing. Some thought that subsidies from the bonds sold to build the Lexington Civic Center at the corner of Broadway and Main would be enough to save the historic Opera House, but success came only after private individuals established an endowment type trust, initially headed by art patrons Linda Carey and W.T. Young. Governor Louie Nunn's wife Beulah worked to secure the Main Street girlhood home of Mary Todd Lincoln (which had also served as a brothel for the famed Belle Brezing) but was not successful until 1977.

Removal of the downtown L&N and C&O railroad tracks began in 1968 upon receipt of the federal and state funds for urban renewal. At the same time, Bart N. Peak and William H. McCann, state representatives from Lexington with strong U.K. connections, drafted House Bill 543, which secured the legal basis for a Lexington–Fayette County merger. Peak, a Fayette County judge from 1958 to 1966, had studied other communities with merged governments and felt sure it could work for Lexington. Most local politicians, including the Lexington area's state senator William Kenton, anticipated that the legislature would focus on the preliminary census numbers indicating that the population was growing past 100,000, and Lexington would soon be ranked as a city of the first class. This designation meant that Lexington would have a completely different governance structure according to the Kentucky constitution. At the time, four councilmen and a mayor—all with equal decision-making votes—led the government while the city manager handled basic administrative functions such as staffing, payroll, and budget.

Merger of public services began in Lexington with the state court–mandated consolidation of the public school system in 1967—described earlier in this chapter. The next significant merger was of the city and county fire departments in 1970. Mayor Charles Wylie and the four councilmen (Fred Fugazzi, Joe Graves, Harry Sykes, and Tom Underwood) worked with County Judge Joe E. Johnson and the county commission to make the transition smooth for all concerned. Since the beginning of the fire companies in Lexington, and certainly under the organizing influences of the ward bosses of the Progressive Era, firefighters were important political blocs that needed to be handled with respect. Of all the Kentucky firefighters, Chief Earl McDaniel of Lexington was held in great esteem. He had been active in national and international associations and is now in the Kentucky Firefighters Hall of Fame. Under his leadership, the Lexington department changed from a small operation with six fire stations to a modern one with nearly twenty stations, and he started the oldest state firefighter school. During McDaniel's tenure, the U.S. Chamber of Commerce twice named him and the Lexington Fire Department the #1 fire department in the nation for a city Lexington's size.

When the City Commissioners did not take up the Peak-McCann idea for merger in 1969–1970, a group of citizens called GO (Governmental Options) started a

Lexington

merger drive under the leadership of William E. Lyons, assistant professor of political science at U.K. who later wrote a monograph of his work on this initiative. Dr. Phillip Crossen, also of U.K., chaired the small group whose members seemed more amenable to the new world of rock festivals and student protests than to the staid and conservative culture of traditional Lexington.

This town-gown culture clash had surfaced more than once. Older residents and the more conservative elite of Lexington saw the younger hippie crowds and their favorite professors as adversaries. Dress had always been an important definer of status in Lexington, and the white-shirt-and-tie crowd avoided mixing with those who sported the new scruffy look of the 1960s and 1970s. Governor Louie Nunn, chairman of the U.K. Board of Trustees during the time when students protested the killings at Kent State University and the invasion of Cambodia, brought out the National Guard with live ammunition in two instances to show military strength over the "hippies:" once as the students were watching the ROTC building burn (no one is sure how it caught fire) and again when the Republican governors convened at the Phoenix Hotel. In both instances, the gatherings were peaceful—some say the governor over-reacted by bringing in soldiers with live ammunition, but clearly many of the city leaders were comforted by the presence of the clean-cut Guardsmen standing at respectful attention. Journalist-photographer Guy Mendes remembers one particularly volatile clash between the U.K. community and Lexington authorities during 1970. Obstetrics-gynecology professor Phillip Crossen allowed students to hold a rock festival on his farm on Armstrong Mill Road to benefit an underground newspaper, *Blue-Tail Fly*, and the Black Student Union. The police raided the party and County Attorney E. Lawson King accused Crossen of promoting indecency: some of the students had been found huddled together under a blanket and the police testified to observing fornication.

With the city-county merger initiative, the U.K. faculty worked together with the Chamber of Commerce, the League of Women Voters, and the Rotary Club. They had been sponsoring programs on city-county consolidation, and the GO group organized a petition drive to put merger up as a referendum. Professor Lyons describes GO as a "small band of citizens" who worked with League of Women Voters volunteers to get the requisite 5 percent of voters to sign the petition. They presented the petition to the county clerk in November 1970, including an endorsement by County Judge Robert F. Stephens who announced in the Fayette County Fiscal Court that he supported the idea of consolidation. Stephens quickly appointed the requisite ten members to a study group including Lyons. Meanwhile the city representatives had yet to be named. The elections of 1970 led to an upset: only Charles Wylie and Harry Sykes were elected from the Wachs/Kincaid-supported ticket. Ray Boggs and Tom Underwood, the other three city commissioners, became a "three man majority," often voting as a bloc against Wylie and Sykes. The city named its representatives on the merger commission in mid-February and there remains today some controversy over Lyons's portrayal of the city's support for creating the charter. Nevertheless, in less than six months a draft charter was on the table for consideration. The city changed from a structure of nearly sixty precincts with four council members elected at-large in a partisan election to twelve districts, each with a representative and three at-large representatives elected in non-partisan elections. The forty-page document took fifteen months to develop and in November 1972 under a new administration with a new mayor, H. Foster Pettit, the citizens of Fayette County and the city of Lexington voted in an overwhelming majority—more than 70 percent—in favor of the Lexington-Fayette Urban County Government Charter. On January 1, 1974, Lexington became the first city in Kentucky to consolidate with its county government to form a single government. At the time there were very few in the nation. Mayor Pettit was re-elected in 1974 and served one term; Mayor James G. Amato served one term from 1978 to 1981; Mayor Scotty Baesler served from 1982 until he took office as a U.S. representative in 1992; Vice-Mayor Pam Miller took on his responsibilities and then won her re-election bid, serving from 1993 to 2002. In the next election Greater Lexington rejected partisan politics: Lexington council member Scott Crosbie, openly supported by the Republican Party, lost in 2003 to Teresa Isaac.

The newly merged city-county government completed the new Vine Street in 1973, and tall new buildings for Bank of Lexington, First Security, and Citizens Union girded the new area. By 1975 the plan for a Lexington Civic Center came to life with its central feature: a new sports arena, originally proposed by City Commissioner and Mayor Pro Tem Tom Underwood. At the time Rupp Arena was the largest in the United States. With its seating capacity of 23,000, it surpassed the Brigham Young University arena by approximately 200 seats. Lexingtonians had been talking about building a downtown convention center since 1916. The university attracted Lexington financial contributions to build the Memorial Coliseum on the campus in 1950, but it held only 11,000. Dr. Ray Holsclaw led the advocacy group inspired by what U.K. fans called the "Alley Cats," those luckless Kentuckians who stood outside Memorial Coliseum trying to find tickets to games. Holsclaw started a Rupp Arena Citizen's Committee, sending out survey cards across the country in hopes of gaining support for the idea. They received over 50,000 survey cards in reply.

Lexington developers Donald and Dudley Webb took the lead in further development of the area around the Civic Center. With the help of the Garvice Kincaid family, the Webbs began construction of the block between Vine and Main across the street from the Civic Center. The new business areas of Vine Center, Lexington Financial Center (Lexington's tallest building), and the Festival Market soon followed. Other entrepreneurs and developers were part of the redevelopment of Lexington's downtown. The Triangle Foundation created the tree-lined Triangle

Lexington

Park in front of the Civic Center, and its cascading fountain and tree-lined walks serve today as a welcoming public space for city art festivals and parade watchers. Established in 1980 and operating under the motto, "Private Initiative for the Public Good," the Triangle Foundation is a private, non-profit group of central Kentucky citizens and corporations who give time and resources to self-initiated capital fund projects for which there are no other monies available. Other Foundation projects include Thoroughbred Park on the corner of Main and Midland Streets, where cars used to sit in long lines waiting for the trains to pass, and the development of the Fayette County Courthouse Plaza along Limestone Street.

By 1985 the downtown renovation efforts included the block across Main Street from the Civic Center. This area included sixteen buildings from the 1880s that had in various times included saloons, hotels, and restaurants. Preserving as much of the original facades as possible, Victorian Square opened with office and retail space, a restaurant named after the prominent Desha family, a children's museum, and an artist "attic" for locals who needed studio and exhibition space. Since the renovation also preserved many of the original metal ceilings, exterior balconies, and ironwork, Lexington's Victorian Square is listed on the National Register of Historic Buildings. The wonderful work by historian Tom Clark and former Chamber of Commerce president Ed Houlihan to bring the Lexington History Museum to the old Fayette County Courthouse, one block away from Victorian Square, is a boon to the downtown revitalization effort.

In addition, the building spree included a series of pedways across the five block area to encourage the feeling of a single Civic Center, with everything accessible by all who attended the large events. In 1985 Lexington was chosen as the site for the national college basketball tournament, the "Final Four," and the new Center seemed a perfect fit. Today, nearly 1,000 businesses have located in Lexington's downtown, and with a median age of thirty-three years, the downtown inhabitants are young and energized for new opportunities. This promising future for Lexington did not happen by accident.

In the late 1990s during her second term, Mayor Pam Miller worked on two main initiatives that have come to be her legacy to the future of Lexington: the protection of a "green belt" of horse farms around Lexington and the revitalization of the downtown city core area. Lexington and Fayette County were one of the first in the nation to establish a growth control ordinance that created an "urban service area" in 1958. Proposed by Wolfgang Roseler, a planning consultant from Cincinnati, the concept convinced the Kentucky Court of Appeals in 1959 that the individual developers could be corralled into certain areas and Lexington's horse farms could be protected by the City of Lexington. The Urban Service Area of roughly seventy-three square miles effectively limited urban developers to the designated area with the rural area being reserved for agricultural use. In a 2004 interview, Helm Roberts remembered his work as a consultant to William H. Qualls, who was executive director of the Lexington Fayette County Planning Commission and fearless advocate for local government control over its green space throughout the 1960s and early 1970s. Roberts wrote legal descriptions for the boundary in an update in 1973 when the City Commission expanded the boundary slightly. As the supply of developable land within the original urban service area became limited, and with the older city core areas neglected by developers, the debate grew up around limitations of Lexington's growth. In 1979 the Kentucky Planning Association awarded Bill Qualls its Highest Honor Award for resisting pressures to relax or eliminate the community's Urban Service Area policy.

A few suburban developments in the rural zone sprang up during that time since the land development rights had already been committed before the implementation of the Urban Service Area. However, this escalated pressure on Lexington's elected officials to re-think the concept of an urban service area. Mayor Miller formed a workgroup to study this issue and in 1998 the city hired William Simons, a consultant from Chicago, to lead discussions and provide guidance on how best to respond during the public hearings held during this time. A highly publicized public campaign by various special interest groups gave Lexingtonians a whole new set of bumper stickers to display. Two in particular—"Growth is Good" and "Growth Destroys Bluegrass Forever"—were highly controversial, pitting developers and rural landowners against urban renewal planners, intellectuals, and preservationists. Mayor Miller brought all the divergent groups to the table, and they met in the Bank One building downtown for three years to help craft what became a very complicated system. Finally adopted formally by a brave Lexington-Fayette County Urban County Council in 2001, the Purchase of Development Rights (PDR) program compensates farmers to remove their land permanently from any development plans and to conserve farmland. This program is still controversial in the eyes of many who had hoped that the Urban Service Area concept would continue to hold up in court against developers desiring a free market environment. Either way Lexington may have been the first to initiate a locally run program to protect the agricultural, cultural, and environmental resources that make the Lexington area unique.

In 1999 Mayor Miller formed a committee to investigate downtown revitalization. This committee produced a report which, among other things, recommended the creation of a workgroup to focus on and direct redevelopment initiatives. This idea was taken up by the Lexington-Fayette Urban County Government, and the nonprofit Lexington Downtown Development Authority, Inc. opened its doors in December 2001. In a 2004 interview, former Mayor Miller emphasized that the Downtown Development Authority has succeeded in planning for new housing units for the downtown area but that the basic downtown traffic patterns need to be adjusted so that downtown can be pedestrian-friendly again. She agrees with urban redevelopment experts who are now telling cities that "congestion is good." The former city officials and downtown businesses who worked so hard at getting the streets cleaned up and widened for multi-lane throughways in the 1960s find this suggestion a step backwards. The right to drive straight through town at twenty-five miles per hour, hitting the synchronized stoplights with just the right timing to allow the driver to never step on the brakes, was hard fought. Time will tell if Lexingtonians can give up their love affair with cars and be willing to walk a few city blocks or invest more in city public transportation to conduct business or be entertained downtown.

Other important development efforts are underway in Lexington as a consequence of Mayor Miller and (at that time) Vice-Mayor Teresa Isaac's leadership. In 1998 HUD awarded Lexington a $19 million grant as part of a nationwide public housing revitalization effort called HOPE VI. The idea was to improve public housing infrastructure and management processes to provide new services such as job training, literacy programs, and financial assistance for occupants whose average income was $5,100. One of the big changes came with the 1999 demolition of Charlotte Court, a twenty-four-acre lot of public housing on the north side of Lexington. This neighborhood of fifty-two apartment buildings had been built in 1941 to accommodate the housing needs of Lexington's poor. Over the years the area became rife with drug-related problems, shootings, and other serious crime. Six hundred residents had to be relocated, but 290 new public housing units were slated to be constructed around Lexington—ninety-five homes have been built in place of the deteriorated apartment buildings at Charlotte Court. The Bluegrass-Aspendale housing units located in the area where the Kentucky Association once had its famed racetrack, are also being reconstructed to accommodate fewer residents in more modern homes. Its wonderful Teen Center under the leadership of Ann Grundy and Bruce Mundy served as an important space for education and ethnic pride.

Lexington has continued its efforts at merger in the twenty-first century with the creation of Commerce Lexington Inc. from the consolidation of the Greater Lexington Chamber of Commerce, Lexington United, and the Partnership for Workforce Development in January 2004. Lexington's Chamber of Commerce, chartered originally in 1881 and reorganized in 1915, had previously taken the lead in organizing mercantile, industrial, financial, and educational interests. While the Chamber in the twenty-first century had many major employers as members, approximately 80 percent of its member businesses contained less than fifty employees. The city's rejuvenated efforts at marketing itself nationally found common cause in the economic development group Lexington United, founded in 1982 to assist in local business expansion as well as to recruit new companies to locate here and invest in the city. In the mid-1990s under the leadership of Mayor Miller, the city created a Partnership for Workforce Development that sought creative ways to bring different educational and training opportunities together in order to raise the educational levels of the labor force and attract new employers.

Expansion

Currently, Commerce Lexington has more than 3,500 business and professional members. They represent nearly 2,000 companies throughout the Central Kentucky Region. This is now the main business organization whose goal is to promote economic development, job creation, and overall growth in Lexington and its neighboring communities.

Further evidence of Lexington's boom is the new mega-churches. Southland Christian Church averaged 170 attendees in 1956. By the 1990s, on a 115-acre site south of town, this church averaged over 7,000 in attendance each weekend. According to its website, by 2001 the church leaders finished phase I of their expansion program with a new "Worship and Activities Center, a Children's Worship Center, a Gathering Atrium, a Benevolence Facility, and additional classroom space." The church's affiliation numbers are difficult to estimate since half the state views its television program, and $1 million, 20 percent of its annual budget, is dedicated to missions each year. Similarly, Immanuel Baptist Church is situated on twenty-two acres in a south-end suburb and serves over 4,000 members as well as providing its services on television. Comparatively, the historic downtown churches such as Pleasant Green Missionary Baptist Church (now the fourth oldest African-American Baptist church in America), First Presbyterian Church, Christ Church Episcopal Cathedral, and Central Christian Church (the descendant of the Cane Ridge and Hill Street Christian churches that created the Disciples of Christ denomination) serve 1,800, 700, 1,600, and 2,000 members respectively.

With the growth of conservative fundamentalist Christianity among the newer white populations came the formation of a Christian school from a collaboration of many churches. The Lexington Christian Academy began as an alternative school for Gardenside Christian Church in 1975, which merged with two other alternative schools in 1989. By the mid 1990s it moved to 120 acres and warehouse space on Reynolds Road on the south side of town. The 200,000 square foot building was one-fourth the size of the neighboring Fayette Mall, Kentucky's second largest mall at the time. The Lexington Christian Academy is one of the most successful schools in the nation in terms of enrollment growth, serving children from twelve Central Kentucky counties and nearly 150 different churches.

This growth is part of a larger national trend and is not what makes Lexington unique. Without the horse industry, Lexington would be any other midwestern or southern city. In a prime location where the surrounding horse farms can rely on the plentiful calcium and phosphorous in the limestone deposits to build the strong skeletons suited for the sport of racing, the rolling, well-drained grasslands are perfect for training young horses to run. And we are not just talking about thoroughbreds: quarterhorses, Arabians, saddlebreds, and standardbreds all contribute to Kentucky's horse population and they all contribute to the horse industry's multi-billion dollar annual goods and services.

Lexington

Besides the beautiful Keeneland, Lexington boasts the fastest harness racing track in the world at The Red Mile. The Kentucky Horse Park a few miles north of Lexington offers an International Museum of the Horse, steeplechases, polo matches, horse shows, and the magnificent Three Day Event when future Olympic equestrian teams are determined from their performances in dressage, the cross-country obstacle course, and stadium jumping. The Horse Park also lets visitors see up close some of the most famous thoroughbreds, Tennessee walking horses, Appaloosas, Morgans, Lipizanners, and a variety of workhorses, miniature horses, and ponies. Horse-drawn carriages tour downtown, and mounted police patrol with some of the best former steeplechasers. Horseback riding is available in many farms around town.

But it is the thoroughbred industry that brings in the big bucks, and Lexington serves as the world's center for financial and legal services for the thoroughbred. Two of the top thoroughbred sales companies operate in Lexington: Keeneland Association and Fasig-Tipton Kentucky, Inc. In 2003, yearlings sold at auction in Kentucky totaled more than $621 million. The record highest price ever paid for a yearling at auction was set in 1985—a bid of $13.1 million for a foal by Nijinsky II out of My Charmer. 75 percent of the Kentucky Derby winners were foaled in Kentucky; the first six winners of the Triple Crown (the Derby, the Preakness, and the Belmont Stakes) came from the Bluegrass area. The Lexington office of the Jockey Club holds the American Stud Book, now a computerized database containing the pedigrees and race results of more than two million horses. During the 1930s the Lexington *Herald* boasted it would give free newspapers on any particular racing day in which no horse bred within a fifty-mile radius of Lexington won a race at a major track. No one remembers this offer ever being taken up.

Lexington's is a growth economy: people are moving into the area, employment is growing, and per capita income levels are increasing to above the national average. At the same time this has not led to a rise in the prices of goods and services: Lexington remains a good place to live with a cost of living index and housing costs below the national average. Energized from former Mayor Pam Miller's approach to more collaborative relationships with the state's flagship institution, the University of Kentucky is poised to make radical changes to the city's growth. The institution's mandate by the state to become a top research institution, coupled with its own vision to serve Kentuckians more effectively, will have a major effect on how Lexington grows in the future. The careful attention that Mayor Teresa Ann Isaac has paid to bringing good housing and a higher quality of life to all segments of our population will pay big dividends as its demographic numbers of ethnic groups changes to accommodate new immigrant groups.

Despite the failure of the Clinton health reform package, the 1990s saw dramatic changes in the health insurance market, and these changes have been reflected in Kentucky. Managed care accounts for nearly half of all Kentuckians with commercial health insurance coverage. The U.K. Hospital, ranked several times now in the Top 20 in the country in cancer care by *U.S. News & World Report*, increasingly collaborates with surrounding health care organizations—the U.K. Children's Hospital serves as the only full-service, tertiary care support for children in eastern Kentucky. The U.K. College of Medicine is ninth in *U.S. News & World Report's* 2003 annual ranking of medical schools' rural medicine programs. The U.K. Center for Rural Health and College of Pharmacy are top ranked nationally.

In addition, the relationships between the horse industry and U.K. have continued most profitably. The Maxwell H. Gluck Equine Research Center, acknowledged as the finest equine research facility in the country, has resulted in a number of discoveries related to vaccination and disease control, blood testing, and breeding efficiency. W.T. Young's $5 million donation helped launch the campaign that built the $58 million library named after him. Young, founder of the highly successful Overbrook Farm in the 1980s where Storm Cat now stands at stud, had been active in many educational and civic concerns including his service as a major benefactor for Transylvania University. He also began an endowment that keeps the land around the U.K. library undeveloped parkland.

Lexington is a thriving business center surrounded—in a very self-conscious way—with the best horse farms in the world. New ethnic groups have joined the city, especially in the Hispanic and Asian communities, and Lexington's restaurants and arts scenes reflect a new cosmopolitanism. In the 2000 issue of the *Places Rated Almanac*, Lexington is eighth in access to health care in North America. Unemployment levels are consistently some of the lowest in the Commonwealth. Some other high rankings Lexington has received from national publications in 2003 include: *Forbes'* Best Places in Terms of Business Costs, 4th place; *Forbes'* Best Places for Business and Careers, 14th place; *Expansion Management Magazine's* Best Places to Locate a Company, 7th place; and *Entrepreneur's* Best Cities for Entrepreneurs (Top Midsize Cities in Midwest), 8th place.

Ranked sixth in the nation in the percentage of population having completed sixteen or more years of school, the city is poised for the new economy of the twenty-first century. At the crossroads of Interstates 75 (north and south) and 64 (east and west), Lexington is in the center of almost everything. And her opportunities are boundless.

BIBLIOGRAPHY

Beard, Louie A. "On the Future of the Turf," *The Blood-Horse* XLIV, No. 21 (November 24, 1945), 1079-1082.

Bolin, James Duane. *Bossism and Reform in a Southern City: Lexington, Kentucky, 1880–1940*. Lexington: University Press of Kentucky, 2000.

Bradford, John. *The Voice of the Frontier: John Bradford's Notes on Kentucky*. Edited by Thomas D. Clark. Lexington: The University Press of Kentucky, 1993.

Breathitt, Edward "Ned" T. Interview by Betsy Brinson in Frankfort, Kentucky, February 23, 2000, as part of the Kentucky Civil Rights Project, Kentucky Historical Society, Frankfort.

Brock, Loretta Gilliam. *A History of the Woman's Club of Central Kentucky*. Lexington: The Woman's Club of Central Kentucky, 1996.

Cone, Carl B. *The University of Kentucky: A Pictorial History*. Lexington: University Press of Kentucky, 1989.

Donovan, Herman Lee. *Keeping the University Free and Growing*. Lexington: University of Kentucky Press, 1959.

Faulconer, J.B. "The Keeneland Story: A Quarter-Century of Racing in the Finest Tradition," *Thoroughbred Press*, n.d. [July 1, 1960], Keeneland Association Library, Lexington.

Filson, John. *The Discovery, Settlement and Present State of Kentucke*. New York: Corinth Books, 1962 (orig. pub. 1784).

Graves, Joe. Interview by author in Lexington, April 8, 2004.

Green, Pat. Interview by author in Lexington, February 14, 2004.

Hanna, Joe. Interview by author in Lexington, February 21, 2004.

Hewitt, Abram S. *The Great Breeders and Their Methods*. Lexington: Thoroughbred Pub., Inc., 1982.

Hollingsworth, Kent. *The Wizard of the Turf: John E. Madden of Hamburg Place*. Lexington: Privately published by Preston Madden, June 1965.

———. *The Kentucky Thoroughbred*. Lexington: University Press of Kentucky, 1976.

Lewis, R. Barry, ed. *Kentucky Archaeology*. Lexington: University Press of Kentucky, 1996.

Lucas, Marion B. *A History of Blacks in Kentucky, Vol. I: From Slavery to Segregation, 1760–1891*. Frankfort: The Kentucky Historical Society, 1992.

Lyons, W.E. *The Politics of City-County Merger: The Lexington-Fayette County Experience*. Lexington: University Press of Kentucky, 1977.

Bibliography

McElfresh, Allen. Interview by Glenna Graves in Lexington, April 7, 1981.

Miller, Pam. Interview by author in Lexington, March 29, 2004.

O'Malley, Nancy. " 'Stockading Up:' A Study of Pioneer Stations in the Inner Bluegrass Region of Kentucky," *Archaeological Report* 127, submitted to Kentucky Heritage Council. Program for Cultural Resource Assessment, University of Kentucky, 1987.

Parrish, Gladys V. "The History of Female Education in Lexington and Fayette County." Thesis (M.A.) University of Kentucky, 1932.

Peter, Robert, M.D. "A Brief Sketch of the History of Lexington, Kentucky and of Transylvania University, Delivered as an Introductory Lecture to the Winter Course in the Medical Department of Transylvania University, on Monday Evening, November 6, 1854." Lexington: D.C. Wickliffe Printer, 1854.

Peter, Robert. *History of Fayette Co., Kentucky.* Edited by William Henry Perrin. Chicago: O.L. Baskin & Co., 1882.

"Proposal for the Establishment of a Model Race Track at Keeneland, Lexington, Ky., A" With illustrations by Bryant Fleming. n.p., n.d. [1935] Keeneland Association Library.

Ranck, George W. *History of Lexington Kentucky, Its Early Annals and Recent Progress.* Cincinnati: Robert Clark & Co., 1872.

Rice, Otis K. *Frontier Kentucky.* Lexington: The University Press of Kentucky, 1993.

Roberts, Helm. Interview by author in Lexington.

Ryan, Dag. *Traces: The Story of Lexington's Past.* Lexington: Lexington-Fayette County Historic Commission, 1987.

Share, Allen J. *Cities in the Commonwealth: Two Centuries of Urban Life in Kentucky.* Lexington: The University Press of Kentucky, 1982.

Staples, Charles R. *The History of Pioneer Lexington (Kentucky) 1779–1806.* Lexington: Lexington-Fayette County Historic Commission, 1973 (orig. pub. 1939).

Stedman, Ebenezer Hiram. *Bluegrass Craftsman: Being the Reminiscences of Ebenezer Hiram Stedman Papermaker 1808–1885.* Edited by Frances L.S. Dugan and Jacqueline P. Bull. Lexington: University of Kentucky Press, 1959.

Talbert, Charles Gano. *The University of Kentucky: The Maturing Years.* Lexington: University of Kentucky Press, 1965.

Underwood, Thomas R., Jr. Interview by author in Lexington, March 2, 2004.

Wharton, Mary E., Edward L. Bowen, et al. *The Horse World of the Bluegrass.* Edited by Bruce F. Denbo. Lexington: John Bradford Press, 1980.

Wooley, Carolyn Murray. *The Founding of Lexington, 1775–1776, Including a Map of the Original Land Grants of the Region.* Lexington: Lexington-Fayette County Historic Commission, 1975.

Wright, John D., Jr. *Lexington: Heart of the Bluegrass.* Lexington: Lexington-Fayette County Historic Commission, 1982.

INDEX

Index